THE
JAGANNĀTHA-VALLABHA NĀṬAKA

THE JAGANNĀTHA-VALLABHA NĀṬAKA —A STUDY

(WITH INTRODUCTON AND TRANSLATION)

DR. (SMT.) RAJALAXMI SWAIN
Lecturer in Sanskrit
Surajmal Saha College, Puri

BHARATIYA KALA PRAKASHAN
DELHI (INDIA)

First Edition : 2002

Published by **C.P. Gautam**
BHARATIYA KALA PRAKASHAN
3421-A, IInd Floor, Narang Colony, Tri Nagar,
Delhi-110035. Phone : 7153083

ISBN : 81-86050-77-9

Laser Type Setting by
A-ONE GRAPHICS
Brahmapuri, Delhi-110053

Printed at
Santosh Offset Press
Delhi

Dedicated to

My Teacher

DR. SIDDHESWAR JENA

as a mark of gratitude

and

humble submission.

—Authoress

CONTENTS

FOREWORD

It gives me great pleasure to write a few words by way of introducing Dr. (Smt.) Rajalaxmi Swain, Lecturer-in-Sanskrit, Surajmal Saha College, Puri (Orissa) to the world of scholarship, through her work : "*The Jagannātha-Vallabha-Nāṭaka :* A Study" with Introduction and Translation" of Rāmānanda Rāya. This represents with some changes her doctoral thesis accepted by the Utkal University, Bhubaneswar (Orissa).

Like other parts of India (Bhāratavarṣa) Orissa has contributed significantly to the growth and development of Sanṣkrit literature and it has produced the unforgettable *gīta-kāvya* literature. Jayadeva (12th century A.D.) has given us very charming, sweet, melodious and immortal *gītakāvya viz* the *Gīta-Govinda.* It is a lyrical poem with dramatic elements and depicts the amorous dalliances of Rādhā and Kṛṣṇa. It has been a source of many later works, dramatic and poetical. Out of approximately 128 imitations of Jayadeva's *Gīta-Govinda,* the *Jagannātha-Vallabha-Nāṭaka* (JVN) is possibly the first imitation in a dramatic form on the same theme by Rāmānanda Rāya (also known as Paṭṭanāyaka, 16th century A.D.) who was a poet, the Kṛṣṇaite devout worshipper and an exponent, naturally, of the Rādhā-Kṛṣṇa philosophy. He was also a high official (governor/minister) of Prataparudra of the solar dynasty of Puri. This play in five acts is also known as *Rāmānanda-Saṅgīta-Nāṭaka,* which goes clearly to suggest that it is a musical play. It contains 21 *rāgas* and the stanzas in these *rāgas* are copiously quoted by later musicologists in their work. The play was written sometime between 1497 A.D. -1509 A.D., possibly before the advent of Caitanya Mahāprabhu to Puri. The latter and Rāmānanda used to meet each other; the latter was much admired by Caitanya Mahāprabhu.

Earlier to the present work under question, the JVN was published more than once and translated into regional languages, but a good edition with an English translation prefixed by a general detailed study has been a desideratum and Dr. (Smt.) Swain has tried to remove this gap by presenting what she calls a "correct text" of the play with English translation (Part-II) and a detailed study of the play in six chapters in Part-1. This text (Part-II) may be said to be a stepping stone to the critical edition. It is obvious that the present work adds to the existing literature on individual studies with text and translation of various plays, drama in general, and to the Gauḍīya Vaiṣṇavism and especially to the Rādhā-Kṛsna-theme play in addition to the contribution of Orissa to the Sanskrit literature.*

In the end I would like to congratulates the authoress for an indepth study and look forward to have many more works from her learned pen in the years to come.

—S.G. Ḳantawala

Place : Vadodara
Date : 23rd June, 2001.
("Rathayātrā"- day)

---

* vide (i) Report of the First international Sanskrit Conference, 1972, Delhi, Vol. I, Pt. I (1975) ed. By V. Raghavan, pp. 368ff, i.e.(a) Tripathi K.B., Contribution of Orissa to Sanskrit literature, pp. 368ff and (b) Rath, B. Contribution of Orissa to the *Gīta-Kāvya* literature pp. 382ff.

(ii) Dasgupta S.N., A History of Indian Philosophy, Vol. IV, 1975, Delhi, pp. 386ff.

PREFACE

Inspired by my father I was interested in research after my Post-Graduate studies. My father Sri Arjun Charan Swain happens to be a close friend of Dr. A.C. Swain, formerly Professor and Head of the Department of Sanskrit, Utkal University, Vani Vihar, Bhubaneswar. In fact I was a student of Professor Swain from 1982 to 1984 during my Post-Graduate studies. As advised by him, I decided to carry on research on an Orissan Manuscript, particularly on the *Jagannātha-vallabha-nāṭaka* of Rāya Rāmānanda in the year 1992.

During the early years of 16th century Rāya Rāmānanda composed this drama on the amorous sports of Rādhā and Kṛṣṇa and it was staged at Puri during the rule of king Pratāparudra (1497-1540 A.D.) Because of its mellifluous musical songs it was highly appreciated by the devotees of Gauḍīya Vaiṣṇavism as they considered the reading, reciting and witnessing this drama a kind of their pious duty. Owing to its popularity this drama was widely circulated at that time and it reached different parts of India. As Gaurāṅga Gopāla Senagupta points out in the Preface to his work *Jagannātha-vallabha-nāṭaka,* Rāmanārāyaṇa Vidyāratna was the first person to get this drama published twice from Murshidabad, Berhampur, Bengal in the year 1874 and 1889. After him many scholars and devotees of Gauḍīya Vaiṣṇavism have translated the drama into their respective mother-tongues. Even before the printing machine came into use, maintains Senagupta, the manuscripts of that drama were available in Viśvabhāratī (Śāntiniketana), Asiatic Society, Sanskrit College Library, Calcutta, Dhaka University Library, Madras Government Library, Bhandarkar Oriental Research Institute, Poona and also in Tubingen University, Germany; but despite this assertion of Senagupta, it is a fact that the manuscript of the *Jagannātha-vallabha-nāṭaka* is now rarely available. Senagupta procures only three manuscripts on the basis of which he has edited the text of the drama published by Baulman Prakashan, Calcutta in the year 1992. With constraints and hardship we have collected only six different texts of the work-three printed texts in Bengali language and three in Oriya language including one manuscript from Orissa State Museum, Bhubaneswar.

The work is divided into two parts. Part I deals with a critical study of the *Jagannātha-vallabha-nāṭaka* whereas Part II contains English translation, Sanskrit text of the play and the bibliography. The Part I consists of six Chapters. In the Chapter I, I have given a short introduction to the summary of the five Acts of the play and a brief description of my collection of six texts of *Jagannātha-vallabha-nāṭaka* on the basis of which a correct text of the play has been prepared. Chapter II deals with the life and the time of Rāya Rāmānanada. Chapter III discusses other works of the play-wright. Chapter IV comprises assessment of the different characters of the drama e.g. Śrīkṛṣṇa the hero, Śrī Rādhā the heroine, *Vidūṣaka* the jester, Madanikā and her friends. Chapter V contains a critical estimate of the drama along with the play-wright's acquaintance with the rules of dramaturgy. And finally in Chapter VI I have tried my best to show the merit of Rāya Rāmānanda as a dramatist, and also his mastery over the science of music.

I am thankful to Sri Karunakar Bisoi, Curator, Orissa State Museum for having provided me with a xerox copy of *Jagannātha-vallabha-nāṭaka* bearing No. SMS 66 in the beginning of my research work.

I am grateful to the Manager, Haridasa Thakur Matha Baba Natabar Das, Puri due to whose kindness I was able to procure from their library xerox copies of two Bengali texts-one by Rāmanārāyaṇa Vidyāratna and the other by Jyotiścandra Śarmā.

I will fail in my duty if I do not keep on record the sincere help and co-operation extended to me by Sudip Chatterjee the Librarian of Jagannatha-vallabha Matha, Puri for he has made many rare books available to me during the period of my research.

Retired Professor S.G. Kantawala of Baroda deserves sincere appreciation for he has provided me with the xerox copy of a relevant Chapter from Bharata's *Nāṭya-śāstra* (G.O.S.). He has also obliged me with a Foreword to this work. I express my indebtedness to Prof. N.Gangadharan of Madras as he has helped me in procuring some necessary books from Ananthacharya Indological Research Institute, Bombay. I am also grateful to Dr. A.C. Sarangi present Professor of Sanskrit, Utkal University and Dr. G.K.Dash, Reader in Sanskrit, Utkal University for solving some grammatical problems noticed in the *Jagannātha-vallabha-nāṭaka*.

I express my deep sense of gratitude to Professor Dr. A.C. Swain who is not only the prime source of inspiration behind my research pursuits, but also who has interpreted the difficult Sanskrit verses of the *Jagannātha-vallabha-nāṭaka* and extended his ungrudging help in rendering the text into English language.

I am greatly indebted to my revered guide Dr. Siddheswar Jena, Reader in Sanskrit, Ravenshaw College (Autonomous), Cuttack for he has shown keen interest in my work from the very beginning and without his thorough supervision this work would not have attained the shape in which I present it now.

I cannot forget the help of my family members—Sri Harihar Samal my brother-in-law, Sri Sitakanta Narendrajit Singh my husband in order to bring the work to its completion. My words fail really to describe their love and symapthy shown to me for as a married lady bound by domestic fetters, I am conscious of my own weakness and limitations.

Lastly I thank Mr. C.P. Gautam, Bharatiya Kala Prakashan, Delhi for bringing out this work in time.

Puri, **—Smt. Rajalaxmi Swain**

June, 2002

ABBREVIATIONS

A.V.	—	*Atharva-Veda*
B.P.	—	*Bhāva-Prakāśana*
Bd. P.	—	*Brahmāṇḍa Purāṇa*
Br. P.	—	*Brahma Purāṇa*
Bhav. P.	—	*Bhaviṣya Purāṇa*
Bhāg. P.	—	*Bhāgavata Purāṇa*
C.C.	—	*Caitanya-Caritāmṛta*
D.R.	—	*Daśa-rūpaka*
G.G.	—	*Gīta-govinda*
H.V.	—	*Harivaṁśa*
J.V.N.	—	*Jagannātha-vallabha-nāṭaka*
K.S.	—	*Kumāra-sambhava*
Mārk. P.	—	*Mārkaṇḍeya Purāṇa*
N.C.	—	*Nāṭaka-Candrikā*
N.D.	—	*Nāṭya-darpaṇa*
N.L.R.	—	*Nāṭaka-lakṣaṇa-ratnakośa*
N.S. (C.S.S.)	—	*Nāṭya-śāstra,* Chaukhamba Sanskrit Sansthan
N.S. (G.O.S.)	—	*Naṭya-śāstra,* Gackward Oriental Series, Baroda
N.S. (K.S.S.)	—	*Nāṭya-śāstra,* Kashi Sanskrit Series
R.V.	—	*Ṛg-Veda*
R.S.	—	*Rasārṇava-sudhākara*
S.D.	—	*Sāhitya-darpaṇa*
S.P.	—	*Śiva Purāna*
U.N.	—	*Ujjvala-nīlamaṇi*

PART I
STUDY OF THE DRAMA

CHAPTER-I

INTRODUCTION

The *Jagannātha-vallabha-nāṭaka* is a drama consisting of five Acts by the play-wright Rāmānada Rāya. It deals with the love of Śrī Rādhā and Śrīkṛṣṇa. After the composition of Jayadeva's *Gīta-govinda* in the latter half of 12th century A.D. the succeeding generations of poets in India have tried their best to imitate it; and in consequence, a large number of poems have not only been written glorifying the love of Śrī Rādhā amd Srīkṛṣṇa, but also some new poems have been composed depicting the love between Śiva and Pārvatī, Rāma and Sītā in a similar manner in slavish imitation of Jayadeva's masterpiece *Gīta-govinda.* In his book *A Study on the Śrīkṛṣṇalīlāmṛtam* Prof. Banamali Rath has pointed out that due to extreme popularity of the *Gīta-govinda* and its captivating effect on its readers nearly some hundred twenty eight imitations have been made throughout India; and the *Jagannātha-vallabha-nāṭaka* being a musical drama is the fourth work written in imitation of the *Gīta-govinda.*[1] After Jayadeva, when *kāvyas* based on the amorous dalliance of Śrī Rādhā and Śrīkṛṣṇa are abundantly available in Sanskrit literature, the *Jagannātha-vallabha-nāṭaka* by Rāmānanda Rāya seems perhaps to be the first drama dealing with the love-sports of Śrī Rādhā and Śrīkṛṣṇa.

The *Jagannātha-vallabha-nāṭaka* begins with three benedictory stanzas praising Lord Kṛṣṇa in his dancing posture and invokes his blessings in the form of bestowing happiness upon the three worlds. At the end of the benediction the stagemanager and the actress enter the stage when their conversation centres round youthfulness, spring season, affliction of women in separation and the blissful stage of companions in union. Next the stage-manager gives a glorious account of the conquests and achievements of Pratāparudradeva in which he refers to the invincible and indomitable valour and prowess of the king. Then the stage-manager makes allusion to the play-wright, his father and the play which is going to be encacted before the audience.

The drama proper begins when we meet with Śrīkṛṣṇa dressed in yellow garb in Vṛndāvana in the company of his favourite friend *Vidūṣaka*. At the advent of the spring laden with flowers and foliage and with the sweet notes of cuckoos from among the thicket of trees, the Vṛndāvana presents an exquisite beauty to the onlookers. Hearing the sound of the flute played by Śrīkṛṣṇa, smitten with love Śrī Rādhā enters the pleasure-garden in the company of a host of her friends, Madanikā and the sylvan deity. Struck at the sight of Śrīkṛṣṇa looking like the lustre of the petal of a blue lotus (*nīlotpaladadala-komala-cchavih*) Śrī Rādhā asks Madanikā about the person; and the latter replies that he is no other than Mukunda the love-incarnate who enamours the hearts of young cowherd-maidens and takes them to his confidence. Śrīkṛṣṇa looks at Śrī Rādhā, and appraising her beauty remarks that neither the lotus nor the moon can stand comparison with her face. *Vidūṣaka* Ratikandala is well-aware of the love-sickness of Śrīkṛṣṇa at the sight of fawn-eyed Śrī Rādhā. Here the first Act comes to an end and it is called *pūrvarāga* or the dawning of love since it refers to the mutual love and attachment of the hero and the heroine at first sight.

The second Act begins with the conversation between Madanikā and Aśokamañjarī. Since the very sight of Śrīkṛṣṇa, Śrī Rādhā has been absent-minded and unmindful of the worldly affairs. Due to the heat of excess love-passion she asks Aśoka-mañjarī to prepare for her a bed of new lotus-leaves. On the other hand, Śaśimukhī is deputed to Śrīkṛṣṇa with a billet doux (*anaṅga-patrikā*) from Śrī Rādhā containing a Prakrit verse on her love-lorn condition.

Śaśimukhī approaches Śrīkṛṣṇa; and there is an exchange of feelings between them under a *Bhāṇḍīra* tree. Madanikā in the meanwhile conceals herself behind the *Bhāṇḍīra* tree and listens to their conversation.

From the love-letter Śrīkṛṣṇa is aware of Śrī Rādhā's depth of love. Though he has the same intensity of love for her, he pretends as if he knows nothing. Suppressing all his feelings he remains callous to it; and he wants to test the strength of mind of Śrī Rādhā. Before Śaśimukhī Śrīkṛṣṇa meekly says that he has neither seen nor followed Śrī Rādhā. It is strange that Śrī Rādhā beholds him in every direction, whereas on the bank of river Yamunā he is all along busy in some playful amusement with cowherd-boys. Expressing still more surprise Śrīkṛṣṇa again says that he is a mere boy; it is unbecoming on the part of Śrī Rādhā, a grown-up lady to make a show of her love before him. If the cowherd-boys come to know of it, they will laugh at him and take him amiss. Moreover, Śrī Rādhā comes of a high prestigious family. It is not desirable that a lady like her should violate the code of conduct befitting her family. With these words Śrīkṛṣṇa ignores the advances of Śrī Rādhā and in the company of *Vidūṣaka* proceeds to bring back the calves. The second Act ends here and it is rightly called *bhāvaparīkṣā* or testing the sentiment of love since Śrīkṛṣṇa desires to test the innate feelings of Śrī Rādhā before their union takes palce.

In the third Act Śrī Rādhā is greatly pained at heart to learn that Śrīkṛṣṇa had turned down her love. Śaśimukhī puts forth all the facts before Śrī Rādhā and advises her to think of Śrīkṛṣṇa no more; but Śrī Rādhā's love for Śrīkṛṣṇa is so deep that she is unable to dissociate herself from the thoughts of the latter. Before Madanikā Śrī Rādhā avers that since the very sight of Śrīkṛṣṇa Cupid has taken possession of her heart, and she is deeply in love with Śrīkṛṣṇa. As she has lost control over her body, she asks her most trustworthy companion Madanikā to suggest some remedy for it. With words of consolation Madanikā then advises Śrī Rādhā not to be hopeless so soon. She discloses to Śrī Rādhā that she has already noticed the love of Śrīkṛṣṇa for her to be equally intense.

Meanwhile Mādhavī who had been sent to Śrīkṛṣṇa by Madanikā just to know his mind, appears on the stage and demands reward for the work she has done. Śaśimukhī forcibly snatches away the portrait from the hand of Mādhavī and to her amazement, notices some letters which indirectly hint at Śrīkṛṣṇa's attachment for Śrī Rādhā. From all these developments though Madanikā is optimistic about union of Śrī Rādhā with Śrīkṛṣṇa, Śrī Rādhā does not believe in it. She is still doubtful of her fortune in getting united with Śrīkṛṣṇa. The last song of the third Act records the feelings of frustration of Śrī Rādhā in this connection; and the Act goes by the name *bhāva-prakāśa* revealing the sentiment of love of both the hero and the heroine.

In the fourth Act Madanikā hides herself behind a *Mādhavī* bower and listens to the conversation between Śrīkṛṣṇa and *Vidūṣaka*. Śrīkṛṣṇa is found to be penitent after having rejected the love-offer of Śrī Rādhā. He regrets that when the young lady confidently expressed her love in him through her companion, he turned it down without a thought. He has indeed abandoned the precious jewel mistaking it for a shell (*hā hā śukti-dhīyā mahā-maṇirabhūt tyakto mayā)*. Desirous of finding out some means Śrīkṛṣṇa asks the *Vidūṣaka* to send for Madanikā. When Madanikā arrives, *Vidūṣaka* relates to her the pathetic condition of Śrīkṛṣṇa as to how the latter is tormented by the shafts of Cupid. Optimistic about the union of her dear companion with Śrīkṛṣṇa, Madanikā avails of this opportunity, and in an aggrieved tone refers to the love-sickness of Śrī Rādhā before Śrīkṛṣṇa that she has already become weak and emaciated due to the pangs of separation. Poor Śrī Rādhā has only loveliness left in her body (*sāpi lāvaṇya-mātra-śeṣā kalyāṇī*). Though she anoints her body with sandal paste, she finds no peace; neither the lotus nor the moon gives her delight; tears uninterruptedly flow down from her eyes. One can notice in her all types of mad behaviour. It is needless to say that Śrī Rādhā is somehow alive. Then Śrīkṛṣṇa requests Madanikā to arrange for their union; and Madanikā gladly takes the responsibility of uniting the heroine with the hero.

Madanikā repairs to Śrī Rādhā and informs the latter about the love-sickness of Śrīkṛṣṇa. She says that like her, Śrīkṛṣṇa's suffering is intense; he is eqaully love-stricken. Nothing is pleasing to Śrīkṛṣṇa, only the union of Śrī Rādhā can save him from the peril.

Breathing a sigh of great relief Śrī Rādhā gets ready to go to the rendezvous. While she proceeds to the secret meeting place, because of her delay Śrīkṛṣṇa apprehends many dangers coming in the way of his sweet-heart. Out of sheer affection for the lady-love he implores the eastern mountain to cover the rays of the rising moon going to spread all around and as such not to cause any obstacle on the path of his beloved. Thus with all anxiety when Śrīkṛṣṇa awaits Śrī Rādhā in the bower of creepers fashioned by him, she enters into it in the company of her friend.

Both *Vidūṣaka* and Madanikā are happy to notice the union of their friends. Leaving them in that lovely bower they proceed elsewhere.

In the fifth Act as Śaśimukhī observes, Madanikā the chief go-between in the union of Śrī Rādhā and Śrīkṛṣṇa enters the stage in a drowsy state. She is found walking with wavering footsteps and bearing a face with reddish eyes resembling the reddish lotus flower.

Śrī Rādhā and Śrīkṛṣṇa the young pair are fast asleep in the bower after spending the sleepless night in course of enjoying unrestrained amorous sports. Madanikā expresses great pleasure at the sight of the young pair in such a state. Śaśimukhī approaches her to enquire of her drowsiness. Madanikā discloses before the former that in course of intently watching the various amorous sports of Śrī Rādhā and Mādhava, she has spent the entire night without any sleep and that is why she feels drowsy. Then Śaśimukhī wants to know the development of affair of the young pair after their entry in the bower. In giving a vivid and glorious account of the love-sports between Śrī Rādhā and Śrīkṛṣṇa, Madanikā says that both of them got united in such a way that there was absolutely no gap in between the two. Each one of them pierced the other with nails and bit with teeth; they had hurt their bodies in such a way that in course of sexual enjoyment to their heart's content, they breathed long and deep sighs of relief; and the pangs of separation existing in between them long since came to an end. Having heard of it Śaśmukhī is all eager to see the most graceful body of Śrī Rādhā blessed with marks of nails and teeth. And

Madanikā readily points out Śrī Rādhā sitting in the front and Śrīkṛṣṇa sitting at a little distance.

When Madanikā proceeds to greet Śrī Rādhā after the union, there is heard some uproar behind the curtain. The demon Ariṣṭa is found to have wrought some havoc on earth. By digging out the earth with his horns and hoofs, by rending the quarters with his thundering sound and by causing fear with the movement of his two meteor-like eyes, he is about to devastate the cowherd village Vraja. With all courage and pride Śrīkṛṣṇa encounters Ariṣṭa, and gives him a smashing blow. By slaying the demon who is a menace to the three worlds, and throwing him out of Vṛndāvana to a great distance, he gives all protection to Vraja and ensures the safety of its residents. When Śrīkṛṣṇa crowned with success appears on the stage, Madanikā goes ahead to greet him. At her request Śrīkṛṣṇa quite exhausted takes rest beneath a *Vakula* tree. And since it is the most opportune moment to reward Śrīkṛṣṇa for his daring act, Madanikā immediately comes there with Śrī Rādhā and presents her to Śrīkṛṣṇa, with the request to grace her friend with his company for ever. As advised by Madanikā, with the hem of her garment Śrī Rādhā fans the body of Śrīkṛṣṇa marked with drops of sweat. Śrīkṛṣṇa admits that Madanikā has done the most pleasing act by presenting Śrī Rādhā to him in time.

The concluding verse of the fifth and last Act of the *Jagannātha-vallabha-nāṭaka* depicts the fruit of listening to the amorous pastime of Śrīkṛṣṇa; and the Act is rightly called *Rādhāsaṅgama* as it gives an account of Śrī Rādhā's union with Śrīkṛṣṇa.

In the *Gīta-govinda* Jayadeva uses eleven different Rāgas[2] for its twenty four songs; on the other hand for twenty one musical songs, Rāmānanda makes use of twenty Rāgas.[3] The Rāga "Sāmagujjarī" is used twice in this drama whereas for the rest nineteen songs nineteen Rāgas are used.

The *Jagannātha-vallabha-nāṭaka* taken up for a critical study here is based upon six texts available to us—(i) Orissa Museum Manuscript written in Oriya script; (ii) Text of Rāmanārāyaṇa

Vidyāratna translated and published by him in Bengali characters, (iii) Text edited and translated into Bengali by Jyotiścandra Śarmā; (iv) Text and translation of *Jagannātha-vallabha-nāṭaka* in Oriya by Pt. Puruṣottama Brahmacārī; (v) Text and Translation of the drama with a Preface of forty pages in Oriya by Smt. Viṣṇupriyā Otā, and (vi) *Jagannātha-vallabha-nāṭaka* edited and translated into Bengali by Gaurāṅga Gopāla Senagupta in the year 1992.

(i) The first manuscript is from the Sanskrit Manuscript section of the Orissa State Museum bearing No. SMS 66. The manuscript is written on plain paper consisting of twenty three pages. It seems to be a copy of the palm leaf-manuscript deposited in the Manuscript Section of Parija Library, Utkal University, Bhubaneswar. This Manuscript is full of scribal errors and only in four places are inserted Prakrit sentences along with their Sanskrit renderings. In the concluding portion of the drama the manuscript contains a beautiful poem consisting of six verses which speak of author's deep devotion to Lord Kṛṣṇa. Though full of defective readings it describes how the five sensory organs of the dramatist are forcibly attracted by Śrīkṛṣṇa the son of the king of Gopa (*śrī gopendrasutaḥ* sa karṣati balāt pañcendriyāṇyāli me /6/).

(ii) The text of Rāmanarāyaṇa Vidyāratna is published by him from Berhampur, Murshidabad, Bengal in 1289 Agrahāyana. Besides containing a verse-translation of Locana Dāsa Ṭhākura, the work contains a translation in Bengali-prose. In contrast to other books and manuscripts, the advantage of this book lies in the fact that it renders all the Prakrit dialogues of the drama into Sanskrit.

(iii) The text of Jyotiścandra Sarmā is another Bengali text in our collection. It is edited and translated by Śarmā himself. Instead of exact literal prose translation of Sanskrit verses as is done by Vidyāratna, Śarmā presents them in dramatic prose pattern which we often come across in Purāṇic plays. Besides, Śarmā translates most of the musical songs of the drama in his own lucid style thereby improving upon the verse-translation of Locana Dāsa Ṭhākura. It is published in 450 Caitanya era and 1342 sāla.

(iv) Pt. Puruṣottama Brahmacārī has edited the text with a literal prose translation of the drama without any versification. The transaltor has made this translation in order to make the drama available to the Oriya readers, especially to the Viṣṇuite devotees. Pt. Brahmacārī in his Oriya version has followed the translation and interpretation of Rāmanārāyaṇa Vidyāratna to a great extent, but he does not care for giving the Sanskrit rendering of the Prakrit portion of the drama. And at many places the Prakrit portion is found to contain many erratic readings. This text is published by Bhakti-Vinoda-Āśrama of Berhampur in the district of Ganjam, Orissa in the year 1979.

(v) Smt. Viṣṇupriyā Otā Lecturer in Oriya brings out the text and translation of *Jagannātha-vallabha-nāṭaka* in Oriya script in 1982. As she admits in the Preface, she depends upon the texts of Vidyāratna and Brahmacārī for her work. Divided into two parts her work consists of an introduction of forty pages. Smt. Otā tranalates some *ślokas* and twenty one musical songs of Rāmānanda in versified form; and as such her translation of *ślokas* and songs, is not faithful to the original text. Despite following Vidyāratna, she does not incorporate Sanskrit rendering of the Prakrit portions. Even though published recently the text abounds in innumerable mistakes.

(vi) Last but not the least, the text of the drama edited and translated into Bengali by Gaurāṅga Gopāla Senagupta is published from Calcutta in 1992. It is the third Bengali text in our collection. In the introduction to his work consisting of forty pages Senagupta deals with the life-history of Caitanya, Rāmānanda Rāya and Locana Dāsa Ṭhākura. For editing the text he has taken help of three books—*Jagannātha-vallabha-nāṭaka* by Vidyāratna, *Jagannātha-vallabha-nāṭaka* by Rasika Mohana Vidyābhūṣaṇa and a manuscript of the play available in the Asiatic Society, Calcutta. Unlike five texts discussed above, we notice here that Senagupta gives different readings in the footnotes of his work. In addition to the translation of the drama into simple colloquial Bengali prose for the easy understanding of the common readers, he has apended to his work the Bengali versification of twenty one musical songs by Locana Dāsa Ṭhākura.

Though a critical edition of *Jagannātha-vallabha-nāṭaka* is not our concern, still we have made an humble attempt to have a correct text of it as far as it is feasible. We have made a thorough comparison of all the six texts avaiable to us; and on the basis of them we have ventured to prepare a correct text of the drama. Our English version of the drama as well as the critical study of it is based upon the correct text prepared by us.

REFERENCES

1. Vide Rath, Banamali, *A Study on the Śrīkṛṣṇalīlāmṛtam,* Ch. VIII "An account of the similar works," pp. 193-211.
2. "Mālava", "Gurjarī", "Vasanta", "Rāmakarī", "Karṇāṭa", "Deśākhya", "Deśavarāḍī", "Naṭa", "Bhairavī", "Varāḍi" and "Vibhāsā".
3. "Naṭa", "Kedāra", "Vasanta", "Goṇḍakirī", "Gāndhāra", "Toḍivarāḍī", "Sāmagujjarī", "Mallāra", "Suhayī", "Deśāga", "Karṇāṭa", "Mālava", "Duḥkhīvarāḍī", "Sāmatoḍī", "Rāmakeli", "Mālavaśrī", "Sukhasinduḍā", "Āhira", "Lalita", and "Maṅgalagujjarī".

CHAPTER-II

RĀYA RĀMĀNANDA : HIS LIFE AND TIME

Rāmānanda Rāya the author of *Jagannātha-vallabha-nāṭaka* is not only a play-wright, but also he is a poet, a pious devotee, a theologian, a philosopher and a great propounder of loving devotion. Well-versed in different traditional scriptures, it is he to whom the loving adoration of the supreme deity with a feeling of close intimacy as existing between the lover and the beloved (*kāntābhāva*) owes its origin. A connoisseur of art and literature he is said to have taken up reins of administration for some years in the far-off Rajamahendri in Deccan during the regime of Pratāparudra the Gajapati king of Orissa. Though Rāmānanda Rāya shines like a bright star in the firmament of Sanskrit literature in the first-half of the 16th century A.D., and his contribution to the field of drama, poetry, music and especially to the development of Vaiṣṇava devotional philosophy cannot be ignored, it is a pity that not much is known about the personal life of this erudite scholar. Contemporary records are hardly available about his life and activities. In his own drama *Jagannātha-vallabha-nāṭaka* he refers to his parentage in brief. Besides, we find scant allusions to him in four more texts such as *Śrīkṛṣṇa-Caitanya-Caritāmṛta* of Murāri Gupta, *Śrīkṛṣṇa-Caitanya-Caritāmṛta mahākāvya* and the *Caitanya-Candrodaya-nāṭaka* of Kavi-Karṇapura Paramānanda Sena, and *Caitanya-Caritāmṛta* of Kṛṣṇadāsa Kavirāja.

Śrīkṛṣṇa-Caitanya-Caritāmṛta of Murāri Gupta is popularly known as *Kaḍacā* or a brief biographical account. Though the date of composition of this biography of Caitanya is recorded to be 1510 A.D., it actually depicts the events of his life till 1530 A.D.[1] In this Sanskrit *kāvya* there is reference to Caitanya's meeting with Rāmānanda Rāya at Kāñcīnagara[2], the narration of his experience of pilgrimage before Rāma Rāya, his advice to the latter and his final departure from Kāñcīnagara for Puri in the company of Viṣṇudāsa.[3]

Based on the work of Murāri, *Śrīkṛṣṇa-Caitanya-Caritāmṛta mahākāvya* of Kavi-Karṇapura Paramānanda Sena consisting of 20 cantos is dated at 1542 A.D. In this *mahākāvya* it is described that at the beginning of Caitanya's South Indian tour, Sārvabhauma Bhaṭṭācārya the great Vedantist in the court of the king Pratāparudra requests Caitanya to meet Rāmānanda on the way; but Caitanya meets Rāmānanda on his return journy (Canto XIII. 33ff) and resides with him for four months (Canto XIII.60). The Sanskrit verse attributed to Rāmānanda *nānopacārakṛta-pūjanam ārtabandhoḥ*[4] and his Brajabuli song *pahile hi rāga nayana bhaṅge bhela*[5] are quoted in full in this *kāvya*.

Kavi-Karṇapura's drama *Caitanya-Candrodaya* in ten Acts is composed in 1572 A.D. Written on the model of *Prabodha-Candrodaya* it is somewhat allegorical in character. Not strictly following Murāri's work and departing in many ways from his own *kāvya*, it seems to be a mature work of Karṇapura and it pays more attention to the later phase of Caitanya's life.[6] In this drama the seventh Act entitled *Tīrthāṭana* (account of pilgrimage) is of much importance for us in so far as it speaks of the meeting of Caitanya with Rāmānanda on the bank of the river Godavari and the latter's exposition of *Hari-bhakti*[7] in course of his conversation with the former. Later after returning from the South Indian Pilgrimage while recounting his experience before Sārvabhauma in the beginning of the eighth Act, Caitanya besides admitting the greatness of Rāmānanda, appreciates his views on *bhakti-tattva*.[8]

The *Caitanya-Caritāmṛta* of Kṛṣṇadāsa Kavirāja is the biography of Caitanya written in Bengali language. Deriving considerable source materials from previous works of Murāri Gupta, Svarūpa Dāmodara and Kavi-Karṇapura etc., it is a full-fledged work as far as Caitanya's earlier and later life is concerned. Written many years later after the death of Caitanya and completed in 1615 A.D., it is not merely a biography but a book of its kind on the entire theology of Bengal Vaiṣṇavism. In contrast to other texts, it is this work which treats the life, personality, and erudition, of Rāmānanda Rāya and some aspects of his family in greater details; and without it we would have been in darkness.

Caitanya-Caritāmṛta II Madhyalīla Ch. 8 depicts in details the long philosophical discourse held between Caitanya and Rāmānanda Rāya at Rajamahendri on the bank of the river Godavari. In the opinion of Professor Asoke Chatterjee Sastri "this celebrated discourse—the self-luminous guiding star in the firmament of Vaiṣṇava philosophy has been eternally shining in the *Caitanya-Caritāmṛta* (Madhya, Ch. VIII).[9] In this dialogue (II. 8.57-291) Caitanya questions Rāmānanda and the latter answers with due reverence to the former.

In the *Caitanya-Caritāmṛta* II.8.292ff it is clearly stated that Caitanya starts discussions and deliberations with Rāmānanda for ten days, and then he moves to far off south on pilgrimage. After the departure of Caitanya from Vidyā-nagara, Rāmānanda misses him, and pays no more attention to his duties. A devotee by nature, the proximity of Caitanya even for a short period brings a significant change in the life of Rāmānanda and he resigns from the post of Governor of Rajamahendri with a view to spending the rest of his life as a *pārṣada* of Caitanya at Puri. He seeks the permission of king Pratāparudradeva and the king unhesitatingly grants his wish. Pratāparudra was so much impressed by the erudition and scholarship of Rāmānanda that even after the resignation of the latter from his post he makes necessary arrangements for his life-long stay at the Jagannātha-vallabha garden in Puri town and allows Rāmānanda to enjoy all the facilities and privileges which he had been enjoying during the tenure of his office.[10]

As scholars unanimously agree, Caitanya is born in Śaka 1407 i.e., 1485 A.D.[11] At the age of twenty four he takes up *sannyāsa* in Śaka 1431 i.e., 1509 A.D.[12] Determined to go to Vṛndāvana for ever, he yields to the wish of his mother for residing permanently at Puri, He comes to Puri in 1510 A.D.[13] At Puri he meets Vāsudeva Sārvabhauma Bhaṭṭācārya, the great Vedantist and foremost logician who was a court Pandit of king

Pratāparudradeva.[14] Caitanya defeats Sārvabhauma and the conversion of the latter is regarded as a matter of great pride and victory for Caitanya. *Caitanya-Caritāmṛta* II. Madhya, Ch.6 refers to the conversion of Sārvabhauma in details. In Ch. 7 of Madhyalīlā of this text when Caitanya decides to go on South Indian pilgrimage, Sārvabhauma requests him to meet Rāmānanda Rāya at Vidyānagara on the bank of the river Godavari.[15] Sārvabhauma meekly admits that unable to understand Rāmānanda's depth of learning and his Vaiṣṇavite leaning, he has, at first, laughed at him.[16] In the same text II.8.16ff, we notice that after meeting Rāmānanda Rāya Caitanya frankly admits that it is through the persuasion of Sārvabhauma[17] that he has made a halt at the spot to meet Rāmānanda. Caitanya also refers to the fact that after converting Sārvabhauma he has failed to know from him anything about *Kṛṣṇa-tattva;* but Sārvabhauma has suggested Rāmānanda's name instead as a knower of this *tattva* though the latter was not present at Puri.[18] Anyhow Caitanya carries on his long and extensive pilgrimage to Southern and Western India for a little less than nearly two years; and on his way back he meets again Rāmānanda Rāya at Vidyānagara and shows him his collection of two important texts namely *Brahma-Saṁhitā* and *Śrīkṛṣṇa-Karṇāmṛta* which fully agree with the views of Rāmānanda on Kṛṣṇa theme.[19] On his return from pilgrimage Caitanya halts at Ālvarnātha temple for sometime and sends his attendant Kṛṣṇadāsa to Puri. All the followers of Caitanya are happy enough to know of his return. On reaching Puri Caitanya narrates his experience before Sārvabhauma and other devotees.[20] At Puri arrangements are made for his permanent residence in the home of Kāśī Miśra. At that time Bhavānanda Rāya the father of Rāmānanda Rāya comes there to pay homage to Caitanya in the company of his four other sons. Sārvabhauma introduces Bhavānanda Rāya to Caitanya, and the latter is very much pleased to know Bhavānanda as the father of Rāmānanda. At the direction of Bhavānanda, his son Vāṇīnātha permanently continues to remain at the service of Caitanya.[21]

Thus the real erudition of Rāmānanda comes to limelight after Caitanya's meeting with him. It is Caitanya who, in fact, notices in Rāmānanda profoundity of devotional love, the germ of

Kṛṣṇaite Vaiṣṇavism and moreover, the idea of loving adoration of the Supreme Lord with intimate feelings of the lover and the beloved (*kāntābhāva*).

Rāmānanda is said to be a disciple of Rāghavendra Purī and a grand-disciple of Mādhavendra Purī.[22] It is a fact that before Caitanya met Rāmānanda at Vidyānagara, Rāmānanda was already a devout Vaiṣṇava and an exponent of Rādhā-Kṛṣṇa philosophy. He had composed his *Jagannātha-vallabha-nāṭaka* prior to the advent of Caitanya in Orissa in 1510 A.D. We have clear evidence in support of this fact that there is no mention of the name of Caitanya even once in his drama when there are frequent allusions to the name of king Pratāprudra his patron almost at the end of each musical song present in the text.

Coming to the *Jagannātha-vallabha-nāṭaka* we see that in the prologue of this drama Rāmānanda refers to Bhavānanda Rāya as his father and speaks of him in glowing terms as follows :

> *Sarva-vidyā-nadī vilāsa-gāmbhīrya-maryādā-*
> *sthairya-prasādādiguṇa-ratnākarasya suraguru-*
> *pranīta-nīti-kadamba-karambita-mantrāśravi-*
> *kṛta-praguṇa-pṛthvīśvarasya śrī Bhavānanda Rāyasya*
> *tanujena śrīhari-caraṇālaṅkṛta-mānasena*
> *ŚrīRāmānandaRāyeṇa kavinā ....Act I.17*

From this description it is evident that Bhavānanda Rāya was a learned and virtuous person; and like an ocean he was a repository of virtues like dignity, propriety of conduct, patience and serentiy etc. The king followed and was guided by his counsel as he strictly adhered to the moral precepts laid down by Bṛhaspati the preceptor of gods. And Rāmānanda Rāya was his son.

As we know from *Caitanya-Caritāmṛta* II.10.49-53, Bhavānanda Rāya had five sons. Saralā Devī and K.N. Mahapatra also speak of five sons of Bhavānanda in their texts.[23] They are Rāmānanda, Gopīnātha Paṭṭanāyaka, Vaṇīnātha Paṭṭanāyaka, Kalānidhi Paṭṭanāyaka and Sudhānidhi Paṭṭanāyaka. Rāmānanda was the eldest of them all. Pleased with the erudition, devotion and poetic calibre of Rāmānanda, Pratāparudradeva the then king of Orissa appointed him as the Governor of Rajamahendri,[24] in the Andhra State. Even Gopinātha Paṭṭanāyaka the brother of Rāmānanda was appointed by the king as the Governor of Medinipur in the north.[25] The two cousins of Rāmānanda namely Śikhi Mahānti and his sister Mādhavī were also good scholars, and Mādhavī Devī had written a drama called *ŚrīPuruṣottamadeva-nāṭaka*.[26] As Mādhavī was quite learned and intelligent, king Pratāparudra appointed her as the scribe in the temple of Lord Jagannātha.[27] Bhavānanda and all his sons were most fortunate to enjoy royal patronage, and engaged in some work or other of the royal household all of them earned their livelihood.[28]

It seems that initially the family surname of Rāmānanda was 'Paṭṭanāyaka', and later they have acquired this tille of 'Rāya' by virtue of their position in the royal court of king Pratāparudradeva. S.K. De holds that Rāmānanda's father Bhavānanda Rāya was probably a local chief, feudatory to Gajapati Pratāparudra.[29] Thus most of the members of Rāmānanda's family continued to bask in the sunshine of royal favour.

About the birth-place of Rāmānanda there is a good deal of controversy among the scholars. In the preface to his work *Jagannātha-vallabha-nāṭaka* Gaurāṅga Gopāla Senagupta holds that previously the fore-fathers of Bhavānanda were the inhabitants of Vardhamana district in Bengal. Due to the prevalence of Muslim rule in Bengal they fled to Orissa where Hindu kings were in power. And they rose to high posts in the royal court there due to their own ability and competence. Probably Rāmānanda Rāya was born at Cuttack.[30] Rasika Mohan Vidyabhusana another Bengali scholar maintains the same view and opines that before the birth of Caitanya Rāmānanda perhaps had his birth at Cuttack,[31] but it is a fact that the village Bentapura[32] in Brahmagiri constituency in the district of Puri, Orissa is the real birth place of Rāmānanda. The village Bentapura of Brahmagiri is near the famous Alvarnātha temple where Caitanya made a halt for sometime just at the beginning of his South Indian pilgrimage and also on his return journey from the South. This village is now at a distance of some twenty kilometres from the famous Puri town. Scholars like

Cakradhara Mahapatra, K.N. Mahapatra and Bhakti Siddhanta Saraswati Goswami support this view in their respective books.[33]

There is some doubt raised by some scholars as regards the caste of Rāmānanda Rāya. In *Caitanya-Caritāmṛta* II.Ch.8 and 10 there is ample reference to it. On his South Indian pilgrimage when Caitanya meets Rāmānanda on the bank of the river Godavari, out of sheer humility the latter tells the former that he is a *śūdra* by birth;[34] where is he, a mere royal servant given to sensual pleasures and where is Caitanya the God-incarnate![35] After Caitanya's return from South India when Rāmānanda's father Bhavānanda surrenders before Caitanya along with his four other sons, Bhavānanda refers to himself as a *śūdra*; with the divine touch of Caitanya, he admits, he and his family are redeemed.[36] On the basis of these confessions they are said to be born in a lower caste. And it leads David Kinsley, to draw the conclusion that "revered devotee Rāmānanda Rāya was a śūdra",[37] but it is untenable. That Rāmānanda came of a respectable *karaṇa* family is an undisputed fact and a fact beyond any doubt.[38] Scholars of Bengal and Orissa like Rasika Mohan Vidyabhusana,[39] Gauranga Gopala Senagupta[40] and K.N. Mahapatra,[41] are unanimous on the point.

It will not be out of place to mention here that the resignation of Rāmānanda Rāya from the post of Governor of Rajamahendri has been seriously viewed by the historians. It is R.D. Banerji who blames and holds Rāmānanda particularly responsible for the fall and decline of Orissan empire. In his *History of Orissa*, Vol. I, p. 332 he writes that "at a time when the Oriya nation needed the services of every honest and capable man for the defence of her political prestige and empire, Rāmānanda Rāya betrayed his trust to his own people by retiring from his position on the weakest frontier of the country, and one may ascribe the fall of Koṇḍavidu, Kondapalle and Rajamahendri to their being left in charge of young and inexperienced officers like the prince Vīrabhadra on the retirement of Rāmānanda". This assessement of Banerji clearly suggests that Rāmānanda was a competent officer and his untimely retirement from the responsible post he held, spelt a disaster for the Oriya nation; but on the other hand we should not close our eyes to the fact that given to devotion and detachment Rāmānanda's heart experienced such bliss and beatitude in the company of Caitanya that after the departure of the Master from Rajamahendri he proceeded in the path of renunciation without delay.

Prabhat Mukherjee also refutes the views of R.D. Banerji about Rāmānanda and he is of opinion that "to find fault with Rāmānanda, Banerji has even distorted true facts".[42] Mukherjee rightly shows that "Rāmānanda resigned the Governorship of Rajahmundry before the Orissa campaign of Krishna Raya. We find him at Puri in 1512. Secondly Rajahmundry was not the frontier province of Orissa at the time of his retirement....At the time of Krishna Raya's invasion Vīrabhadra and Tirumala Rautaraya were the governors of the Southern Provinces of Koṇḍviḍu and Udayagiri and they stubbornly resisted the enemy".[43] Mukherjee further alleges that "R.D. Banerji brushes aside these details and writes that Rāmānanda was in the charge of 'the weakest frontier' of the kingdom".[44] But according to Mukherjee's opinion the southern side was not the weakest frontier, but "the northern one was the weakest frontier of Orissa through which the Muslims made their aggressive inroads and finally destroyed the independence of the country".[45]

Besides, in the *Caitanya-Caritāmṛta* III.9.122 we come across a casual remark against Rāmānanda that he never cared to maintain the record of income and expenditure. The corresponding verse in the text is as follows :

Rājamahindāra rājā kainu Rāma-Rāya/
ye khāila, ye bā dila, nāhi lekhā-dāya//

According to *Caitanya-Caritāmṛta* this was the statement of king Pratāparudra. And on the basis of this statement Rāmānanda's integrity stands questioned by some historians.[46]

But in the context of serious allegations levelled against his brother Gopīnātha Paṭṭanāyaka, the Governor of Medinipur who was found guilty of embezzling a large amount of the Royal Treasury and had fallen in arrears to the extent of two lakhs of *kāhāṇas* of cowries,[47] we think that this may be a passing reference of the king about Rāmānanda. Temperamentally a poet and a devotee, Rāmānanda was perhaps indifferent to the maintenance of any account of the revenues of the state, and Pratāparudra might be unhappy over this.

In his learned introduction to *'Padyāvalī'* De points out, 'after returning from pilgrimage Caitanya settled permanently at Puri at about Śaka 1430 (1517 A.D.).[48] With a few selected disciples he spent the remaining sixteen years of his life in daily worship and adoration. Rāmānanda joined him and became a close associate of Caitanya. Both of them, holds Saralā Devī, used to go to the lotus pond called Narendra to take their bath. After bath standing outside close to the Garuḍa pillar they were accustomed to have a *darśana* of Lord Jagannātha. It is in the recesses of the Rādhākānta Matha that both of them were engaged in discussions and deliberations on *Kṛṣṇa-bhakti-tattva*.[49] As pointed out by De, Caitanya passed away in Āṣāḍha Śaka 1455 (June-July 1533 A.D.)[50] at the age of forty eight. And both Rāmānanda and Pratāparudra survived him. Pratāparudra survived for six more years and died in 1540 A.D.[51]

The historians have fixed the period of Pratāparudra beginning with 1497 A.D. and closing with 1540 A.D.[52] As Rāmānanda had already become the Governor of Rajamahendri prior to the advent of Caitanya in Orissa in 1510 A.D. and he had spent the remainder of his life in devotion and renunciation after the death of Caitanya,[53] so the period consisting of the last two decades of 15th century and the 1st half of 16th century is most possibly his approximate time in view of the dearth of any concrete and definite records. It is needless to say that this view finds support with Bhakti Siddhanta Saraswati Goswami when the learned Gosvāmin maintains that "his time can be safely admitted from the eighth decade of the fifteenth century to the succeeding fourth decade of the Christian Era.[54]

REFERENCES

1. For details vide De, S.K. *Early History of the Vaiṣṇava Faith and Movement in Bengal,* Ch. II, pp. 35-36
2. Gosvami, Madanamohan, *Śrīkṛṣṇa-Caitanya-Caritāmṛtam* or *Murāriguptera Kaḍacā* (only Bengali Translation), III. Canto 15.1.
3. *Ibid.*, III. Canto 16.9-12.
4. Goswami, Prankishor, *Srī Kṛṣṇa-Caitanya-Caritāmṛta mahākāvya,* Canto XIII.42.
5. *Ibid.*, Canto XIII.46.
6. For details see De, S.K. *Early History of the Vaiṣṇava Faith and Movement in Bengal,* pp. 44-45.
7. Bhagavān — *kā vidyā* ?
   Rāmānandaḥ — *haribhaktir eva na punar vedādi-niṣṇātatā*
   Bhagavān — *kīrtiḥ kā* ?
   Rāmānandaḥ — *bhagavatparo'yamiti yā khyātir na dānādijā*
   Bhagavān — *kā śrīḥ* ?
   Rāmānandaḥ — *tat-priyatā* na vā dhana-jana-grāmādi-bhūyiṣṭhatā
   Bhagavān — *Kiṁ duḥkhaṁ*
   Rāmānandaḥ — *bhagavat-priyasya viraho no hṛd-vraṇādi-vyathā//8*
   Bhagavān — *bhadram / ke muktāḥ* ?
   Rāmānandaḥ — *Pratyāsattir haricaraṇayoḥ sānurāge na rāge prītiḥ premātiśayini harer bhakti-yoge na yoge / āsthā tasya praṇayarabha-sasyopadehe na dehe yeṣām te hi prakṛti-sarasā hanta muktā na muktāḥ //9*
   Bhagavān — *bhavatu / kiṁ geyaṁ -*
   Rāmānandaḥ — *vraja-keli-karma -*
   Bhagavān — *kiṁ iha śreyaḥ -*
   Rāmānandaḥ — *satāṁ saṅgatiḥ /*
   Bhagavān — *kiṁ smartavyaṁ -*
   Rāmānandaḥ — *aghārī-nāma-*

Bhagavān — kim anudhyeyaṁ-
Rāmānandaḥ — *murāreḥ padam /*
Bhagavān — *kva stheyaṁ -*
Rāmānandaḥ — *Vraja eva /*
Bhagavān — *kiṁ śravaṇayor ānandi -*
Rāmānandaḥ — *Vṛndāvana-krīḍaikā /*
Bhagavān — *kiṁ upāsyam atra -*
Rāmānandaḥ — *mahasī śrīkṛṣṇa-rādhābhidhe / 10*
Caitanya-Candrodaya-nāṭaka, Act VII, 8-10

8. Śrīkṛṣṇa Caitanyaḥ - *Sārvabhauma!....kevalam eva Rāmānanda-Rāyaḥ/ sa tvalaukika eva bhavati/* × × × ×
kintu Bhaṭṭācārya - *Rāmānanda-matam eva me rucitam/* *Caitanya-Candrodaya-nāṭaka,* Act VIII, p. 255.
9. Sastri, Asoke Chatterjee, *Caitanya,* p. 46.
10. *tomāra ye barttana tumi khāo se barttana/*
niścinta hayān bhaja Caitanyera caraṇa//
C.C. II, Madhya Ch. II.22
11. De, S.K. *Padyāvalī,* Introduction, p. XVII.
12. *Ibid.*, p. XXII.
13. Mukherjee, Prabhat, *The History of Medieval Vaiṣṇavism in Orissa*, Ch. XI, p.174.
14. See Sastri, Asoke Chatterjee, *op.cit.*, p.44.
15. *Rāmānanda Rāya āche Godābarī-tīre/*
adhikārī hayena tenho Bidyānagare//
śūdra-biṣayi-jñāne upekṣā nā karibe/
āmāra bacane tānre abaśya milibe// C.C. II. 7.62-63.
16. *alaukika bākya ceṣṭā tānra nā bujhiyā/*
parihāsa kariyāchi tānre baiṣṇaba baliyā// C.C. II. 7.66
17. *Sārvabhauma Bhaṭṭācārya kahila tomāra guṇe/*
tomāre milite more karila yatane//
*tomā milibāre mora ethā āgamana/ C.C.*II.8.30-31a
18. *Sārvabhauma saṅge mora mana nirmala haila/*
Kṛṣṇa-bhakti-tattva kaha, tān hāre puchila//
tenho kahe-āmi nāhi jāni Kṛṣṇa-kathā/
*sabe Rāmānanda jāne, tenho nāhi ethā// C.C.*II.8.125-126

19. *tīrtha-yātrā-kathā-prabhu sakala kahilā/*
karṇāmṛta, brahma-saṁhitā, dui punthi dilā//
prabhu kahe-tumi yei siddhānta kahile/
ei dui punthi sei saba sākṣī dile// *C.C.*II.9.323-324.
20. Kavirāja, Kṛṣṇadāsa—*C.C.*II.9.338ff.
21. *Ibid.*, II.10.36-38, 49-61.
22. De, S.K., *Padyāvalī,* Introduction, p.XXV.
23. Devī, Saralā, *Rāya Rāmānanda* (Oriya), p.7, 154; Mahapatra, K.N. *A Descriptive Catalogue of Sanskrit Manuscripts of Orissa,* Vol. II. p. CXV.
24. Mahapatra, Cakradhara, *Utkala Itihāsara Eka Ajñāta Adhyāya,* Ch. 3, pp. 36-37.
25. *Ibid.*, p.37.
26. Mahapatra, K.N., *op.cit.,* p.CXVI.
27. Devī, Saralā, *op. cit.,* p.151.
28. *Ibid.*, p.154
Cf. also Senagupta, Gaurāṅga Gopāla, *Jagannātha-vallabha-nāṭaka,* preface, P.2.
29. De, S.K. *Padyāvalī,* Introduction, p.XXV.
30. Senagupta, Gaurāṅga Gopāla, *Jagannātha-vallabha-nāṭaka,* Preface, pp.1-2.
31. Vidyabhusana, Rasika Mohan, *ŚrīRāya Rāmānanda* (Bengali) Ch.2, p.16.
32. Just to ascertain the truth behind it, during my visit to the village Bentapura in Brahmagiri constituency, I met the family members of Rāmānanda Rāya. One of them, a school teacher informed me that they happen to be the descendants of Gopīnātha Paṭṭanāyaka, the brother of Rāmānanda. They are *karaṇa (kāyastha)* by caste and they are still using Paṭṭanāyaka as their surname. Rāmānanda was unmarried and on his return from Rajamahendri he had never been to his home.
33. Mahapatra, Cakradhara, *op. cit.*, Ch.3, p.34.
Mahapatra, K.N., *op.cit.,* P.CXV.
Goswami, Bhakti Siddanta Saraswati- *Rāi Rāmananda* (English), Ch.I, p.3.
34. *tathāpi puchila-tumi Rāya Rāmānanda?/*
tenho kahe, sei han dāsa śūdra manda// *C.C.*II. 8.21.

35. *Kāhāan tumi—sākṣāt-īśvara nārāyaṇa/ kāhān muin—rājasebī biṣayī śūdrādhama//* C.C.II.8.35.
36. *Rāya kahe -āmi śūdra, biṣayī adhama/ tabu tumi sparśa—ei īśvara lakṣaṇa // C.C.* II.10.54
37. Rosen, Steven J., *Vaiṣṇavism*—"Śrī Caitanya's Pilgrimage to South", p. 181.
38. Vide Supra our footnote No.32.
39. Vidyabhusana, Rasika Mohan—*Srī Rāya Rāmānanda* (Bengali) p. 16.
40. Senagupta, Gaurāṅga Gopāla, *Jagannātha-vallabha-nātaka,* Preface, p. 2.
41. Mahapatra, K.N. *op. cit.*, p.CXV.
42. Mukerjee, P., *The History of the Gajapati Kings of Orissa,* Appendix-H.P. 104.
43. *Ibid.*
44. *Ibid.*
45. *Ibid.*, pp. 104-105.
46. *Ibid.* p. 105.
47. *dui-lakṣa-kāhāṇa tāra ṭhāin bākī haila/* *C.C.* III. 9.19a
48. De, S.K., *Padyāvalī,* Introduction, p.xxix.
49. Devī, Saralā, *op.cit.*, p. 84.
50. De, S.K., *Padyāvalī*, Introduction, p.xxx.
51. Mukherjee, P., *The History of Medieval Vaiṣṇavism in Orissa*, Ch.XI, p.177.
52. *Ibid.*
53. Banerji, R.D., *History of Orissa.* Vol. I, p. 332.
54. Goswami, Bhakti Siddhanta Saraswati, *op.cit.*, Ch. I, p. 6.

CHAPTER -III

OTHER WORKS OF RĀYA RĀMĀNANDA

Except *Jagannātha-vallabha-nāṭaka* though no other Sanskrit text of Rāmānanda has yet come to our notice, still he is said to have written a few other works of importance which are discussed in this Chapter.

Padyāvalī is an anthology of Sanskrit verses on Kṛṣṇa and Kṛṣṇalīlā compiled by Rūpa Gosvāmin. This compilation contains-386 verses composed by about 125 poets. In the critical edition of this text as pointed out by De, Rāmānanda Rāya is the author of verse No.13.[1] Prior to Rūpa Gosvāmin it is Kavikarṇapura Paramānanda Sena who refers to this Sanskrit verse in his *Śrī Kṛṣṇa-Caitanya -Caritāmṛta mahākāvya*, Canto XIII.42 and following him Kṛṣṇadāsa Kavirāja also quotes it in *Caitanya-Caritāmṛta* II. Madhyalīlā Ch. 8.69. The Sanskrit verse is as follows :

nānopacārakṛtapūjanam ārtabandhoḥ
premṇaiva bhaktahṛdayaṁ sukhavidrutaṁ syāt/
yāvat kṣudasti juṭhare jaraṭhā pipāsa
tāvat sukhāya bhavato nanu bhakṣyapeye//

The verse is however not traceable in the *Jagannātha-vallabha-nāṭaka* of Rāmānanda Rāya.

In *A Descriptive Catalogue of Sanskrit Manuscripts of Orissa,* Vol.II Rāmānanda Rāya is stated to have written a work called *Tikapañcakam.* As Sri Kedarnath Mahapatra, the then Curator of Orissa State Museum points out,[2] the manuscript of it was with Prof. (Dr.) A.B. Mohanty of Cuttack, but after the lapse of so many years it has not yet come to the notice of the scholars.

Another work called *Marmanirūpaṇam* is attributed to

Rāmānanda Rāya. It is said to be dealing with the love-sports of Rādhā and Kṛṣṇa, but the work is nowhere referred to except in the biography of Rāmānanda[3] written by Saralā Devī.

Rāmānanda was a skilled hand at composing poems in Brajabuli language. Prior to the emergence of standard Oriya, Hindi and Bengali languages, there was in vogue a mixed language called Brajabuli containing words borrowed from the above three languages and the Maithilī language. It is said that this mixed artificial language prevailed in the states of Bihar, Assam, Bengal and Orissa before 15th century A.D. Vidyāpati the most renowned poet of Mithilā (1352-1448 A.D.) and Caṇḍīdāsa the noted poet of Bengal (Circa 14th to 15th century) wrote songs in Brajabuli language dealing with Rādhā's illicit love with Kṛṣṇa; and their songs were very appealing to the masses. In course of time it became a common practice with the later Vaiṣṇava devotees to write devotional songs based on Rādhā-Kṛṣṇa līlā. Due to the extreme popularity of Brajabuli songs, Rāmānanda was not free from its impact. He has given enough evidence of his skill and merit in composing songs in Brajabuli language.

We are well aware of the fact that on the advice of Sārvabhauma Bhaṭṭācārya, Caitanya met Rāmānanda Rāya on the bank of the river Godavari in the far off Deccan. He put questions and elicited from him answers on many aspects such as the loving-devotion (*prema-bhakti*) *Kṛṣṇa-tattva* and *Rādhā-tattva* etc. At the end of their discussion when Caitanya asked Rāmānanda to tell something more, as Kṛṣṇadāsa Kavirāja Gosvāmin rightly points out, the latter recited a song of his own[4] composed in Brajabuli language. Kavikarṇapura Paramānanda Sena refers to this song in his *Śrīkṛṣṇa-Caitanya-Caritāmṛta* mahākāvya Canto XIII. 46. Caitanya extremely thrilled with the depth of the meaning of the song, acquired clear understanding of the Rādhā-Kṛṣṇa philosophy. By covering the face of Rāmānanda with his hand[5] he prevented him from reciting any more. The song reads as follows:

pahile hi rāga nayana-bhaṅge bhela
anudina bāḍhala, abadhi nā gela/
nā so ramaṇa, nā hāma ramaṇī

dunhu-mana manobhaba peṣala jāni/
e sakhi, se saba prema kāhinī
kānu-ṭhāme kahabi bichurala jāni/
nā khonjalun dūtī, nā khonjalun ān
dunhu keri milane madhya ta pāncabāṇa/
ab sohi biraga, tun hu bheli dūtī
su-purukha-premaki aichana rīti/

—*C.C.* II. 8.194

This short Brajabuli song is quite suggestive of Rādhā-Kṛṣṇa *prema-tattva* and is an invaluable gem of Vaiṣṇava poetic literature. Caitanya was overwhelmed with joy to listen to this song and the later philosophy of Caitanyaism came to be founded on it. Prior to Rāmānanda no Vaiṣṇava Gosvāmins of Bengal composed songs in Brajabuli language. And this song under discussion is regarded as the earliest Vaiṣṇavite composotion in this language. According to critics, it is not only the first Brajabuli poem, but also Rāmānanda was the first Vaiṣṇava poet of the Brajabuli language. Of all the Brajabuli songs written on Rādhā-Kṛṣṇa theme at that time, this song of Rāmānanda was the first and the song by Yasoraj Khan[6] the Muslim devotee of Bengal, was the second. Sukumara Sen the eminent critic of Brajabuli literature rightly remarks that "it should be more properly reckoned as the earliest Brajauli poem written in Orissa and it must be remembered that he was an Oriya".[7] He further maintains that "so far as the contemporary evidence goes, this poem is the earliest Brajabuli composition handed down to us, with the only exception of the poem byYasoraj Khan".[8]

Apart from the above song, some sweet devotional songs of Rāmānanda are noticed in an old Bengali Vaiṣṇava anthology like the *Pada-kalpataru* of Vaiṣṇavadāsa. Rāmānanda is also the author of two more song-books in Brajabuli language namely *Daṇḍa-velā* and *Daṇḍātmaka-līlā*. In the year 1945 on the basis of a palm-leaf manuscript collected from Orissa Priyaranjan Sen edited *Rāya Rāmāndera-bhaṇitāyukta-padāvalī* in Bengali character. This *Padāvalī* consisting of 60 songs is nothing but *Daṇḍātmka-līlā* which aims at depicting the different activities of Rādhā and

Kṛṣṇa during the sixty four divisions *(daṇḍa)* of the day and the night. Recently in 1992 *Daṇḍa-velā* of Rāmānanda has been edited by Pramila Misra, Directorate of Culture, Orissa, Bhubaneswar on the strength of two palm-leaf manuscripts available in the Manuscript Section of Orissa State Museum. This *Daṇḍa-velā* comprises 30 songs and in mellifluous Brajabuli language it describes as to how Kṛṣṇa is engaged in various activities from dawn to dusk during the thirty two *daṇḍas* of the day. The activities of Kṛṣṇa relate to his rise early in the morning *(nidrā-tyāga)*, assemblage of his friends like Madhumaṅgala, etc., repairing to the *goṣṭha*, milking the cows *(go-dohana)* bathing *(snāna)*, besmearing the body with sandal paste and unguents *(śri-aṅga-maṇḍana)*, preparation of dishes, taking food in the compnay of friends *(bhojana)* and so on till his meeting with Rādhā at the close of the day.

Both *Daṇḍa-velā* and *Daṇḍātmaka-līlā* deal with the same theme. They deal with the different activities of Kṛṣṇa and Rādhā at different *daṇḍas* of the day whether it is thirty two or sixty four, but the language and style of presentation is not similar in these two works. It is due to this reason that in the preface to her work the editor Misra doubts the authorship of these two texts by one and the same author. She, however, remarks that the problem requires thorough study and investigation.[9]

Credit goes to Rāmānanda for having witten *Rādhā-janma*, Gaura-janma and *Śukla-dvitīyā-milana* in Brajabuli language. *Rādhā-janma* consisting of twenty nine songs deals with the birth of Rādhā, the spouse of Kṛṣṇa; *Gaura-janma* contains eleven songs; it depicts the birth of Caitanya who gets the permission of his mother for taking up *sannyāsa*. *Śukla-dvitīyā-milana* contains only six songs and narrates the union of Rādhā with Kṛṣṇa. These three texts together with *Daṇḍa-velā* and *Daṇḍātmaka-līlā*[10] go by the name of *Rāya Rāmānanda Padyāvalī* published by the Directorate of culture, Orissa in 1992.

The songs of Rāmānanda Rāya collected from different parts of Orissa have been published in certain journals and magazines of the State in a somewhat scattered manner. The authorship of two more works—*Nāyikā-bheda* and *Sūrya-pūjā* is also attributed to Rāmānanda. Thought three palm-leaf manuscripts available so far deal with the same theme, their language and mode of presentation differs from each other; and the question of authoriship by one and the same person raises some doubt.[11]

From the foregoing discussion it seems very clear that Rāmānanda was undoubtedly a great poet in Brajabuli language in his time. The Pradyumna Miśra episode as narrated in *Caitanya-Caritāmṛta* III. Antyalīlā Ch. 5 clearly shows that he had consisderable ability in dramatic art and science of music. Rāmānanda took pleasure in instructing dance and music to young damsels, besmeared their bodies with perfumes and unguents, even dressed and decorated them with attractive precious garments, and yet he was over and above narrow human passion. The composition of twenty one musical songs in the *Jagannātha-vallabha-nāṭka* and the song thirty one[12] of *Daṇḍātmka-līlā* containing lines such as -

dhiktā dhiktā dhiktā tātānā rītānā rītānā/
jhanana jhanana jhaṅkṛ.../

unquestionably prove his talent in the science of music.

As Kṛṣṇadāsa Kavirāja states, Caitanya was not only pleased with the devotional love of Rāmānanda, but also he was struck with wonder to notice his vast learning. Caitanya highly admired his knowledge of poetics, dramaturgy and *Rasa-śāstra*. And it is because of this that he got the works of Rūpa Gosvāmin examined by Rāmānanda (*C.C.*III. 1. 118ff). Rūpa Gosvāmin used to read out his works before Rāmānanda and the latter's assessment of Rūpa's works was given weightage by Caitanya. Nevertheless, the use of Prakrit language in the *Jagannātha-vallabha-nāṭaka* shows Rāmānanda's mastery of it like that of Sanskrit. Thus there is the least doubt that Rāmānanda had deep knowledge in the various branches of Sanskrit language and literature.

As pointed out above, though Rāmānanda used to instruct the musical songs of his own drama to the young damsels or say *deva-dāsīs* so as to enact the same before Lord Jagannātha, he did not have any sexual laxity on his part; rather he could remain detached and dispassionate all through. With his thoughts centered on Kṛṣṇa as a cowherd maiden (*gopī*) he was ever in perpetual union with the Lord. And Kavirāja Gosvāmin pays highest tributes to the personality of Rāmānanda when he proclaims that Rāmānanda was not an ordinary human being, he was as if *Kṛṣṇa-bhakti* incarnate.

Rāmānanda Rāya kathā kahile na haya/
mānuṣya nahe Rāya, Kṛṣṇa-bhakti-rasamaya//

—*C.C.* III. 5.71

In another context in *Caitanya-Caritāmrta* II. 7.65 Kṛṣṇadāsa Kavirāja considers Rāmānanda to be the pinnacle of wisdom and loving devotion. In his words-

pāṇḍitya āra bhakti-rasa dunhera tenho sīmā/

Not only this, because of the extreme popularity of Caitanyaism, in latter years when Caitanya came to be identified with and regarded as an incarnation of Kṛṣṇa,[13] an incarnation of Rādhā[14] and also as the dual incarnation of both Kṛṣṇa and Rādhā[15] by his followers, Rāmānanda as a close associate of Caitanya was also looked upon as an embodiment of Visākhā,[16] the female companion of Rādhā by the Vaiṣṇava Gosvāmins of succeeding generations.

REFERENCES

1. De, S.K. *The Padyāvalī,* The Text, p.6. Notes on Authors, p.225.
2. Mahapatra, K.N., *A Descriptive Catalogue of Sanskrit Manuscripts of Orissa,* Vol.II, p.CXVI.
3. Devī, Saralā, *Rāya Rāmānanda* (Oriya), p.89.
4. Bhaktivedanta Svami, A.C., *Caitanya-Caritāmṛta II,* Madhya-līlā, Ch. 8, 194.
   cf. Devī Saralā, *op.cit.,* p.14.
5. *eta bali- āpana kṛta gīta eka gāhila/*
   preme prabhu svahaste tānra mukha acchādila//
   C.C. II. Madhyalīlā, Ch.8, 193.

6. Yasoraj Khan enjoyed the royal patronage under Hussain Shah, the then ruler of Bengal who ascended the throne in 1493 A.D. and died in 1518 A.D. Yasoraj turned to be a devotee of Caitanya when the latter permanently settled at Rādhākānta Matha at Puri.
7. Vide Devī, Saralā, *op.cit.* p. 158.
8. *Ibid.*, p. 155.
9. Misra, Pramila, *Rāya-Rāmānanda Padyāvalī,* bhūmikā, p. 4.
10. Of course *Daṇḍātmka-līlā* has not been separately published in *Rāya Rāmānanda Padyāvalī.* The songs showing similarity of theme with *Daṇḍa-velā* have been pushed back to the footnotes by the editor whereas the rest twenty nine songs appear in the Appendix of the anthology (songs 6-34).
11. Vide Misra, Pramila, *op.cit.,* bhūmikā, pp. 4-5.
12. It is the song thirty one as appearing in the Appendix of *Rāya Rāmānanda Padyāvalī,* p.101 edited by Smt. Pramila Misra, Directorate of Culture, Orissa, but chronologically it may not be the song thirty one of *Daṇḍātmaka-līlā.*
13. Vide Sarasvati, Prabodhananda, *Caitanya-Candrāmṛta*, I.1 See also De, S.K., *Early History of the Vaiṣṇava Faith and Movement in Bengal,* p. 435.
14. Vide *C.C.* II.8.279.
    Rādhikāra bhāba-kānti kari aṅgīkāra/
    nija rasa āsvādite kariyācha abatāra//
    See also De, S.K., *Early History of the Vaiṣṇava Faith and Movement in Bengal,* pp. 426-427.
15. Vide *C.C.* II.8.282.
    tabe hāsi tānre prabhu dekhāila svarūpa/
    rasa-rāja, mahā-bhāba-dui eka rūpa//
    See also De, S.K., *Early History of the Vaiṣṇava Faith and Movement in Bengal,* pp. 427, 435.
    Goswami, Bhakti Siddhanta Saraswati—*Rāi Rāmānanda* (English) p. 3.
16. Goswami, *Ibid.*

CHAPTER-IV

CHARACTERS IN THE PLAY

In Chapter I a detailed Act-wise summary of the *Jagannātha-vallabha-nāṭaka* has been given. Now we take up a discussion on the characters in the play. Except *Sūtradhāra* and his wife *Naṭī* altogether there are eight dramatic personages in this play. They are—Śrīkṛṣṇa, Ratikandala, Śrī Rādhā Madanikā, Vana-devatā (the sylvan deity), Śaśimukhī, Mādhavī and Aśokamañjarī. Of them the first two are male characters and the last six are female characters. Like each and every play having its appropriate hero and heroine, Lord Kṛṣṇa is the hero and Śrī Rādhā is the heroine of this play. Ratikandala plays the role of *Vidūṣaka* or conventional jester. Madanikā acts as the chief go-between. Though there is reference to Vana-devatā twice[1] in the play, her role cannot be exactly determined. Besides, the companions of Śrī Rādhā like Śaśimukhī, Mādhavī and Aśokamañjarī work together for the dramatic denounment.

ŚRĪKṚṢṆA

As has been already pointed out, Śrīkṛṣṇa is tne nero of the play. Dressed in yellow garments, carrying feathers of peacock on his head and *tilaka* mark on the forehead, having moon-like countenance and putting an ever new smile in the face, he looks most handsome and charming. With a flute in his hand, lustrous ear-ornaments hanging from the ears and with captivating side-long glances he is the centre of attraction for the cowherd-maidens. Endowed with thirty two auspicious marks his divine character as the Lord of gods seems to be firmly established.

First of all Śrīkṛṣṇa satisfies the general characteristics of a *nāyaka* or hero. The *Daśa-rūpaka* of 10th century A.D. defines the term *netā* (*nāyaka* so designated) as follows :

netā vinīto madhuras tyāgī dakṣa priyamvadaḥ/
raktalokaḥ śucir vāgmī rūḍha-vaṁśaḥ sthiro yuvā//
buddhy utsāha smṛti prajñā kalā-māna samanvitaḥ/
śūro dṛdhaśca tejasvī śāstracakṣuśca dhārmikaḥ//

—*D.R.* II.1-2.

The *Sāhitya-darpaṇa* a rhetorical text datable to first half of 15th century A.D. refers to the traits of *nāyaka* in the following verse-

tyāgi kṛtī kulīnaḥ suśrīko rūpa yauvan otsāhī/
dakṣo 'nuraktalokas tejo vaidagdhya śīlavān netā//

—S.D.III.30

To put in a nutshell, a *nāyaka* or hero has a number of qualities to his credit. He must be young, handsome, graceful, generous, prompt, valiant, amiable and well-born. Endowed with intelligence, energy and a sharp memory he is also supposed to be firm, modest, steadfast, righteous, skilled in arts and science and beloved of his people.

Coming to Śrīkṛṣṇa we notice that he is *tyāgī* (of sacrificing nature) when he goes forward to fight with the dreadful demon Ariṣṭa even at the cost of his life. His firmness *(dṛḍhatā)* is evinced when by raising aloft his bold and proud arms he gives the guarantee of safety to the cowherd village Vraja. He gives a clear proof of his gallantry and heroism *(vīratva)* by killing the mighty bull-demon who was, as it were, a menace to the three worlds. He is considered to be *kṛtī* (a man of successful achievement) not only by gaining victory over the so called demon, but also by winning the love of Śrī Rādhā in the final Act of the drama. His *kulīnatā* (high lineage) is well attested to by his birth in the glorious race of the Yadus. His handsomeness is evident from his physical splendour arising out of shining yellow garments and lustrous ear-ornaments. Śrīkṛṣṇa's eloquence (*vāgmitā)* is noticed in his very act of evading the love-offer of Śrī Rādhā in the first instance on the ground of *pātivratya* and *kula-dharma* (maintenance of chastity and family virtues). His righteousness (*dhārmikatā*) is noticed when he directs Śaśimukhī to advise Śrī Rādhā to desist from her improper passionate desire as it goes against the existing social order. Thus in the *Jagannātha-vallabha-nāṭaka* Śrīkṛṣṇa conforms to the common characteristics of a *nāyaka*.

All the texts on rhetorics starting with Bharata's *Nāṭya-śāstra* (200 B.C.) and ending with the *Sāhitya-darpaṇa* of Viśvanātha Kavirāja (1st half of 1500 A.D.) speak of four types of *nāyaka*—*dhīrodātta, dhīra-lalita, dhīra-śānta* or *dhīra-praśānta* and *dhīroddhata*.[2] Now let us consider as to in which category Śrī Kṛṣṇa is to be put.

At first sight Śrīkṛṣṇa seems to be care-free; he is light-hearted; his only business is to secure the love of Śrī Rādhā; he takes pleasure in decorating his body with sandal paste, garlands, beautiful garments and precious ornaments; moreover in the first Act of the play[3] his appreciation of the beauty of Vṛndāvana and his extreme fondness in playing the flute show him as a lover of art. Except it no seriousness is noticed in his character. According to the characteristics as laid down in the texts on rhetorics this is the conduct of a *dhīra-lalita nāyaka*.[4] A *dhīra-lalita nāyaka* acts as a gay thoughtless person bereft of any sense of responsibility. In the *Gīta-govinda* Śrīkṛṣṇa is portrayed as a *dhīra-lalita nāyaka*. It is evident from songs 3 and 4 of Canto I of the *Gīta-govinda* in which Śrīkṛṣṇa is depicted as engaged in amorous sports with different cowherd-maidens. In a distressed voice with a pensive look Śrī Rādhā consoles her female-messenger that she is not to be blamed if deceptive Kṛṣṇa does not keep his appointment; he wantonly delights in loving many women.[5] Since the *Jagannātha-vallabha-nāṭaka* deals with the same theme of the love-sports of Śrī Rādhā and Śrīkṛṣṇa and it concludes with the union of the hero and the heroine, Śrīkṛṣṇa deserves to be classed as a *dhīra-lalita nāyaka*. But in course of encountering the demon Ariṣṭa Śrīkṛṣṇa's chivalrous fight and heroic feats besides his firm determination of protecting Vraja and its residents[6] suggest his indomitable and invincible strength and prowess; this novel characteristic in the conduct of Śrīkṛṣṇa elevates him to the position of a *dhīrodātta nāyaka*. The *Bhāva-prakāśana* a rhetorical text of 1175-1250 A.D. clearly maintains that a *dhīrodātta nāyaka* must have the ambition of winning the battle *(udātto vijigīṣuḥ syāt...B.P.* IV.119).

However, *Daśa-rūpaka* (II.4b-5a) defines *dhīrodātta nāyaka* as follows :

> *mahāsattvo'tigambhīraḥ kṣamāvān avikatthanaḥ/*
> *sthiro nigūḍh āhaṅkāro dhīrodātto dṛḍhavrataḥ//*[7]

Śrīkṛṣṇa is a great valiant hero *(mahāsattva)* for it is he who mercilessly took away the life of the demon Ariṣṭa when from the forest Vṛndāvana he sportively kicked him off like a ball.[8] Śrīkṛṣṇa is highly serious and grave *(ati-gambhīra)* as he has never succumbed to the first love-offer of Śrī Rādhā. With a view to testing her stamina he has rejected her submission under the pretext of being a mere immature boy knowing little of love and dalliance.[9] Since the Lord is never boastful of his activities and achievements, he is rightly held to be *avikatthana;* but due to modesty his sense of pride is latent in him *(nigūḍhāhaṅkāra)*. He is also endowed with a spirit of tolerance *(kṣamāvān)*. Besides, he is firm, steadfast *(sthira)* and determined *(dṛḍhavrata)* as it has been explicit from his unwavering resolve and proud proclamation that by all means he would protect the residents of Vraja from the attack of Ariṣṭa. Thus in the *Jagannātha-vallabha-nāṭaka* Śrīkṛṣṇa conforms to all the features that a *dhīrodātta nāyaka* is supposed to possess.

No doubt the *Nāṭya-śāstra*. the *Daśa-rūpaka*, the *Nāṭaka-lakṣaṇa-ratnakośa, Bhāva-prakāśana,* and *Rasārṇava-sudhākara* etc., are important texts on rhetorics. And the *Sāhitya-darpaṇa* which covers all the aspects of poetics and dramaturgy happens to be the full-fledged latest text datable to the 1st half of 15th century A.D. Notwithstanding the impact of these rhetorical works on contemporary *kāvyas* and dramas, for doing justice to the character of Śrīkṛṣṇa it becomes necessary to refer to the *Nāṭaka-Candrikā* (a text on dramaturgy) written by Rūpa Gosvāmin of 16th century A.D. In this text Rūpa Gosvāmin speaks of three divisions of *nāyaka* as *divya, divyādivya* and *adivya* and he takes Śrīkṛṣṇa, Rāmacandra and Yudhiṣṭhira as representing the three different types respectively. But he concludes that it is Śrīkṛṣṇa who is the foremost of all these three different heroes *(eṣu Kṛṣṇo guṇādhikaḥ)*. The characteristics supposed to be present in all types of heroes as per the orthodox classification (*dhīrodātta dhīra-lalita* etc.) are present in him and in the drama dealing with love and amorous themes he deserves place to be a *nāyaka.*[10] In his other rhetorical text *Ujjvala-nīlamaṇi* Rūpa Gosvāmin expresses the same view as regards Śrīkṛṣṇa.[11]

The texts on rhetorics like *Nāṭya-śāstra, Daśa-rūpaka* etc., also speak of a further classification of *nāyaka* as *dakṣiṇa, anukūla, dhṛṣṭa* and *śaṭha.* It cannot be taken as a classification of *nāyaka* but this classification is based upon the attitude and behaviour of the lover towards his lady-love. In our *Jagannātha-vallabha-nāṭaka* Śrīkṛṣṇa is pictured as a monogamist, and he is attached to no other cowherd-maiden except Śrī Rādhā, so he is to be safely regarded as an *anukūla nāyaka.*[12]

Thus Śrīkṛṣṇa is a *dhīrodātta* and *anukūla nāyaka* in this play.

ŚRIRĀDHĀ

Śrī Rādhā plays the role of principal heroine *(nāyikā)* in the play. She is youthful and exquisitely beautiful. She is such a paragon of beauty that in the words of our dramatist "neither the lotus nor the moon can be compared to the face of this fawn-eyed lady. Except the lotus and the moon the creator has even created no other object to stand comparison with her sweet lovely charming countenance".[1]

In the play we notice that just at the sound of the flute of Śrīkṛṣṇa sporting in Vṛndāvana, Śrī Rādhā with all anxiety enters the pleasure-garden with her friends. Struck with love-sickness with elephant-like gait she is slow in her movement. As she and her companions steadily move towards the grove, she is delighted at the first sight of Śrīkṛṣṇa endowed with the beauty of a blue-lotus petal *(nīlotpala-dala-komalacchaviḥ*-I.43.). Smitten with love Śrī Rādhā becomes callous to everything all around; she does not look at the moon nor does she hear the sweet-note of the cuckoos; she avoids the company of her friends; away from public view she likes to remain in seclusion; and in course of conversation with others she continues to give meaningless replies; thus all the actions of Śrī Rādhā that follow are enough to indicate her amorous propensity. From her love-letter and from Śaśimukhī when Śrīkṛṣ ṇa learns that Śrī Rādhā is deeply inclined to him, pertinently thrice he questions on the status of Śrī Rādhā- (i) it does not behove Śrī Rādhā firm in the observance of domestic virtues and norms *(kulācalā)* to abandon her family glory and pride *(kula-sthiti)*.[2] (ii) She is an adherent of family norms and traditions *(kula-pālikā)*, so naturally her husband is very dear to her; it is improper and unwise to show her attachment otherwise.[3] (iii) For women of noble birth (*kula-vanitānām)* it is a heinous crime to have affairs with other people; is it not a matter of great surprise that she violates the code of conduct usually followed in family circles?[4] Now from this conversation of Śrīkṛṣṇa with Śaśimukhī it is evident that Śrī Rādhā is already married though the name of her husband has not been specified in our drama. Somebody else other than Śrīkṛṣṇa is her husband whom we do not know.

Coming to the texts on dramaturgy, we see that the rhetoricians speak of three types of *nāyikā* (heroine) *svā* or *svīyā anyā* or *parakīyā* and *sāmānyā* or *sādhāraṇā*.[5] It seems that they have perhaps made this division of heroines keeping in view the sex-relationship of man and woman. *Svīyā* is one's own wife, other man's wife is *parakīyā* whereas a common place woman or courtezan *(gaṇikā)* is called *sādhāraṇā*.

Parakīyā nāyikā is of two types—*uḍhā* or *paroḍhā,* and *kanyakā*.[6] In defining *paroḍhā* Singabhūpala author of *Rasārṇava-sudhākara* of 14th century A.D. says—she is called a *paroḍhā,* who, though already married, longs for sex enjoyment with another person.[7] Viśvanātha Kavirāja the author of *Sāhitya-darpaṇa* is of the same view and he holds that a *paroḍhā* or *anyoḍhā* addicted to wanderings is devoid of modesty; she violates the domestic norms and brings all dishonour to the family.[8] On the other hand, a young bashful girl or maiden who is still under the care and control of her parents is designated as *kanyā* or *kanyakā*.[9]

As per the rules of dramaturgy, Śrī Rādhā cannot be the principal heroine of this *nāṭaka*. As has been already discussed, she belongs to another person, and somebody else happens to be her husband. And in keeping with the age-long mythological tradition of our country, Śrīkṛṣṇa also has his own wives in the harem. Of course in this play he is attached to none except Śrī Rādhā. Now when Śrī Rādhā makes approaches to Śrīkṛṣṇa, as per aesthetic norms, it is considered to be tantamount to the approach of a *parakīyā* to an *upa-pati* (paramour). As the rhetoricians hold, a *svīyā* or husband's own wife deserves the role of a principal heroine in a play. A *paroḍhā* or other man's wife can only play the role of an *upa-nāyikā* or secondary heroine. They again maintain that if an *upa-pati* (paramour) and a *paroḍhā* come to play the role of the hero and the heroine in a *nāṭaka,* there cannot be full realization of the main sentiment *(pradhānarasa);* there will be *rasābhāsa* instead. Instead of free and fair union as in case of a husband and his own wife *(svīyā),* the *upa-pati* and *paroḍhā* would always plan for secret meetings far away from public view. Since the love between *upa-pati* and *paroḍhā* is beset with obstacles and they meet with many a hurdle in the way of their union, the main sentiment is not fully realised by the audience. Moreover, the display of *upa-pati's* amours with *upa-nāyikā* (secondary heroine) on the stage creates a bad impression on the audience. Particularly in the Sanskrit dramas rooted in Indian culture it is totally unethical and unwholesome. And that is why a *paroḍhā nāyikā* is hardly permitted to play a leading role in the *nāṭaka* depicting a principal sentiment. Hence an amour with *paroḍhā* is not allowed to form the subject of dominant sentiment in a drama.[10]

But it is Rūpa Gosvāmin who does not agree to this view of the traditional rhetoricians. In his *Nāṭaka-Candrikā* he is of opinion that the above principle of amour with *paroḍhā* which cannot be the main sentiment of a drama, is applicable only to common heroes and heroines, but not to Śrīkṛṣṇa or Śrī Rādhā who are beyond the pale of it.[11] Śrīkṛṣṇa is not ordinary hero nor even Śrī Rādhā an ordinary heroine. In his *Ujjvala-nīlamaṇi* in two separate Chapters (Chs.3 & 4) he discusses this point. On the authority of ancient religious texts he points out that in Dvārakā Śrīkṛṣṇa is said to have sixteen thousand one hundred and eight wives. Of them Rukmiṇī, Satyabhāmā and Jāmbavatī, etc., were prominent. Though all these wives happen to be *svīyā nāyikās* of Śrīkṛṣṇa, in the opinion of Rūpa Gosvāmin it is not improper to treat the maidens of Gokula attached to Śrīkṛṣṇa as also his *svīyā nāyikās*. The maidens of Gokula have chosen Śrīkṛṣṇa as their husband according to the *Gāndharva* rites. It is not something unusual. Therefore they deserve to be regarded as *svīyā nāyikās*. They are known as *parakīyā* only because of the unmanifest character of their marriage and the secrecy of their love in the *prakaṭa līlā* of Śrīkṛṣṇa.[12]

In support of his point of designating the cowherd-maidens as *svīyā-nāyikās* of Śrīkṛṣṇa Rūpa Gosvāmin quotes from *Śrīmad Bhāgavata* (X.33.38). The residents of Vraja were not jealous of Śrīkṛṣṇa for his engagement in love-sports with the cowherd-maidens. Each and every resident of Vraja enjoyed the company of his wife as they were deluded by the illusory power of Śrī Kṛṣṇa.[13] Thus the cowherd-maidens remained immaculate in character though they regularly participated in amorous sports (*rāsa-krīḍā*). Endowed with the sweetness of highest love (*mahā-prema-mādhurya*) they are even in a better position than *svīyā-nāyikās* like Rukmiṇī, Satyabhāmā, Jāmbavatī and others.[14] Of all the cowherd-maidens the eternal consort Śrī Rādhā is the most favourite beloved of Śrīkṛṣṇa. Rūpa Gosvāmin identifies her with *hlādinī-mahāśakti* of the magical and mystical philosophy of *Tantra*.[15]

Even though it is taken for granted that the love-sports of the cowherd-maidens (*paroḍhā*) with Śrīkṛṣṇa (*upa-pati*) cannot be depicted as the main sentiment as it leads to *rasābhāsa*, Rūpa Gosvāmin points out that the delineation of the love-sports of Śrīkṛṣṇa and the cowherd-maidens is the most excellent erotic sentiment.[16] According to him that is the highest type of love where there is secrecy of affairs, social obstruction and rare opportunity for union.[17]

It will not be out of place to refer here to the development of the concept of Śrī Rādhā who occupies such a prominent place in the drama of Rāya Rāmānanda. S.C. Mukherjee and B.S. Miller have vividly discussed the origin and development of the concept of Śrī Rādhā in their works.[18] Until the *Gīta-govinda* of Jayadeva (12th century A.D.) this concept had little developed. Even in the

Śrīmad Bhāgavata Purāṇa (Rāsapañcādhyāya X.29-33) which contains an account of the love-sports of Śrīkṛṣṇa and the *gopīs,* there is no clear reference to the name of Śrī Rādhā as the most beloved of Śrīkṛṣṇa. In the entire text only once do we come across a veiled reference to her name in the verse *-anayā-Rādhito* nūnaṁ bhagavān Harirīśvaraḥ (*Bhāg. P.* X.30.28), which literally means- 'Lord Hari (Śrīkṛṣṇa) has surely been adored by this maiden'. So the interpretation of this verse as done by the Vaiṣṇavites is doubtful.[19] Besides the Purāṇa-texts like *Padma* (VI. Uttarakhaṇḍa, Chs. 245-252), and *Brahma-Vaivartta* (Part II, Chs. 7-32, 52-55, 63-129) depicting the love of Śrī Rādhā and Śrī Kṛṣṇa in detail, are of late origin.

It seems that Jayadeva has not borrowed the idea of Śrī Rādhā from a single source, but he depends upon many stray verses and obscure references[20] as available to him from different texts to finally shape the figure of ŚrīRādha. And the findings of Miller appropriately lead her to remark that "Jayadeva had invented "Rādhā". Although he clearly did not invent her, he did create a unique heroine for Indian devotional literature".[21] After Jayadeva (1200 A.D.) and Nimbārka[22] (1350 A.D.) who made the worship of Śrī Rādhā most exclusive in his cult, it is needless to say that Śrī Rādhā comes to occupy the position of the highest type of devotee in the Vaiṣṇava doctrine; she becomes the central theme of the later *parakīyā* thought of the school. It is the Vaiṣṇavas particularly the Caitanyaites of 1600 A.D. who elevate her status and make her a symbol of human soul's passionate love for the Supreme Being, that is, Śrīkṛṣṇa. In the *Jaganātha-vallabha-nāṭaka* in course of depiciting the love episode of Śrī Rādhā and Śrīkṛṣṇa Rāmānanda has not failed to bring home to his readers this idea which may be clear from the following analysis of the drama.

In the Act I.36 just at the sound of the flute of Śrīkṛṣṇa, Śrī Rādhā abandons all her modesty and enters the pleasure garden. Here the sound of the flute represents the clarion call of the Supreme Being to the individual soul that Śrī Rādhā stands for. This concept is corrobarated in Act III. 5,[23] where Śrī Rādhā admits that in the sound of the flute she repeatedly listens to the voice of the supreme spirit resembling the chant of the sweet *Sāmaveda;* she starts meditating upon her association with Śrīkṛṣṇa endowed with the glow of the rising sun and the moon. In consonance with Vaiṣṇava philosophy, it is nothing more than human soul's irresistible temptation to be united with the supreme God Śrīkṛṣṇa. In the words of Kinsley, "Rādhā represents the human devotee who gives up everything in order to cling to the Lord, and Kṛṣṇa represents God, irresistibly beautiful and attractive. The aim of Kṛṣṇa devotees is to develop or uncover the Rādhā dimension within themselves, that tendency within all human beings to devote themselves entirely and passionately to Kṛṣṇa".[24]

The texts on dramaturgy[25] speak of eight conditions of a heroine depending upon her relation with a lover. Each class of heroine as discussed above-be she a *svīyā, parakīyā* or *sādhāraṇā* may undergo these eight states. Thus she may be *svādhīna-bhartṛkā* (absolute mistress), *vipralabdhā* (deceived) *khaṇḍitā* (enraged), *kalahāntaritā* (separated by quarrel), *virahotkanṭhitā* (distressed by lover's involuntary absence), *vāsaka-sajjā* (awaiting in full dress) *abhisārikā* (moving towards the lover) or *prosita-priyā* (when her lover is absent abroad).

In the Gīta-govinda Jayadeva has depicted seven such states of Śrī Rādhā in relation to her lover-hero Śrīkṛṣṇa. In this connection we may cite the remarks of Miller who holds that "Rādhā plays the classical heroine in seven of the eight stylized psychological states of relation to the hero *(nāyikāvasthā)* that are delineated by the theorists of Indian drama. Each of the states is identified in the text by Jayadeva with reference to its technical name or to its characteristic sign".[26] In the *Jagannātha-vallabha-nāṭaka* which has closely follwed the theme of *Gīta-govinda* and has, with slight variation, dramatised it, Rāmānanda gives the picture of four such conditions of Śrī Rādhā as *vāsaka-sajjā, vipralabdhā, abhisārikā* and *svādhīna-bhartrkā*. It will be evident from the discussions that follow.

First of all though the dramatist has not mentioned the term *vāsaka-sajjā* in his text, it cannot escape the attention of the reader so far as the description goes on in the last two verses of Act III.

Śrī Rādhā says to Madanikā that "the bower is humming with swarms of bees, the jasmine flowers and the bees are gently moving, the sun has touched the western mountain; the moon is about to rise,[27] and her body longs for the company (*sanga-sukham aṅgam api-JVN.*III.34). This statement suggests that Śrī Rādhā, ready in the so called naturally decorated bower, has been really waiting for the arrival of her lover. It refers to the *vāsakā-sajjā*[28] state of the heroine as laid down by the dramaturgists in their texts.

Even when the lover after sending a female messenger or fixing the appointment at a rendezvous does not turn up, the heroine is regarded as *vipralabdhā*[29] (deceived). In the Act IV. 35ff of the drama Śrī Rādhā is noticed to have put on befitting dress, and she is fully prepared to proceed to the rendezvous to get united with Śrīkṛṣṇa. For this she has passed through a good part of the dreadful forest though the path is everywhere covered with utter darkness, but Madanikā the chief go-between has not yet returned with the final message from Śrīkṛṣṇa. In this situation Śrī Rādhā feels upset and broken-hearted; in a pensive look she tells her companion Mādhavī that she is indeed deceived by them (*sahimāhavi; vippalambhīdahmi bhavadīhim* -Act IV. 36).

Then we meet with Śrī Rādhā as an *abhisārikā*; and the picure of *abhisārikā* Śrī Rādhā has been lively portrayed by the dramatist. In course of wading through the dark and dense forest so as to reach the rendezvous, Śrī Rādhā on the way meets Madanikā. Madanikā advises her to gratify Śrīkṛṣṇa in the bower of creepers. Accordingly along with Madanikā Śrī Rādhā advances towards the secret bower. As enjoined by the texts on dramaturgy, she is called an *abhisārikā* who, smitten with love, goes herself to meet the lover or compels the lover to come to her for the sake of dalliance.[30] At the instigation of Madanikā here Śrī Rādhā willingly proceeds to the bower to meet Śrīkṛṣṇa and that is why she is rightly called an *abhisārikā*.[31]

Morevoer Śrī Rādhā may be considered as a *svādhīna-bhartṛkā* after her union with Śrīkṛṣṇa in the last Act of the drama. A *svādhīna-bhartṛkā* is defined to be one who has her husband in subjection. That woman captivated by whose love and pleasing qualities the husband continues to remain by her side, blessed and gleeful is indeed a *svādhīna-bhartṛkā.*[32] Unlike the *Gīta-govinda* or other Purāṇa texts that describe the love-sports of Śrīkṛṣṇa with the cowherd-maidens, this drama speaks of Śrīkṛṣṇa as attached to nobody else but Śrī Rādhā. Only Śrī Rādhā enjoys Śrīkṛṣṇa's proximity; both the bodies become one having no difference in them (*militam idaṁ kila tanu-yugalaṁ punar api na kañcana bhedam*-Act V.24). In course of narrating their affairs to Śaśimukhī, Madanikā remarks that she considers the scene of full-fledged love-sports of Rādhā and Mādhava (Śrīkṛṣṇa) to be a marvel (*Rādhā-Mādhava-keli bharād aham adbhutam ākalayāmi* -Act. V.33ff). After killing the demon Ariṣṭa when Śrīkṛṣṇa tired and exhausted is resting beneath the *Vakula* tree, on the advice of Madanikā, Śrī Rādhā fans him with the hem of her garment and alleviates the pain and exertion of his body (Act V.57-58). It shows that it is Śrī Rādhā alone who enjoys the bliss of union with her lover, and there is none to rival her. The lover is readily at hand, he is under her full control. Being the only beloved of Śrīkṛṣṇa there is enough justification to regard her as *svādhīna-bhartṛkā* in the drama.

VIDŪṢAKA

The *Vidūṣaka* is a conventional character in Sanskrit dramas. He is a confidant and close friend of the hero. It is his primary duty just to produce laughter on the stage. He knows the knack as to how to create humour and make a situation free from tension. *Vidūṣaka's* tongue knows no restraint, and through his sheer irrelevant vulgar speech he makes himself an object of ridicule before the audience. He is also famous for his gluttony in Sanskrit dramas. He directs his sharp satire at every shortcoming and inconsistency, and thus makes fun of every character in the play. Vidūṣaka's love and regard for the hero is so high that he always stands by his side; and the hero takes him into his confidence in all matters. Either in weal or woe, adversity or prosperity he never deserts the hero; rather gladly he offers him his services as and when necessary. Though easily irritable, *Vidūṣaka* is easily appeased.

It is Bharata the author of *Nāṭya-śāstra* (200 B.C) who deals with the nature and characteristics of the *Vidūṣaka* in detail. *Vidūṣaka* is bald-headed, hunch-backed, tawny-eyed, double-tongued, mis shapen dwarf, having projecting teeth.[1] Endowed with wit and presence of mind he makes sweet charming interesting talk.[2] The very gait of *Vidūṣaka* produces laughter on the stage and it may be shown in three ways- (i) by physical deformity like bald-headedness, crippledness, misshapen face and having long protruding teeth, etc; (ii) by the use of unmeaningful irrelevant vulgar speech; and (iii) with unusual dress like rags, skin or by smearing the body with ink, ashes, etc. If he walks like a bird looking up and down with wide strides, it also becomes an object of laughter due to limbs.[3]

According to Bharata, corresponding to four classes of hero like *dhīroddhata, dhīra-lalita, dhīrodātta* and *dhīra-praśānta* there are four types of *Vidūṣaka e.g.*, (i) *Liṅgin* (ascetic), (ii) *Dvija* (Brahmin), (iii) *Rājajīvin* (royal employee) and (iv) *Śiṣya* (pupil) respectively. Gods and kings are respectively *dhīroddhata* and *dhīra-lalita* heroes. Ministers and commanders of royal army are said to be *dhīrodātta whereas Brahmins and merchants are regarded as* dhīrapraśānta. An ascetic acts as a *Vidūṣaka* for dhīroddhata, a Brahmin plays this role for *dhīra-lalita,* but a *dhīrodātta* hero takes a royal employee as his *Vidūṣaka* whereas a pupil is employed as *Vidūṣaka* by the *dhīra-praśānta* hero.[4]

The *Nāṭya-darpaṇa* of Rāmacandra and Guṇacandra a text of later half of 12th Century A.D. follows Bharata's *Nāṭyaśāstra* in toto in this connection; but it deviates from Bharata on one point that while Bharata allows a Brahmin for the king and a pupil for the merchant to do the job of *Vidūṣaka,* the *Naṭya-darpaṇa* allows all the three such as an ascetic, a Brahmin or a royal employee to play the role of *Vidūṣaka* for the king and the merchant.[5]

Like the *Nāṭya-śāstra* Ch. XXXV.71, the *Nāṭya-darpaṇa* gives an interesting etymological explanation of the word "Vidūṣaka". It says the *Vidūṣakas* are so called because they completely destroy (*viśeṣeṇa dūṣayanti, vināśayanti*) peace by conflicts and conflicts by peace in case of heroes in separation and cause the separation to be forgotten by affording pleasure (*vipralambhaṁ tu vinoda-dānena vismārayantīti Vidūṣakāḥ*).[6]

The definition of *Vidūṣaka* in the texts like *Daśa-rūpaka* 974-995 A.D.). Bhāva-prakāśana (1175-1250 A.D.) *Rasārṇava-sudhākara* (1330 A.D.) and *Sāhitya-darpaṇa* (1st half of 1500 A.D.) is very precise. According to them the *Vidūṣaka* is a person who produces laughter through his deformed physical appearance, dress and speech.[7] Taking delight in quarrels he is conscious of his own business i.e., eating.[8]

Coming to our text *Jagannātha-vallabha-nāṭaka* we notice that the Vidūṣaka is a close and reliable friend of Śrīkṛṣṇa the principal hero of the play. He works with all sincerity in order to unite the hero with the heroine. And he is a Brahmin by birth. Keith points out that "theorists offer no explanation of the anomaly of a Brahmin in such a curious position".[9] but it is obvious that in the existing Sanskrit dramas all dramatists engage a Brahmin for the queer job of *Vidūṣaka*. In the play the *Vidūṣaka* four times refers to his Brahminhood. In Act II.5, Act IV.5, 12 and 33 it is clear that he is a Brahmin by birth. Particularly in Act IV.12 we come across his distinct statement when he says-"ahme bāhmaṇā ujjuā phuḍaṁ jjevva bhaṇāma" (we Brahmins are straight forward; we speak clearly and distinctly).

Nomenclature is an important factor in Sanskrit dramas. Even though names do not carry any value in actual life, in olden times importance was attached to it and the name was given taking into consideration the caste, status and creed of the person concerned. So names were different in case of different characters in keeping with their nature and activities. And because of this, the texts on dramaturgy have specified the nomenclature of the characters in some measure. Texts like *Bhāva-prakāśana. Rasārṇava-sudhākara* and *Sāhitya-darpaṇa* have their specific nomenclature for the *Vidūṣaka*. The *Bhāva-prakāśana* (IX.87) suggests that a *Vidūṣaka* should have names such as Vātsyāyana, Śākalya, Maudgalya, Vasantaka or Gālava etc.[10] The *Rasārṇava-sudhākara* (III.329) says that names like Śrīvatsa, Gautama, Kautsa, Gārgya, Maudgalya, Vasantaka or Kāpileya are to be borne by a *Vidūṣaka,*[11] but *Sāhitya-darpaṇa* a latest text on rhetorics is of the view that the name of a *Vidūṣaka* should be connected with some flower or the spring.[12] In other words, a *Vidūṣaka* should assume name such as "Rasālaka" pertaining to a flower and "Mādhavya" pertaining to the spring season just as noticed in Kalidāsa's *Abhijñāna-śākuntalam.*[13] In our text *Jagannātha-vallabha-nāṭaka* only once we come across the peculiar name of *Vidūṣaka* as Ratikandala when Śrīkṛṣṇa after entering the Vṛndāvana forest addresses him as such and invites his attention to the enthralling beauty of the forest.[14]

The *Agni Purāṇa* maintains that *Pīṭhamarda, Viṭa* and *Vidūṣaka*—these three are called the *narma-sacivas* of the hero in achieving his end.[15] Of the three, *Vidūṣaka* is by nature fickle-minded and quarrelsome. Clever and prompt in action he is ever fond of food.[16] His love of food is a stale and stereotyped feature in any Sanskrit drama. As far as food is concerned, he is so greedy that he gets abundant pleasure in eating. In the Act I of *Jagannātha-vallabha-nāṭaka* when Śrīkṛṣṇa invites his attention to enjoy the beauty of the forest Vṛndāvana, he thinks of the dining hall where fine rice, sweet smelling ghee, sweetmeats and curds are available in plenty. In his wods, the forest Vṛndāvana may be enjoyable for his friend Śrīkṛṣṇa, but for him the enjoyable place is a dining hall where the choicest delicacies are available.[17]

Off and on *Vidūṣaka* speaks of food. In Act II.29ff Śaśimukhī hands over the love letter of Śrī Rādhā to Śrīkṛṣṇa. He reads aloud the letter and comes to know that Śrī Rādhā suffers from the torment of Cupid. Then instantly the *Vidūṣaka* advises Śaśimukhī to present two sweetmeats to Śrīkṛṣṇa; only then he would proceed to vanquish Cupid.[18]

For amusing the audience the *Vidūṣaka* ridicules and belittles everybody, but in the *Jagannātha-vallabha-nāṭaka* we notice him to be a man of learning. His knowledge of ancient scriptures is factual and laudable. In the drama *Vidūṣaka's* scriptural knowledge appears to be sound and flawless in connection with the description of the solar orb. In course of describing the sun at the mid-day the *Vidūṣaka* says that the sun seems to be rotating just as it continued to rotate when it was put to lathe by Viśvakarman.[19] In course of passing her days in the company of her lord the sun-god, Saṁjñā was very much tormented by the sharp piercing rays of her lord. Aware of it Viśvakarman the divine architect cut the sun-god to size; he placed him on his lathe and ground the sun-god in such a way that a very minor portion of the splendour remained. This reference to the legend of Viśvakarman putting the sun-god to his lathe for cutting him to size as narrated in the different texts[20] is a proof of the correct knowledge of the *Vidūṣaka*.

Unable to bear the torment of love Śrī Rādhā makes an approach to Śrīkṛṣṇa through Śaśimukhī; on some pretext or other Śrīkṛṣṇa rejects her love (Act II.34-35). Commenting on the desperate condition of Śrī Rādhā the *Vidūṣaka* through a beautiful comparison sings aloud a verse[21]-'Agitated by the schorching heat of the sun the female swan seeks shelter under the shade of the bunch of lotus-flowers, but shaken by the wind the bunch of lotus-flowers moves away, thus failing to provide rest under its shade. Here Śrī Rādhā smitten with love by Cupid is compared to the female-swan, and the shade of the lotus flowers is no other than Śrīkṛṣṇa who is supposed to alleviate her suffering.

Sāhitya-darpaṇa, the latest text on rhetorics very clearly maintains that in the affairs of love *Viṭa, Ceṭa* and *Vidūṣaka* etc., are the assistants of the hero. Devoted to the hero *(bhaktaḥ)*, they are skilful in jests and they remove the pride of angry ladies. Without showing any indifference they take keen interest in the purpose of the hero, so they are rightly said to be his sincere assistants.[22]

In keeping with this rule in our drama under discussion we see that *Vidūṣaka* Ratikandala is a sincere friend of Śrīkṛṣṇa, and honestly he tries his best for fulfilling his desire. In Act IV, overtaken by Cupid Śrīkṛṣṇa feels intensely dejected and depressed. He finds no hope of union with Śrī Rādhā. In Act II he has already turned down the request of *Vidūṣaka* who persuaded him to accept Śrī Rādhā.[23] In course of time a sense of frustration prevails over Śrīkṛṣṇa. Aware of this pitiable condition of Śrīkṛṣṇa *Vidūṣaka* takes up his cause and firmly resolves to come to his rescue. He apprises Madanikā of the intense suffering of his friend and requests her to fetch Śrī Rādhā all at once. But when Madanikā does not believe in his words, *Vidūṣaka* asserts that as a *nisṛṣṭārtha dūta*[24] he is prepared to approach Śrī Rādhā and fetch her to his friend. Madanikā keen to study the attitude of Śrīkṛṣṇa still questions him on the truth of the version of *Vidūṣaka*. When Śrīkṛṣṇa gives a nod in support of his friend, *Vidūṣaka* once again assures Madanikā that, being a Brahmin, he stands a surety[25] for it; and she need not be afraid of any kind of deception. In this way after effecting the union of his friend with Śrī Rādhā, of course in collaboration with Madanikā he departs from the scene.

In the texts on dramaturgy though there are certain rules as regards the dress and costumes a *Vidūṣaka* is supposed to put on, we do not get any such indication in our drama except the question of language. Bharata is of opinion that a *Vidūṣaka* is to converse in Prakrit language and that too in eastern Prakrit.[26] Other rhetoricians like Sāgaranandin and Viśvanātha Kavirāja follow this rule.[27] In keeping with this time-honoured tradition in our drama we notice that the *Vidūṣaka* is always found to be using Prakrit language in his conversation. Though a Brahmin by birth, perhaps the Prakrit language is preferred by the dramatist for making the caricature more lively and appealing to the audience.

Thus in the *Jagannātha-vallabha-nāṭaka* we notice that the *Vidūṣaka* points out the just or unjust acts of the hero. Without any fear he openly expresses the weakness of Śrīkṛṣṇa. When Śrīkṛṣṇa is intent upon suppressing his feelings of love for Śrī Rādhā, the *Vidūṣaka* discloses his inner feelings. On the face value though Śrīkṛṣṇa abuses *Vidūṣaka* for his careless and irrelevant talk, he appreciates his skill in the innermost recess of his heart. As a sincere friend the *Vidūṣaka* always stands by Śrīkṛṣṇa.

MADANIKĀ AND OTHER COMPANIONS OF ŚRĪRĀDHĀ

According to texts on dramaturgy the heroine of the play is supposed to have some bosom-friends and companions upon whose co-operation she depends for her union with the lover. On behalf of the heroine these friends and companions carry out her mission and materialise her plan. Just as the hero of a drama depends upon *dūtas* (messengers), a heroine resorts to *dūtīs* (female-messengers) for fulfilment of her desire.

Bharata the author of *Nāṭya-śāstra* (200 B.C.) describes the essential traits of a female-messenger in the following verses;

> *protsāhaneṣu kuśalā madhura-kathā dakṣiṇā ca kālajñā/*
> *lasahā saṁvṛta-mantrā dutītyebhir guṇaiḥ kāryā//*
> *tayā protsāhanaṁ kāryaṁ nānā-darśana-kāraṇam/*
> *yathokta-kathanaṁ-caiva tathā bhāva-pradarśanam//*
> *kula bhoga-dhanādhikyaṁ kāryaṁ caiva vikatthanam/*
> *dūtī nivedayet kāryam arthānāṁ caiva bhāṣaṇam//*
>
> —*N.S.* (K.S.S.) Ch. XXV.12-24.

A woman proficient in the art of encouragement, sweet in words, skillful *(dakṣiṇā),* acting (suitably) to the occasion, charming in behaviour and keeping the secrets should be engaged as a female-messenger. By mentioning various causes, communicating the exact words of the hero and describing his condition she should encourage the heroine. The female-messenger is supposed to make an exaggerated statement about the hero's birth, wealth and his capacity for intercourse. Besides she should freely relate the purpose of her visit.

After Bharata other rhetoricians like Rāmacandra and Guṇacandra the twin authors of *Nāṭya-darpaṇa* (1150-1170 A.D.) and Śāradātanaya the author of *Bhāva-prakāśana* (1175-1250 A.D.) speak of the attendants of the heroine and their attributes and activities[1] almost in the same manner as we meet with in *Nāṭya-śāstra* Ch. XXV.9-10.

In course of giving the list of female-messengers like *sakhī* (friend), *naṭī* (actress), *dāsī* (slave-girl) and *dhātreyī* (nurse), etc. *Sāhitya-darpaṇa* the latest text on rhetorics (1st half of 1500 A.D.) states that skill in arts, perseverance, devotion to the heroine, power of knowing the mind, sharp memory, sweetness, readiness to understand a joke *(narma-vijñāna)*, fluency of speech etc., are the essential qualifications of a female messenger.[2]

In the *Jagannātha-vallabha-nāṭaka* so far as the heroine Śrī Rādhā is concerned, we meet with her four close friends-Madanikā, Śaśimukhī, Mādhavī and Aśokamañjarī. Madanikā is the chief go-between in the love-affairs of Śrī Rādhā and Śrīkṛṣṇa. She is bent upon uniting the hero and the heroine. Śrī Rādhā falls in love with Śrīkṛṣṇa at first sight. In the Act II of the drama we notice that thereafter she suffers from the pangs of separation; in such a situation Madanikā sincerely takes up her cause and sends Śaśimukhī a female-messenger to Śrīkṛṣṇa with a love-letter of Śrī Rādhā. Madanikā also deputes another emissary named Mādhavī to Śrīkṛṣṇa with a portrait of Śrī Rādhā in order to captivate him. Not contented with this, she herself proceeds to the foot of the banyan tree (*Bhāṇḍīra-taru)* where she secretly listens to the conversation between Śrīkṛṣṇa and Śaśimukhī. On the other hand, excessively tormented by Cupid when Śrī Rādhā intensely longs for the company of Śrīkṛṣṇa as it becomes somewhat intolerable on her part, she requests her close friend Aśokamañjarī to prepare a bed of fresh lotus-leaves for a soothing touch.

In the estimation of Madanikā, Śaśimukhī is a *nisṛṣṭārthā dūtī*[3] and Madanikā is confident of her success in the undertaking, but unfortunately Śaśimukhī returns disappointed. Śrīkṛṣṇa advises her to desist from her efforts, but on the other hand, Mādhavī who had been to Śrīkṛṣṇa with a portrait of Śrī Rādhā returns with a hopeful message.[4] She demands a reward for her job. In the Act IV convinced of the genuine longings of Śrīkṛṣṇa for Śrī Rādhā Madanikā sends Śrī Rādhā to meet her lover in the rendezvous, and thus she plays the principal role of a mediator in the union of the hero and the heroine.

REFERENCES

ŚRĪKṚṢṆA

1. *JVN,* Act I.38ff; Act III.1.
2. *N.S.* Ch.34.17; *D.R.* II.3a;
   *N.D.*I. 6a; *N.L.R.* 39;
   *B.P.*IV.138; *S.D.* III.31.

3. *sakhe Ratikandala; paśya paśya rāmaṇīyakaṁ Vṛndāvanasya J.V.N.* I.25.
4. *niścinto dhīralalitaḥ kalāsaktaḥ sukhī mṛduḥ—D.R.* II.3
śṛngārī dhīralalitaḥ kalāsaktaḥ sukhī mṛduḥ - N.D. I.9a
saṇgit āntaḥpur āsakto yuddhādisvatinād ṛtaḥ/
amāty āyattasiddhiḥ syāt śṛṅgārī lalitaḥ smṛtaḥ// B.P. IV.117
niścinto mṛdur aniśaṁ kalāparo dhīralalitaḥ syāt/ S.D. III.34a
5. *nāyātaḥ sakhi nirdayo yadi śaṭhas tvam dūti kim dūyase/*
svacchandaṁ bahuvallabhaḥ sa ramate kim tatra te dūṣaṇam/
G.G. Canto VII, song XV.30.
6. *Kṛṣṇaḥ- (sāṭopam upasarpan) abhayaṁ ghoṣa nivāsinām (sagarva bāhum udyamya)/40*
dṛpyad dānava śīrṇa śaila valaya kṣauṇīmahālambane vairivyākule śakra śāntikamakha proddāmayūpe'pi ca/
asmin Kṛṣṇabhuje'pi jāgrati bhayaṁ nityaṁ tad ek āsrayān ghoṣasthān api saṁspṛśed...//41 J.V.N. Act. V.40-41.
7. The definition of *dhīrodātta nāyaka* as given in the *Daśarūpaka* (974-995A.D.) has been verbatim taken over by the author of *Bhāva-prakāśana* (1175-1250 A.D.); and a similar definition is noticed in the *Sāhitya-darpaṇa* of Viśvanātha (1st half of 15th century A.D.).
avikatthanaḥ kṣamāvān atigambhīro mahāsattvaḥ/
stheyān nigūḍhamāno dhīrodātto dṛḍhavrataḥ kathitaḥ//
S.D. III.32
8. *kṣiptvā kandukalīlayā tam adhunā Vṛndāvanād dūrato/*
hatv āriṣṭam ariṣṭam etad akarot śrīmān mukundo jagat//
*J.V.N.*V.46
9. *Kṛṣṇaḥ—(punar api patrikāṁ vācayitvā) sakhi ! samyg idaṁ nāvakalitam* × × × × *yadi ca kulācalay āpi kulasthitir anay āparihara-ṇīyā/ kim iti tadā mayi ratir ativikalā bāle kila karaṇīyā//J.V.N.*II.35.2
10. *svayaṁ prakaṭit aiśvaryo divyaḥ Kṛṣṇādir īritaḥ/*
divyo'pi naraceṣṭātvād divyādivyo Raghudvahaḥ//7//
adivyo Dharmaputrādir eṣu Kṛṣṇo guṇādhikaḥ/
nāyakānāṁ guṇāḥ sarve yatra sarvavidhāḥ smṛtāḥ//8//
lālity odāttayor atra vyaktyā śobhābharo'dhikaḥ/
ten aiṣa nāyako yuktaḥ śṛṅgār ottara nāṭake//9//
Nāṭaka-Candrikā, I.7-9.

11. *Ujjvala-nīlamaṇi*—Ch.I.5-10, 17-21.
12. *anukūla ekaniratah*—*S.D.* III.37

ŚRI RĀDHĀ

1. *yad api na kamalaṁ niśākaro vā*
   bhavati mukha-pratimo mṛgekṣaṇāyāḥ/
   racayati na taṭhāpi jātu tābhyām
   upamitir anya-pade padaṁ yad asya// *J.V.N.* I.46
2. *yadi ca kulācalayāpi kulasthitiranayā pariharaṇīya*
   J.V.N. II.35.2a
3. *dayito dayitastasyā bāleyaṁ kula-pālikā/*
   akāṇḍe kimasau mugdhe dhattām ācāra-viplavam//
   J.V.N. II.42
4. *kula-vanitānām idam ācaritam/*
   para-puruṣādhigame guru duritam//
   sā yadi na gaṇayati kula-caritram/
   kim iti vayaṁ kalayāma na citram// *J.V.N.* II.46.2, 3.
5. *svānyā sādhāraṇastrīti tadguṇā nāyikā tridhā*—*D.R.* II.15a
   svā'nyā sādhāraṇā ceti trividhā nāyikā matā—*B.P.* IV.135
   svakīyā parakīyā ca sāmānyā ceti sā tridhā—*R.S.* I.94
   atha nāyikā tribhedā svānyā sādhāraṇā strīti—*S.D.* III.56
6. *anya-strī kanyakoḍhā ca* -*D.R.* II.20
   uḍhā ca kanyakā ceti dvidhaivānyaṅganā bhavet—*B.P.* IV.137
   anyāpi dvividhā kanyā paroḍhā ceti bhedataḥ—*R.S.* I.106.
   parakīyā dvidhā proktā paroḍhā kanyakā tathā—*S.D.* III.66a
7. *paroḍhā tu pareṇoḍhā pyanya-sambhoga-lālasā/R.S.* I.109
8. *yātrādi-nirat ānyoḍhā kulaṭā galita-trapā/* *S.D.* III.66b
9. *tatra kanyātv anuḍhā syāt salajjā pitṛ-pālitā*—*R.S.* I.107a
   kanyā tvajātopayāmā salajjā nava-yauvanā—*S.D.* III.67a
10. *nānyoḍhāṅgirase kvacit*—*D.R.* II.20
    Cf. Keith, A.B., *Sanskrit Drama,* p.308.
11. *yat paroḍhopapatyośca gauṇatvaṁ kathitaṁ budhaiḥ/*
    tattu Kṛṣṇaśca gopīśca vineti pratipāditam// N.C.V.10
    Cf. *laghutvam atra yat proktaṁ tattu prākṛtanāyake/*
    na Kṛṣṇe rasaniryāsa svādārtham avatāriṇi// *U.N.* I.18
12. *tāsu śrī yaduvīrasya sahasrāṇy asya ṣoḍaśa/*
    aṣṭo ttara śat āgrāṇi Dvāravatyāṁ suviśrutāḥ//6//

tatṛ āpi Rukmiṇī Satyā Jāmbavaty arkanandinī/
Śaibyā Bhadrā ca Kauśalyā Mādrī tyaṣṭau gaṇāgrimāḥ//8//
yāśca gokulakanyāsu patibhāvaratā Harau/
tāsām tad vṛtti niṣṭhatvān na svīyātvam asāmpratam//13//
gāndharva rītyā svīkārāt svīyātvam iha vastutaḥ/
avyaktatvād vivāhasya suṣṭhu pracchannakāmatā//15//
U.N. Ch.III

13. *nāsūyan khalu Kṛṣṇāya mohitās tasya māyayā/*
manyamānāḥ svapārśvasthān svān svān dārān Vrajaukasaḥ//
Bhāg. P. X.33.38
14. *etāḥ sarvātiśāyinyaḥ śobhā-sādguṇya-vaibhavaiḥ/*
Ramādibhyo' pyuru prema-mādhurya-bharabhūṣitāḥ//
U.N. III.38
15. *hlādinī yā mahāśaktiḥ sarva-śakti-varīyasī/*
tatsāra-bhāva-rūpeyamiti tantre pratiṣṭhitā//
U.N. IV.6
16. *atr aiva paramotkarṣaḥ śṛṅgārasya pratiṣṭhitaḥ/*
U.N. I.17
17. *bahu vāryate khalu yatra pracchanna-kāmukatvañca/*
yā ca mitho durlabhatā sā paramā manmathasya ratiḥ//
U.N. I.17
18. Mukherjee, S.C. *A Study of Vaiṣṇavism in Ancient and Medieval Bengal,* Appendix-A, pp.183-192.
Miller, B.S., *The Gīta-govinda of Jayadeva,* Introduction, 5 Rādhā: Consort of Kṛṣṇa's Spring time passion, pp.26-37.
19. For details vide Mukherjee, S.C., *op.cit.,* Appendix-A, pp.189-191.
20. See Miller, B.S., *op.cit.,* Introduction, 5 Rādhā, p.29ff.
21. *Ibid.,* p.37.
22. Mukherjee, S.C., *op.cit.,* Appendix-A, p.183.
23. *śrāvaṁ śrāvaṁ susāma śruti samita parabrahma vaṁśī prasūtaṁ darśaṁ darśaṁ trilokī vara taruṇa kalā keli lāvaṇya sāram/*
dhyāyaṁ dhyāyaṁ samudyad dyumaṇi kumudinī bandhurociḥ sarociscchāyaṁ śrīkānta saṅgaṁ...
—*J.V.N.* Act. III.5
24. Kinsley, David, *Hindu Goddesses,* Ch.6, "Rādhā", p. 82.

25. N.S. (C.S.S.) XXIV.210-219, *D.R.* II.23-27, *B.P.* IV.158-167 *R.S.* I.121-150; *N.L.R.* 336-342, *S.D.* III.72-86.
26. Miller, B.S., *op. cit.*, 5, Rādhā, pp.36-37.
27. *nikuñjo' yam guñjan madhukara-kadamb ākulataraḥ*
    prayātaḥ prāyo' yam carama-giri-śṛṅgaṁ dina-maṇiḥ/
    marun mandaṁ mandaṁ taralayati mallī-madhukarān
    kim anyad vaktavyaṁ vidhur api vidhātā samudayam//
    J.V.N. III.33
28. *ucite vāsake yā tu rati-sambhoga-lālasā/*
    maṇḍanaṁ kurute hṛṣṭā sāvai vāsaka-sajjitā//
    N.S. (C.S.S.) XXIV.212
    Cf. *kurute maṇḍanaṁ yasyāḥ sajjite vāsaveśmani/*
    sā tu vāsaka-sajjāsyād vidita-priya-saṅgamā//
    S.D. III.85
29. *yasyā dūtīm priyaḥ preṣya dattā saṅketam eva vā/*
    nāgataḥ kāraṇen eha vipralabdhā tu sā bhavet//
    N.S. (C.S.S.) XXIV.217.
    Cf. *samayaṁ cāpi saṅketaṁ dattvā preṣya ca dūtikām/*
    anāgatas ced vyāsaṅgād vipralabdhā tu sā smṛtā// B.P. IV.160
    priyaḥ kṛtvāpi saṅketaṁ yasyā nāyāti saṁnidhim/
    vipralabdhā tu sā jñeyā nitāntam avamānitā//
    *S.D.*III.83
30. *hitvā lajjān tu yā śliṣṭā madena madanena ca/*
    abhisārayate kāntaṁ sā bhaved abhisārikā//
    N.S. (C.S.S.) XXIV.219
    Cf. *rūpa-yauvana-sampannā* × × × ×
    uddīpyamāna pañceṣu pañcabāṇavraṇārditā/
    yā'bhisārayate kāntaṁ sā bhaved abhisārikā//
    B.P. IV.167
    abhisārayate kāntaṁ yā manmatha-vaśaṁvadā/
    svayaṁ vābhi saraty eṣā dhīrair ukt ābhisārikā//
    S.D. III.76
31. Rūpa Gosvāmin makes a two-fold division of *abhisārikā: Jyautsnī* and *Tāmasi*. *Jyautsni abhisārikā* proceeds to meet her lover even in the moon-lit night whereas it is *Tāmasī abhisārikā* who prefers making advances during thick darkness.

yābhisārayate kāntam svayaṁ vābhisaraty api/
sā jyautsnī tāmasī yāna-yogyaveṣābhisārikā//
U.N. *nāyikābheda,* 68

32. *Surat ātirasair baddho yasyāḥ pārśve tu nāyakaḥ/*
sāndr āmoda-guṇa-prāptā bhavet svādhīna-bhartṛkā//
N.S. (C.S.S.) XXIV.214

Cf. *āsann āyattaramaṇā hṛṣṭā svādhīnabhartṛkā/ D.R.* II.24
yasyā rati rasāsvāda mudito dayitaḥ sadā/
sad aivāste tayā sākaṁ esā svādhīnabhartṛkā// B.P. IV.162
yasyāś citrarati kriḍālālasaḥ pārśve tiṣṭhati patiḥ sā svādhīnabhartṛkā—N.L.R. 338
kānto ratiguṇ ākṛṣṭo na jahāti yad antikam/
vicitra-vibhram āsaktā sā syāt svādhīna-bhartṛkā//
S.D. III.74

VIDŪṢAKA

1. *vāmano danturaḥ kubjo dvi-jihvo vikṛtānanaḥ/*
khalatiḥ piṅgalākṣaśca sa vidheyo vidūṣakaḥ//
N.S. (K.S.S.) Ch. XXXV.57

2. *prakṛty utpanna-pratibho narmakṛtā narma-garbha-nirbhedyaḥ/*
yas tu vibhūṣita-vacano vidūṣako nāma vijñeyaḥ//
N.S. (K.S.S.) Ch. XXXV.71

3. *vidūṣakasy āpi gatir hāsya traya samanvitā/*
aṅga-vākya-kṛtaṁ hāsyaṁ hāsyaṁ nepathyajaṁ tathā//
danturaḥ khalatiḥ kubjaḥ khañjaś ca vikṛtānanaḥ/
ya īdṛśaḥ praveśaḥ syād aṅgahāsyaṁ tu tad bhavet//
yada tu khagavat gacched ullokita vilokitaiḥ/
atyāyatapadatvācca aṅgahāsyo bhavet sa tu//
vākya-hāsyaṁ tu vijñeyam asambaddha-prabhāṣaṇāt/
anarthakair bahuvidhais tathā c aślīla bhāṣitaiḥ//
cīra-carma-maṣī-bhasma-gairikādyais tu maṇḍitaḥ/
yas tādṛśo bhaved viprā hāsyo nepathyajas tu saḥ//
N.S. (K.S.S.) Ch. XIII.136-140

4. *atra catvāra eva syur nāyakāḥ parikīrtitāḥ/*
madhyam ottama-prakṛtau nānālakṣaṇa-lakṣitāḥ//16//
dhīroddhatā dhīra-lalitā dhīrodāttāstathaiva ca/
dhīrapraśāntakāścaiva nāyakāḥ parikīrtitāḥ//17//

devā dhīroddhatā jñeyāḥ syur dhīra-lalitā nṛpāḥ/
senāpatiramātyaśca dhīrodāttau prakīrtitau//18//
dhīrapraśāntā vijñeyā brāhmaṇā vaṇijastathā/
eteṣāṁ tu punar jñeyās catvārastu vidūṣakāḥ//19//
liṅgi dvijo rājajīvī śiṣyaśceti yathā-kramam/
deva-kṣitibhṛt āmātya brāhmaṇānāṁ prayojayet//20//

N.S. (G.O.S.) Ch. XXIV.16-20

5. *N.D.* IV. 168.
See also Trivedi, K.H.—*The Nāṭya-darpaṇa of Rāmacandra and Guṇacandra-A Critical Study,* p.187.
6. *N.D.* IV.168.
7. *hāsyakṛt ca vidūṣakaḥ—D.R.* II.9.
vikṛtāṅga vaco veśair hāsyakṛt syād vidūṣakaḥ/
B.P. IV.128
vikṛtāṅga vaco veśair hāsyakāri vidūṣakaḥ—R.S. I.92
8. ....*karma vapur veṣabhāṣādyaiḥ/*
hāsyakaraḥ kalaharatir vidūṣakaḥ syāt sva-karmajñaḥ//
9. Keith, A.B., *The Sanskrit Drama,* p. 311.
10. *Vātsyāyanaśca Śākalyo Maudgalyaśca Vasantakaḥ/*
Gālavaścetyevam ādināmānaḥ syur vidūṣakāḥ//
B.P. IX.87
11. *Śrīvatso Gautamaḥ Kautso Gārgyo Maudgalya ityapi/*
Vasantakaḥ Kāpileya ityākhyeyo vidūṣakāḥ// R.S. III.329
12. *kusuma-vasantādyabhidhaḥ... ..../*
syāt sva-karmajñaḥ// S.D. III.42
13. Sastri, K.M., *Sāhitya-darpaṇa* with Lakṣmī Commentary, Footnotes on *Vidūṣaka,* pp.103-104.
14. *Kṛṣṇaḥ—sakhe Ratikandala! paśya paśya rāmaṇīyakaṁ Vṛndāvanasya . J.V.N.* Act I.25
15. *pīṭhamardo viṭaś caiva vidūṣaka iti trayaḥ/*
sṛṅgāre narma-sacivā nāyakasy ānunāyakāḥ//
Agni Purāṇa, Ch. 339.39
16. *svabhāva-capalo netuḥ priyāyāḥ kalaha-priyaḥ/*
dakṣiṇaḥ kāryavic caiva sarvadā bhojana-priyaḥ//
B.P. IX.90
17. *bho vaassa! tujjha edaṁ Vundāaṇaṁ ramanijjaṁ mama uṇa*

bhoaṇālao jjeva jattha kahimpi siharinī kahimpi rasālā kahimpi surahi ghioṁ kahimpi sālibhaoṁ.

J.V.N. Act I.27

18. *bho di! ahmaṇaṁ piava, assassa hatthe laḍḍua-jualaṁ tue dādavvaṁ. piavaassa tattha gadua maaṇaṁ nirākarissadi*

J.V.N. Act II.32

19. *ārovia cakkabhamiṁ bhamido jaha vissakammaṇā sūro/ ajjavi taha sakkāra bhamidaṁ raimaṇḍalaṁ takkemi//*

J.V.N. Act I.50

20. *R.V.* X.17.1-2; *A.V.*-18.1.53, 18.2.33; *Bṛhad-devatā* Ch. 6.33-7.1-7; *Nirukta*-XII.10-11; *Viṣṇu P*.III.2.2-12; *Vāyu P*. II.22.32-86; *Bd.P.* II.59.33-86; *H.V.* 8.1-40; *Br. P.* 6.1-54; *Bhav.P.* I.79. 17b-83; *S.P.*V. *Umā-Saṁhitā* 35.1-42; *Mārk.P.*—Chs. 77-78, Chs. 106-108.

21. *raiara-calidā haṁsī maggai chāaṁ kamala gucchassa/ mārua-dhuaara-āttā pekkhasi jaṁ taṁ niāredi//*

J.V.N. Act II.37

22. *śṛṅgāre' sya sahayā viṭa-ceṭa-vidūṣakādyāḥ syuḥ/ bhaktā narmasu nipuṇāḥ kupita-vadhūmāna-bhañjanāḥ śuddhāḥ//*

S.D. Ch. III.40

23. *(karṇe) bho vaassa! tuhmehiṁ pi sā siviṇe vāra sahassaṁ diṭṭhā. ehniṁ kīsa atthijjanto appā atthāvijjadi?*

J.V.N. Act II.43

24. A *nisṛṣṭārtha dūta* is a type of messenger who having understood the mind of both the sides, gives his witty and considered reply in a given situation and performs his assignment well and neatly.

25. *Vidūṣakaḥ—bhodi ujjue! saccakaṁ jjevva edaṁ, ettha ahaṁ jjevva paḍibhū bahmaṇo* *J.V.N.* Act IV.33.

26. *prācyā vidūṣakādīnām...* *N.S.* (K.S.S.) Ch. XVIII.38

27. *śaurasenīm atha prācyām avantīṁ karhi cit paṭhet// etam eva vaṇik śreṣṭhibālakāśca vidūṣakāḥ/* *N.L.R.* 246b-247a *prācyā viduṣakādīnāṁ...* *S.D.* Ch. VI.161

MADANIKĀ AND OTHER COMPANIONS OF ŚRĪ RĀDHĀ

1. *N.D.* IV (Viveka), 191ff.
   B.P. IV (Adhikāra) 130-134.
2. *kalā-kauśalam utsāho bhaktiś cittajñatā smṛtiḥ/*
   mādhuryaṁ narma-vijñānaṁ vāgmitā ceti tad-guṇāḥ//
   S.D. Ch. III.129b-130a
3. Vastyāyana (400 A.D.) the author of *Kāmasūtra* refers to eight types of female messengers. In defining *nisṛṣṭārthā dūtī* the first type of female-messenger he says—nāyakasya *nāyikāyāśca yathā-maniṣitam artham upalabhya sva-buddhyā kārya-sampādinī nisṛṣṭārthā (Kāmasūtra* V.4.46). In contrast to *parimitārthā dūtī* (female-messenger of measured speech) or *patrahārī dūtī* (a mere conveyer of message) a *nisṛṣṭārthā dūtī* is one who, having understood the mentality of both the hero and the heroine through her intelligence tackles the situation cleverly and performs the undertaking well and neatly.
4. *mā śaṅkiṣṭhāḥ sumukhi vimukhi-bhāvam etasya, na syād ānandāya prathama-mukulā padminī kasya. kāmam/*
   āghrāya aiva praśithila-dhṛtir gandham asyās tathāpi nālambeta kṣaṇam api yuvā kiṁ nu madhyastha-bhāvam//
   J.V.N. Act III.27

CHAPTER-V

JAGANNĀTHA-VALLABHA-NĀṬAKA —A CRITICAL ESTIMATE

In our introduction (vide supra p.1) we have pointed out that out of some hundred twenty eight imitations of Javadeva's *Gīta-govinda*, the *Jagannātha-vallabha-nāṭaka* of Rāya Rāmānanda is possibly the first imitation in dramatic form based on the same Kṛṣṇa theme. What Jayadeva delineated in a lyrical poem, is presented here in the form of a drama.

Like every other Sanskrit play the *Jagannātha-vallabha-nāṭaka* begins with a nāndī (benediction) and a *prastāvaṇā* (prologue). According to the rules of Sanskrit dramaturgy a *nāndī* is required to be performed in order to avert evil and obstacles.[1] The very purpose behind it is to enable a dramatic performance come to a successful close so that during the performance neither the actors nor the spectators meet with any obstacles or impediments. We Indians always believe in divine blessing and protection; without divine blessing and protection no activity would be successful. So nāndī is a benediction or an invocation of blessings[2] at the beginning of a literary or dramatic performance. To offer salutations to the divinity and seek his blessings for the success of the undertaking is an integral part of *nāndī*. Besides invoking some blessings from some divinity, a *nāndī* as the definition demands, should be suggestive of the main theme or the main idea of the plot.[3] It should also include a reference to the moon, the conch, the lotus and the water-lilies etc., because these are auspicious objects.[4]

The *nāndī* of our *Jagannātha-vallabha-nāṭaka* comprises three verses, the first two being in *pṛthvī* metre and the third one in *śārdūlavikrīḍita* metre. Consisting of four lines each the verses are followed by a musical song sung with Rāga 'Naṭa'. The alluring dance of Śrīkṛṣṇa is described in the first verse. By speaking of the delusion arising in the side-long glances of the cowherd-maidens *(gopāṅganā-dṛgañcala-bhavo bhramaḥ)* at the sight of Śrīkṛṣṇa the second verse hints at the plot and the characters of the drama. With allusions to the moon (*sita-dyutiḥ*), the lotus (*ambhoruham*) in the second verse and the white water-lily (*kairava*), the *cakravāka* bird (*koka*) and the moon in the guise of the face of Śrīkṛṣṇa, the slayer of Madhu (*Madhuripor vaktrāpadeśaḥ śaśī*) in the third verse, the auspiciousness is not only brought in, but also the principle of dramaturgy seems to have been honoured by the play-wright. In the musical song that follows, under the pretext of Śrīkṛṣṇa having amorous sports with the cowhered-maidens (*manasija-keli-nanditamānasaṁ...indusundara-vallavī-mukhalālasam*) there is a veiled reference to the eternal love-sports of the supreme soul with the individual soul.

Nāndī is followed by *āmukha* or *prastāvanā* (prologue). The *prastāvanā* is a short preface to the dramatic events that follow subsequently. As held by Bhat, "the present *prastāvanā* of a Sanskrit drama is a heritage from Bharata's pūrvaraṅga, adapted with necessary variation and modification by the dramatists themselves".[5] It consists of a striking conversation which the *Sūtradhāra* or stage-manager holds with his wife (*Naṭī*) or *Vidūṣaka* or *Pāripārśvaka*[6] on some pertinent matter which, to some extent, is suggestive of the plot of the play. It introduces the author and the play by giving their names and other details, creates interest of the spectators, invites their attention and ultimately introduces the play proper.

The prologue of the *Jagannātha-vallabha-nāṭaka* is found to be quite up to the mark in every respect. It gives us not only the name of the play and the play-wright, but also reliable information about the latter's father, his patron and their accomplishments. In course of the conversation between *Sūtradhāra* and *Naṭī* reference is made to a tired intoxicated bee, which in the vernal evening collects honey from every lotus and eventually falls asleep inside the lotus-filament[7] thereby indirectly hinting at *parakīyā-prīti* of Śrīkṛṣṇa and leading to the beginning of the drama proper. We thus notice that the prologue consisting of a lucid conversation rouses the interest, captivates the attention of the spectators and introduces to them the author and his play.

Brevity is another good point to be noted about the prologue of this play. It is nautral that the spectators would be impatient if a play-wright, forgetting the limits of a prologue, introduces in it any impertinent and irrelevant matter and makes it unnecessarily lengthy. It is, in fact, the duty of every play-wright to see that his prologue is short and precise. Happily enough, our play-wright Rāmānanda shows his sense of propriety by avoiding in his prologue the introduction of any such matter and thus making it short and sweet.

According to the authors on dramaturgy *prastāvanā* is of five different types. It is often very difficult to say of which to these five varieties a particular *prastāvanā* really belongs. The *prastāvanā* of our play may be classified as *prayogātiśaya* type since by the application of one topic here another topic is introduced and the entry of dramatic person is thereby effected.[8] The song of *Naṭī* refers to the fatigued and intoxicated bee which falls asleep inside the lotus-filament; it reminds the *Sūtradhāra* of the yellow-garbed Śrīkṛṣṇa who drinks the nectar from the lips of cowherd-maidens and takes rest on the bosom of a grown-up maiden, her breasts serving the purpose of a pillow.[9] And immediately after this we notice Śrīkṛṣṇa appearing on the stage. It may also be taken as *avalagita* variety because through the setting of one thing another thing has been performed.[10]

Sanskrit works[11] on dramaturgy speak of five types of *sandhi*. The *sandhis* are the divisions of the main plot and they are said to be *mukha, pratimukha, garbha, vimarśa*[12] and *nirvahaṇa*[13] in a drama. Though the *Daśarūpaka* of Dhanañjaya (Circa 974-995 A.D.) propounds the *yathāsaṁkhya* theory and maintains that five *arthaprakṛtis* namely *bīja, bindu, patākā*, etc., together with five *avasthās* like *ārambha, prayatna, praptyāśā* and so on serially give rise to five *sandhis*,[14] T.G. Mainkar in his work *Sanskrit*

Theory of Drama and Dramaturgy (The theory of *saṁdhis* and *saṁdhyaṅgas* in Bharata's *Nāṭya-śastra*) has thoroughly discussed this problem and has rightly shown that "Bharata has not said anything as regards the interrelation of either *sandhis* on one hand and the constituents of the plot (*arthaprakṛtis*) or the stages of action (*avasthās*) on the other" (p.14). The learned critic points out the lacunae in the *yathāsaṁkhya* theory and holds that such a correlation cannot work invariably in all cases.[15] Continuing his discussion on the same problem Prof. Bhat opines that of the five constituents of plot (*arthaprakṛti*) it is the first *arthaprakṛti* 'bīja' and the last *arthaprakṛti* 'kārya' that coincide with the first stage of action and the last stage of action respectively, but the remaining three *arthaprakṛtis* namely *bindu, patākā* and *prakarī* cannot be serially connected with the respective stages of action.[16] However, the rhetoricians uphold the validity of the concept of *sandhi* in the construction of the dramatic plot. And in a full-fledged play the five *avasthās* can be easily ascertained.

Coming to out Jagannātha-vallabha-nāṭaka we see that the five *sandhis* namely *mukha, pratimukha, garbha, vimarśa* and *nirvahaṇa* are present in this play. In the first Act the *mukhasandhi* (protasis) begins when Śrī Rādhā attracted by the physical charm and beauty of Śrīkṛṣṇa asks Madanikā—*ajje maaṇie : ko eso nīluppala-dala komala chai kaṇaa ṇiara sariccha vasaṇo īsia alambia kandharaṁ mahura mahuraṁ venuṁ vādei*—I.43. Similarly in Act I.46 Śrīkṛṣṇa is attracted to see the charming figure of Śrī Rādhā. So both Śrī Rādhā and Śrīkṛṣṇa chance to meet in the *Vṛndāvana* forest and fall in love with each other at first sight. Thus their mutual longing for each other is the *bīja* (seed) that is sown and their ardent desire for achieving the end marks the *ārambha* (the first stage of action) in the *mukhasandhi*.[17] The *mukhasandhi* continues to Act II.14-15 where both Aśokamañjarī and Madanikā discuss the love of Śrī Rādhā.[18]

The *pratimukha sandhi* (epitasis) is that in which the first cause or seed laid in the *mukhasandhi* has sprouted but not in a very perceptible manner.[19] In the second Act aware of Śrī Rādhā's love-lorn condition Madanikā deputes Śaśimukhi to Śrīkṛṣṇa with a love-letter in her hand, but with the motive of testing Śrī Rādhā's depth of love Śrīkṛṣṇa refuses to entertain it. The *pratimukha-sandhi* starts from Act II. 16ff, when Madanikā clarifies before Aśokamañjarī that she infers Śrī Rādhā's love-sickness from her aversion to the moon, the sweet-note of cuckoos and from her meaningless reply to the companions.[20] *Vidhuta* being a subdivision (*sandhyanga*) of *pratimukha* is present here in the sense that Śrī Rādhā's offer of love is outright turned down by Śrīkṛṣṇa under some pretext. *Vidhuta* means the rejection of a request in the first instance.[21] The *pratimukha-sandhi* continues up to Act III.9 when advised by Śaśimukhi to divert her mind from the thoughts of Śrīkṛṣṇa with tears in her eyes Śrī Rādhā pines for remedy, for Śrīkṛṣṇa neither understands love nor the pangs of separation in love.[22] Thus there is some development of the plot after the seed is sown in the first Act, and this development is partially perceptible and partially imperceptible. So far as the stage of dramatic action is concerned, the second Act represents the *prayatna-avasthā*[23] as urged by her eagerness of achieving the principal object i.e., Śrī Rādhā's union with Śrīkṛṣṇa, Madanikā sends Śaśimukhi to Śrīkṛṣṇa with Śrī Rādhā's love-letter depicting her love-lorn condition.

At the very outset of the third Act though Śrī Rādhā is disappointed at the refusal of her love by Śrīkṛṣṇa, Madanikā advises her to have patience. In fact she had sent Mādhavī to Śrīkṛṣṇa as an emissary with a portrait of Śrī Rādhā; and Mādhavī had succeeded in her mission. The message that Śrīkṛṣṇa sent through Mādhavī[24] creates a ray of hope in Śrī Rādhā. Madanikā is confident of their union. On the other hand, Śrī Rādhā is diffident as Śrīkṛṣṇa is at a distance. The *garbha sandhi* (catastasis) continues from Act III.10 till the end of the Act. Here the aim of the drama is centralised, the seed (*bīja*) undergoes visible development.[25] Though fraustrated at the refusal of love by Śrīkṛṣṇa, the companions of Śrī Rādhā do not give up their hope, but renew their struggle for achieving the goal. Out of the five *avasthās,* this Act contains third avasthā-prāptyāśā as we see here the possibility of achieving the desired end notwithstanding the presence of some obstacles.[26]

In keeping with the rules of dramaturgy, the fourth *sandhi vimarśa* represents that part of the plot where the means of gaining the end is developed more than that in the *garbha*, but is impeded by some serious obstacle like curse etc.[27] The word *vimarśa* is constituted of prefix 'vi' and *'mṛṣ'* meaning to think. It is so called because here the hero of the plot thinks, reflects or even doubts the attainment of fruit though it is near at hand. Thus there is still a cause of despair. From the beginning of the fourth Act of the *Jagannātha-vallabha-nāṭaka* we find *vimarśa sandhi* where Śrīkṛṣṇa is seen to be repenting for refusing the love of Śrī Rādhā[28] and he is in a state of doubt and suspicion as regards his final union with the heroine. He seeks the help of Madanikā; and Madanikā shoulders the entire responsibility of uniting the heroine with him. Though the final union is fast approaching, Śrīkṛṣṇa is still doubtful of the arrival of Śrī Rādhā[29] just because she is somewhat delayed in her presence in the rendezvous. So far as the stage of action is concerned, it corresponds to the fourth stage *niyatāpti* because with the removal of obstacles the spontaneous cooperation of Madanikā leads to the definite goal.[30]

Finally the *nirvahaṇa sandhi* (catastrophe) begins after the presence of Śrī Rādhā in the rendezvous in the last part of the fourth Act.[31] According to the definition, when the topics relating to the seed scattered in the first four *sandhis* are unified in one, leading to the last nemesis, that part of the drama is called nirvahaṇa.[32] In other words, it is the dramatic denoument which the drama ultimately aims at. After the arrival of Śrī Rādhā in the pleasure—aparment formed of the bower of creepers *(nikuñja-kelisadana)*, there is the long-cherished union of the loving pair. The fifth Act gives a vivid picture of the different phases of amorous sports of both Śrī Rādhā and Śrīkṛṣṇa beginning with verse 17. At this stage the play-wright also indroduces *adbhuta rasa* after the final engagement of the hero and the heroine. In keeping with the rules of dramaturgy, the presentation of *adbhuta rasa*[33] is indispensable in the *nirvahaṇa sandhi*. In the last part of the fifth Act when the drama is heading to its final end, the sudden unexpected appearance of the demon Ariṣṭa with horns and hoofs, and with eyes looking like the flame of a meteor, creates a sense of wonder *(vismaya)*[34] in the audience and presents *adbhuta rasa* on the stage.[35] Finally, after slaying the demon, Śrīkṛṣṇa is permanently rewarded with his union with Śrī Rādhā. Of the five *avasthās* in the fifth Act we notice *phala-yoga* the last stage of action as the fruit or ultimate object is completely achieved.[36]

As regards the Bharaṭavākya (epilogue) it may be said that there is no mention of valedictory verse in the *Nāṭya-śastra* of Bharata and the term in only noticed is the Sanskrit dramas. The learned critic Prof. Bhat in his article "A perspective on nāndī" has vividly discussed all the aspects of the problem and has rightly shown that "in the process of evolution and change, the original *nāndī* of Bharata bifurcated into a benediction and a valediction".[37] He observes that "Salutation to deities, prayer for divine protection and general observance of religious worship were the ideas expressed in the opening benedictory verse called the *nāndī*; and the ideas about the happy rule of the king, prosperity of religion and nation, and the general well-being and happiness of the people found expression in the valedictory verse, which came to be called the Bharatavākya".[38] For instance, most of the plays of Bhāsa a dramatist of second century A.D. end with a concluding verse expressing the pious hope that Rājasiṁha (the lion-like king) may continue to rule over the vast expanse of this whole earth.[39] In keeping with this age-long dramatic practice, our author closes his play with a verse of four lines in *śārdūla-vikrīḍita* metre (Act V.62).

Now let us discuss a pertinent question as to which category of *rūpaka* the *Jagannātha-vallabha-nāṭaka* consisting of five Acts does belong. In the prologue of this drama the author calls it a *saṅgīta-nāṭaka*[40] which means a musical drama. Kṛṣṇadāsa Kavirāja in his *Caitanya-Caritāmṛta* II.2.77 mentions—*Rāyer nāṭakagīti* thereby obviously referring to the *Jagannātha-vallabha-nāṭaka* and its songs which greatly delighted Caitanya. At the direction of Gajapati Pratāparudradeva the patron of the author, the drama seems to have been composed and staged[41] in the early part of the 16th century A D.

About this drama S.K.De maintains that "is is a pretty little amourette, modelled obviously on the Nāṭikā type of Sanskrit plays",[42] but his view need not be mistaken to mean that the drama under review is a *nāṭikā*. According to the definition of the dramaturgical texts, a *nāṭikā* the first division of *Upa-rūpaka* is based upon an imaginary plot; consisting of four Acts it has abundance of female characters and a *dhīra-lalita* as its hero. Śṛṅgāra being the prominent sentiment it is dominated with music and songs.[43] In the *Jagannātha-vallabha-nāṭaka* multiplicity of female characters, dominance of music and songs and the presence of *śṛṅgāra* as the prominent sentiment go in favour of designating it as a *nāṭikā*. On the other hand Śrīkṛṣṇa the hero of the play is of *dhīrodātta* type (vide supra pp. 33-34) the drama comprises five Acts, and its main sentiment is *śṛṅgāra* supported by other subordinate sentiments. Finally in the words of the author it is a *nāṭaka (iti śrī Rāmānanda-Rāya-viracitaṁ śrī Jagannātha-vallabha-nāma nāṭakaṁ samāptam)*.

The rhetorician Viśvanātha (1st half of the 15th century A.D.) who precedes Rāmānanda (early part of the 16th century A.D.) nearly by a century, has taken up the definition of *nāṭaka* in his *Sāhitya-darpaṇa*. In a *nāṭaka* the first division of *rūpaka,* the theme should be a well-known one borrowed either from history or from ancient story or mythology or some folklore; the plot should contain five successive *sandhis*; it must display a variety of sentiments having Acts from five to ten; the hero—a *dhīrodātta* type must be valiant *(pratāpavān)* and majestic and must hail from a well-reputed family; the righteous hero adhering to the path of truth and justice may be either a divine or semi-divine or human figure; out of the nine sentiments *(rasa)* either *śṛṅgāra* or *vīra* will occupy the predominant position and other sentiments will be subservient to the principal sentiment; in the concluding part of the *nāṭaka* i.e., in the last *nirvahaṇa sandhi* the *adbhuta rasa* (sentiment of astonishment) will be inserted.[44] In the *Jagannātha-vallabha-nāṭaka* the theme is mythological; the hero Śrīkṛṣṇa is a divine figure; *śṛṅgāra* is the predominant sentiment attended by all other subordinate sentiments; and it has not only five Acts, but also five *sandhis* as referred to above. Besides, the *adbhuta rasa* is present in the last *nirvahaṇa sandhi* of this play. In the cowherd village Vraja there suddenly appears the demon Ariṣṭa who produces a thundering sound; and Śrīkṛṣṇa forcefully encounters him which excites awe and wonder in the audience. Since this drama fulfills all the necessary conditions of a *nāṭaka* as laid down in the rhetorical texts[45] we can safely say that it is a *nāṭaka* and there should be no further controversy on it.

Besides, the drama *Jagannātha-vallabha-nāṭaka* was originally planned on the model of the *Gīta-govinda*. There is the least doubt that the author was very much influenced by the lyrical charm of the *Gīta-govinda*. Desirous of presenting the traditional theme of *Kṛṣṇa-līlā* in a dramatic form, he perhaps liked to introduce songs, set to different tunes after the manner of the *Gīta-govinda*. And that is why twenty one musical songs have been made use of in this drama, there being four in each Act, excepting five in Act V. Of the twenty one musical songs only two songs are sung with 'Sāmagujjarī Rāga' and the rest nineteen songs resort to other individual Rāgas like 'Naṭa', 'Kedāra', 'Vasanta', 'Goṇḍakirī', etc. And it is needless to say that the association of songs and music has essentially turned this drama into a *saṅgīta-nāṭaka* or musical drama though there is no such classification or division of *rūpaka* in the extant dramaturgical texts. We support the view of Professor De when he observes that "perhaps the play was meant as a musical and spectacular entertainment, its characteristic feature being the introduction of Padāvalīs or songs, set to different tunes.... It invests the play with a delightful operatic atmosphere and... justifies the description that it is essentially a small *Saṁgīta-nāṭaka*"[46] So we do not rule out the playwright's own view when he himself designates his creation as a *saṅgīta-nāṭaka*.

Next we pass on to the point as to why the author has named his play as *Jagannātha-vallabha-nāṭaka*. As the theme of the play relates to *Kṛṣṇa-līlā* or the love-sports of Śrīkṛṣṇa and Śrī Rādhā, instead of various other names why the play-wright particularly prefers this title or why he has a fascination for it.

To this question we would like to submit that since Rāmānanda was a staunch follower of Vaiṣṇavism, probably he has seen no difference between Jagannātha and Śrīkṛṣṇa. To him the two divinities are one and the same; and at the time of composition of this drama before the advent of Caitanya to Puri (1510 A.D.), Jagannātha was regarded as Śrīkṛṣṇa in the holy land of Śrīkṣetra. As pointed out by Rajaguru after Anantavarman Coḍagaṅgadeva conquered Utkal in 1112 A.D., with a view to satisfying the followers of three famous cults namely Śaiva, Śākta and Vaiṣṇava, the renowned king introduced the worship of trinity in the temple of Śrī Puruṣottama. From an inscription of the Nṛsiṁha temple located in the premises of present Jagannātha temple it is known that Anantavarman Coḍavaṅgadeva was not only a great warrior, but also he was well-versed in Vedic lore, religious scriptures, Sanskrit language and literature. In his royal court there was much dispute among the adherents of three different faiths like Viṣṇuism, Śivaism and Śaktism. And the learned king in order to solve this problem seems to have installed three images representing the divinities of the three cults.[47]

Śaṅkara's philosophy of absolute monism came to be in vogue most possibly from 9th century A.D. Rāmānuja's advent in 11th century A.D. made qualified monism popular in South India. Because of contradiction in these two schools, most of the followers of Vaiṣṇavism got inclined towards the doctrine of Nimbārka (1350 A.D.). In those days the followers of Nimbārka were in the habit of worshipping Śrīpuruṣottama in the form of cow-herd Kṛṣṇa. Due to the dominance of Viṣṇuite cult, Śrīpuruṣottama was not only viewed as Kṛṣṇa, but also he came to be adored through 18-syllabled *mantra klim Kṛṣṇāya Govindāya Gopījana-vallabhāya svāhā* and 12-syllabled Vāsudeva *mantra Om namo bhagavate Vāsudevāya*. Even the image of Bālakṛṣṇa (Kṛṣṇa as a boy) has been installed at the foot of *Kalpavaṭa* (the wish-fulfilling banyan tree) in the very premises of the main Puri temple and the devotees are supposed to pay, first of all, a visit to this image before they start circumambulating the holy shrine. In 12th century A.D. Jayadeva's *Gīta-govinda* depicting the love-sports of Śrī Rādhā and Śrīkṛṣṇa overwhelmed the public mind and led the great king Anantavarman Coḍagaṅgadeva introduce the daily recitation of its songs before the image of Śrīpuruṣottama through the *deva-dāsīs*. And there came a time when the followers of Vallabhācārya (1479 A.D.) who used to adore Rādhā-Kṛṣṇa, came to regard the divine couple as "Jagannātha".[48] It is exactly in keeping with this tradition that when Caitanya came to Puri in 1510 A.D., he took Jagannātha as no other than Kṛṣṇa and danced before the Lord in a state of ecstatic frenzy thinking himself to be his dear spouse Rādhā.[49]

As already discussed, the three images which Anantavarman Coḍagaṅgadeva had installed just to satisfy the followers of three different cults, were known as Śrīpuruṣottama, Śrīsaṅkarṣaṇa and Goddess Subhadrā. The name "Jagannātha" had not come into popular use till the end of 12th century A.D. All the contemporary records like inscriptions, copper plates and some Sanskrit texts refer to the name "Puruṣottama" only; but in 1300 A.D. "Puruṣottama" came to assume the popular name "Jagannātha". First of all, we come across the term "Jagannātha" in the inscription of Śrī Kūrmeśvara temple datable to 1230 A.D.[50] Truly speaking, during the reign of Anaṅgabhīmadeva III (1211-1238 A.D.) the name of Śrī Puruṣottama had changed to Śrī Jagannātha.[51] And it is needless to say that since that time this name has been popularly accepted by the people in place of the earlier name "Śrī Puruṣottama".

After the removal of the white plaster from the outer walls of the Puri temple, a number of sculptures depicting the childhood pranks of Kṛṣṇa now come to the notice of the visitors. These sculptures include cow-herd Kṛṣṇa holding a flute in *tribhaṅga* pose, lifting the Govardhana hill, killing the demon Dhenuka, his love-sports with the cow-herd maidens and his journey to Mathurā in the company of Balarāma etc. The Gaṅga rulers got these sculptures carved out through professionals and had fitted them in the body of the temple. On the strength of these proofs, Rajaguru[52] believes that the earlier four-armed image of Śrī Puruṣottama which was installed by Coḍagaṅgadeva, came to be looked upon by the followers of Nimbārka and Vallabhācārya as Bāla Kṛṣṇa (Kṛṣṇa as a boy). The Bālakṛṣṇa assumed the name "Jagannātha" from 1230 onwards and his worship continues as such till to date. So passing through a long period of history the name "Jagannātha" has become popular.

At the time of composition of the *Jagannātha-vallabha-nāṭaka* in the early part of 1600 A.D., this tradition was prevalent at Śrīkṣetra and Lord Jagannātha was considered as non-different from Kṛṣṇa. Aware of this tradition, Rāmānanda seems to have a predilection for this name—"Jagannātha" and that is why he has named his play as *Jagannātha-vallabha-nāṭaka* meaning thereby the drama dear to Śrī Jagannātha alias Kṛṣṇa.

REFERENCES

1. *tathāpyavaśyaṁ karttavyā nāndī vighnopaśāntaye*
   - *S.D.* VI. 23b
2. *āśīr vacanasaṁyuktā stutir yasmāt prayujyate ... ... tasmāt nāndīti saṁjñitā—S.D.* VI.24
3. *āśīr namaskriyārūpaḥ ślokaḥ kāvyārtha-sūcakaḥ nāndīti kathyate*—Quoted by commentators and attributed to Mātṛgupta.
   Cf. *raṅgaṁ prasādya madhuraiḥ ślokaiḥ kāvyārtha-sūcakaiḥ D.R.* III.4
4. *māṅgalya-śaṅkha-candrābja-koka-kairava-śaṁsinī/padair yuktā dvādaśabhir astābhir vā padairuta//* S.D. VI. 25
5. Bhat, G.K.—*Sanskrit Drama: Problems and Perspectives*—Section V. Ch. 22, A Perspective on Nāndī, p. 298.
6. *naṭī vidūṣako vāpi pāripārśvaka eva vā/*
   sūtradhāreṇa sahitāḥ saṁlāpaṁ yatra kurvate//
   citra-vākyaiḥ sva-kāryotthaiḥ prastutākṣepibhi mithaḥ/
   āmukhaṁ tat tu vijñeyaṁ nāmnā prastāvanāpi sā//
   S.D. VI. 31-32
7. *pratikamala-madhūni-pānamatto dvirephaḥ/*
   svapiti kamala-koṣe niścalāṅgaḥ pradoṣe// J.V.N. Act. 20
8. *yadi prayoga ekasmin prayogo'nyaḥ prayujyate/*
   tena pātra-praveśaś cet prayogātiśayas tadā// S.D. VI.36

Cf. *eṣo'yamityupakṣepāt sūtradhāra-prayogataḥ/ pātrapraveśo yatraiṣa prayogātiśayo mataḥ//* D.R. III. 11

9. *yato gopāṅganā-śatādhara-madhupānanirbhara-keliklam āl asā-paghanaḥ kvacit prauḍha-vadhūs tanopadhānīya- maṇḍita-hṛdayaparyyṅka-śāyī pītāmbaro nārāyaṇaḥ smāritaḥ/*
J.V.N. Act I. 20

10. *yatraikatra samāveśāt kāryam anyat prasādhyate/ prayoge khalu taj jñeyaṁ nāmn āvagatitaṁ budhaiḥ//*
S.D. VI. 38

11. *N.S.* (K.S.S.) XXI. 37-43, *D.R.* I. 24 ff, *S.D.* VI. 75-81a.

12. In the *D.R.* it is named as *avamarśa.*

13. In both *D.R.* and *S.D.* this *sandhi* is called *upasaṁhṛti.*

14. *arthaprakṛtayaḥ pañca pañcāvasthā-samanvitaḥ/ yathāsaṁkhyena jāyante mukhādyāḥ pañca sandhayaḥ//*
D.R. I.22

This is to say—

1) *Bīja* and *ārambha* are united to form the *mukha.*
2) *Bindu* and *prayatna* are united to form the *pratimukha.*
3) *Patākā* and *praptyāśā* are united to form *garbha.*
4) *Prakarī* and *niyatāpti* are united to form *vimarśa* or *avamarśa.*
5) *Kārya* and *phalāgama* are united to form *nirvahaṇa* or *upasaṁhṛti.*

15. For details see Mainkar, T.G.—*Sanskrit Theory of Drama and Dramaturgy,* Ch. I, pp. 4-15.

16. Vide Bhat, G.K.—*Sanskrit Drama: Problems and Perspectives* Section V, Ch.24, pp.337-339.

17. *yatra bījasamutpattir nānārtha-rasa-sambhavā/ prārambheṇa samāyuktā tanmukhaṁ parikīrtitam//*
S.D. VI.76b-77a

18. Aśokamañjarī—*adha kadhaṁ tāe lajjātaralāe hiaaṁ tue ṇṇādaṁ?*
Madanikā—*vatse : tāvadeva trapāvarmma bālānāṁ hṛdaye sthiram/*
yāvad viṣamabāṇasya na patanti śilīmukhāḥ//
J.V.N. Act. II. 14-15

19. *phala-pradhānopāyasya mukhasandhi-niveśinaḥ/*
lakṣyālakṣya ivodbhedo yatra pratimukhaṁ ca tat//
S.D. VI. 77b-78a
20. *śaśini nayanapāto nādarād unmadānāṁ*
rutam anu ca pikānāṁ karṇarodhaś chalena/
prativacanam apārthaṁ yat sakhīnāṁ kathāsu
smara-vilasitam asyās tena kiñcit pratītam// J.V.N. II.16
21. *kṛtasyānunayasyādau vidhutaṁ tvaparigrahaḥ// S.D.* VI.90
22. *premacchedarujo' vagacchati Harir nāyaṁ na ca prema vā/*
J.V.N. III.9
23. *prayatnastu phalāvāptau vyāpāro 'titvarānvitaḥ/ S.D.* VI. 72a
24. *mā saṅkiṣṭhāḥ sumukhi vimukhibhāvam etasya, na*
syādānandāya prathama-mukulā padminī kasya kāmam
aghrāyaiva praśithiladhṛtir gandham asyās tathāpi
nālambeta kṣaṇam api yuvā kiṁ nu madhyasthabhāvam?
J.V.N. Act III.27
25. *phala-pradhānopāyasya prāg udbhinnasya kiñcana/*
garbho yatra samud-bhedo hrāsānveṣaṇavānmuhuḥ//
S.D. VI. 78b-79a
Cf. *ud bhedas tasya bījasya prāptiraprāpti eva vā/*
puṇas cānveṣaṇaṁ yatra sa garbha iti saṁjñitaḥ//
N.S. (K.S.S.) XXI. 41
26. *upāyāpāya śaṅkābhyāṁ prātyāśā prāptisambhavaḥ/*
D.R. I. 21a, *S.D.* VI. 72b
27. *yatra mukhyaphalopāya udbhinno garbhato'dhikaḥ/*
śāpādyaiḥ sāntarāyaśca sa vimarśa iti smṛtaḥ//
S.D. VI. 79b-80a
28. *sā ced utpala-locanā sahacarī vaktrena me nirbharaṁ*
premāṇaṁ prakaṭī-cakāra tad ayaṁ hāso mayā kalpitaḥ/
hā hā śukti-dhiyā mahā-maṇir abhūt tyakto mayā daivato
yāyāllocanagocaraṁ punar iyaṁ punyairagaṇair mama//
J.V.N. IV.3
29. *kim eṣā matvā mām aparicitabhāvaṁ vimukhatāṁ*
prayātā, viśyāsaṁ kimu sahacarī vāci na gatā?/
atha bhrāntā vartmany atitimirabhājīha vipine
na śaktā tanv aṅgī smaraśarahatā vā pracalitum// J.V.N. IV.45
30. *apāyābhāvataḥ prāptir niyatāptis tu niścitā/ S.D.* VI.73a
Cf. *apāyābhāvataḥ prāptir niyatāptiḥ suniścitā/ D.R.* 21

31. *Govindasya nikuñja-keli-sadane bhūṣābhavad Rādhikā/*
J.V.N. IV.50
32. *bījavanto mukhādyarthā viprakirṇā yathāyatham/*
ekārtham upanīyante yatra nirvahaṇaṁ hi tat//
D.R. 48b-49a, *S.D.* 80b-81a
33. *nirvahaṇe kartavyo nityaṁ hi raso'dbhutas tajjñiḥ/*
N.S. (K.S.S.) XX.47b
kuryān nirvahaṇe'dbhutam—D.R. III.34
kāryo nirvahaṇe'dbhutaḥ—S.D. VI.10b
34. Wonder or surprise is the permanent mood of *adbhuta rasa.*
35. *śṛṅgābhyāñca khurāñcalena ca balād eṣa kṣmām ullikhan*
kalpānta stanayitnu-garjita ghanadhvānair diśo dārayan/
ulkārcciḥ—pratimallam akṣiyugalaṁ krodhād iv āndolayan-
eṣa vyāpadi majjayan Vrajam abhūd daivād Ariṣṭo'grataḥ//
J.V.N. V.39
36. *samagra-phala-sampattiḥ phala-yoga yathoditaḥ—D.R.* 21ff.
sā' vasthā phalayogaḥ syād yaḥ samagra-phalodayaḥ
- *S.D.* VI.73b
37. *Bhat, G.K.—Sanskrit Drama: Problems and Perspectives,* p.302.
38. *Ibid.* pp.302-303.
39. *imām api mahīm kṛtsnāṁ Rāja-siṁhaḥ praśāstu naḥ/*
40. ....*Śrī Jagannātha-vallabha nāma gajapati Pratāparudrapriyaṁ Rāmānanda—saṅgīta-nāṭakaṁ nirmāya samarpitam abhineṣyāmi/ J.V.N.*I.17
41. ....*kālāgni-rudreṇa śrīmat Pratāparudreṇa*...
*kam api prabandham abhinetum ādiṣṭo'smi/ J.V.N.*I.13
42. *De, S.K.—Early History of Vaiṣṇava Faith and Movement in Bengal,* pp.578-579.
43. *N.S.* (K.S.S.) XX.62-63, *D.R.* III.43-48; *S.D.* VI.269-272.
44. *nāṭakaṁ khyāta-vṛttaṁ syāt pañca-sandhi samanvitam/*
vilāsarddhy ādi guṇavad yuktaṁ nānā-vibhūtibhiḥ//
sukha-duḥkha-samudbhūti nānārasa nirantaram/
pañcādikā daśaparās tatrāṅkaḥ parikīrttitāḥ//
prakhyātavaṁśo rājarṣir dhīrodāttaḥ pratāpavān/
divyo'tha divyādivyo vā guṇavān nāyako mataḥ//

eka eva bhaved aṅgī śṛṅgāro vīra eva vā/
aṅgam anye rasāḥ sarve kāryo nirvahaṇe'd bhutaḥ//

S.D. VI.7-10

45. Vide *N.S.* (K.S.S.) Ch.XX.10-28, 40-48; *D.R.* III.22-38; *S.D.* VI.7-11.
46. De, S.K. *op.cit.*, pp.579-580.
47. Rajaguru, S.N.—"Śrīmandirara śilpakalāre Vaiṣṇava saṁskṛti" (Oriya) *Srimandir,* June 1995, pp.16-17.
48. Rajaguru, S.N. *op.cit., Srimandir,* p.19.
49. *Ibid.*
50. Rajaguru, S.N.—*Inscriptions of Orissa,* Vol.V, Part I, No. 58, pp.98-99;
    Dash, K.C. "Puruṣottama O Jagannātha" (Oriya) *Srimandir,* p.13.
51. Dash, K.C., *Ibid.*
52. Rajaguru, S.N., *op.cit.* (Oriya), *Srimandir,* June 1995, p. 19.

CHAPTER-VI

RĀYA RĀMĀNANDA AS A DRAMATIST

The *Jagannātha-vallabha-nāṭaka* of Rāya Rāmānanda is a small drama. It depicts the traditional stereotyped theme of the love-sports of Śrī Rādhā and Śrīkṛṣṇa in five Acts. In the preceding Chapter it has been discussed that even though small in size, it fulfills the necessary conditions of a *nāṭaka* as laid down in the works on dramaturgy.

As we know, Śrīkṛṣṇa occupies a prominent place in Sanskrit literature of both ancient and medieval times. In the great Epic *Mahābhārata* he is portrayed as a great hero, a skilful statesman and as a *karma-yogin*. After the Epic age the vast anonymous Purāṇa literature continues to keep the tradition of the Mahābhārata alive. The Purāṇas sing aloud the glory and greatness of Śrīkṛṣṇa in a very lucid and charming style. Of them the *Harivaṁśa* (II. Viṣṇu Parvan, Ch.48ff) the *Viṣṇu* (Part V), the *Brahma* (Chs.182-211), the *Padma* (VI. Uttara-khaṇḍa, Chs. 245-252), the *Brahma-vaivartta* (part II. Chs.7-32, 52-55, 63-129) and the *Bhāgavata* deal with the life and heroic feats of Śrīkṛṣṇa, but in contrast to all other Purāṇas the theme presented in the *Bhāgavata Purāṇa* enjoys utmost popularity because of the delineation of the erotic sports with the fervour of devotion *(bhakti)*. And that is why most of the classical Sanskrit poets who compose *kāvyas* on Kṛṣṇa legend prefer to be more close to the theme of the *Bhāgavata Purāṇa* than that of any other Purāṇa.

During the classical period the Śiśupālavadha of Māgha is the first *mahākāvya* to deal with the theme of Śrīkṛṣṇa. Consisting of 20 cantos this *mahākāvya* datable to 700 A.D. depicts the heroic exploits of Śrīkṛṣṇa in a very ornate pedantic style. Then in the 12th century A.D. there comes the *Gīta-govinda* the mellifluous lyrical poem of Jayadeva that describes the various love-sports and amorous dalliances of Śrīkṛṣṇa and his spouse Śrī Rādhā. For its lyrical charm and sweet melody this *Gīta-govinda* exercises a tremendous influence on the later poets and play-wrights. In consequence a number of *kāvyas* and dramas have come into existence in subsequent classical Sanskrit literature. As already pointed out, Prof. Banamali Rath enumerates some 128 works written after 1200 A.D. in imitation of the *Gīta-govinda* (vide supra Ch.I,p.1). In her study of three Kṛṣṇa *kāvyas* Raj Kumari Kubba has given a list of works based on the Kṛṣṇa themes written between 1200 A.D.-1900 A.D.[1]

As far as the Kṛṣṇa dramas in Sanskrit literature are concerned, in the classical period Bhāsa's *Bāla-caritam* is the first drama based on Kṛṣṇa legend. In five Acts Bhāsa deals with the wonderful feats of Kṛṣṇa the cowherd boy beginning with his divine birth and ending with the death of Kaṁsa. According to Kubba, the drama *Jāmbavatī-kalyāṇa* dealing with the marriage of Śrīkṛṣṇa with Jāmbavatī is written by Kṛṣṇadevarāja the king of Vijayanagara in 1500 A.D. She also refers to another drama *Satyabhāmā-vilāsa* by Śeṣakṛṣṇa which belongs to 1600 A.D., but with the present state of our knowledge we cannot decide whether these two dramas mentioned by her are earlier to the *Jagannātha-vallabha-nāṭaka*. On the contrary we are rather sure that the drama of Rāyā Rāmānanda was composed between 1497-1510 A.D. before the arrival of Caitanya at Puri (vide supra p. 14). Besides the *Jagannātha-vallabha-nāṭaka* some Kṛṣṇa dramas are available in Orissa dealing with the divine sports of Śrī Rādhā and Śrīkṛṣṇa. The one-Act play *Pīyūṣa-laharī* and the *Vaiṣṇavāmṛta nāṭaka* by Jayadeva Ācārya dealing with the *vasanta rāsa* and *rāsa-līlā* of Rādhā-Kṛṣṇa respectively are assigned to the period between 1525-1535 A.D.[2] The *Samṛddha-mādhava-nāṭaka* of Kavibhūṣaṇa Govinda which also depicts in seven Acts the famous love-episode of Rādhā-Kṛṣṇa belongs to 1760 A.D.[3] Besides, in course of giving a long list of imitations of the *Gīta-*

govinda Professor Rath has referred to a *nāṭikā* called *Gopālakeli-Candrikā*. Its author Rāmakṛṣṇa is a man of Gujarat.[4] And in her study Kubba refers to another Kṛṣṇa drama namely *Pārijāta-haraṇa* by Kumāra Tātācārya. The subject matter of this drama relates to the Pārijāta tree that was brought from the heaven by Śrīkṛṣṇa.[5] Thus we notice that our drama *Jagannātha-vallabha-nāṭaka* under discussion does not enjoy an insignificant position in the history of Kṛṣṇa-dramas written in Sanskrit literature.

In this drama Rāmānanda seems to be very apt in depicting the feelings of love-in-separation *(viraha)*. While narrating the pangs of separation either of the hero or the heroine, he gives a lively picture arousing sympathy in the spectators. When Śrī Kṛṣṇa refuses his love to Śrī Rādhā, in the Act III with tears in her eyes Śrī Rādhā asks Madanikā about the remedy. Śrī Rādhā meekly submits that Śrīkṛṣṇa neither understands love nor even the pangs of separation-in-love. Cupid never pays heed to proper or improper place. The God of love has no sympathy even for women who are weak and frail. One cannot realise the sorrows and sufferings undergone by another. Life is just a flowing stream, and the youth is so transitory. Who knows what providence has in store for her?[6]

Equally tormenting is the love-lorn condition of Śrīkṛṣṇa when in Act IV he requests Madanikā to come to his rescue. Having refused the love of Śrī Rādhā at first instance, Śrīkṛṣṇa realises to have committed a great blunder. Unable to bear Śrī Rādhā's separation any more, he resorts to Madanikā and seeks her active cooperation. Madanikā approaches Śrī Rādhā and gives a realistic picture of the sufferings that Śrīkṛṣṇa undergoes. Śrīkṛṣ ṇa reproaches the moon, throws away the sandal paste, and casts aside the pearl-necklace; he is afraid of dew-drops; he does not even talk to his favourite attendants; because of his separation from her (Śrī Rādhā), in a desperate and depressed state what is there which Śrīkṛṣṇa does not do?[7]

The world-renowned poet Kālidāsa was famous for the use of similes in his *kāvyas (upamā Kālidāsasya)*. His similes have a great appeal and a great impact on his readers and the later writers.

In the *Kumārasambhava* V.85 he gives an appropriate striking simile when Pārvatī the daughter of the mountain-king at the sight of Lord Śiva with one foot raised to walk away, could neither move nor stay, like a river being obstructed by a mountain in its course.[8] Though our play-wright Rāmānanda cannot, like Kālidāsa, go to such heights of excellaence, still he has attempted a similar picture while describing Śrī Rādhā as an *abhisārikā* and it is worth-mentioning. At the instigation of Madanikā when Śrī Rādhā is proceeding to the rendezvous in the twilight hour and she is just in the mid-way, the moon, all on a sudden, makes its appearance in the eastern horizon. At this Śrī Rādhā has been perplexed to decide whether she would move ahead or go back. In the words of Rāmānanda -

asmin śakradiśaṁ śaśāṅka-hatake saṁdūṣayaty unmanā/
nāgantum na ca gantum adya caturā kiṁ vā kariṣyaty asau//
J.V.N. IV.47

Though small in size, the *Jagannātha-vallabha-nāṭaka* contains some moral sayings that give vent to general truth of life. In Act III.30 we come across such a general statement when Madanikā says "it is very difficult to join the sprout of love once it is shattered by mistake.[9] It simply suggests that love is a two-way traffic, a reciprocal affair; it is an affair between the lover and the beloved; if any misunderstanding creeps in, it nips in the bud. Act V.28 provides us with another instance of this type when Madanikā explains to Śaśimukhi about the nature of sexual love. She says that a teacher imparts teaching to a student; through continuous practice the student masters the teaching. But so far as sexual love is concerned, there is no need of a teacher, one learns it automatically.[10]

On a comparison of the Rāgas of the *Jagannātha-vallabha-nāṭaka* with those of the Gīta-govinda we notice that in the latter for twenty four songs Jayadeva has used eleven Rāgas namely 'Mālava', 'Gurjarī', 'Vasanta', 'Rāmakarī', 'Karṇāṭa', 'Deśākhya', 'Deśavarāḍī', 'Naṭa', 'Bhairavī', 'Varādī' and 'Vibhāsa' but for twenty one songs in his drama Rāmānanda has resorted to twenty Rāgas such as 'Naṭa', 'Kedāra', Vasanta', 'Goṇḍakirī', 'Gāndhāra',

'Toḍivarāḍi', 'Śāmagujjarī', 'Mallāra', 'Śuhayī', 'Deśāga', 'Karṇāṭa', 'Mālava', 'Dukhīvarādī', 'Sāmatoḍī', Rāmakeli', 'Mālavaśrī', 'Sukhasinduḍā', 'Āhirā', 'Lalita' and 'Maṅgala-gujjarī'. Of the twenty one songs, nineteen songs are set to a specific Rāga each whereas only two songs are sung with 'Sāmagujjarī' Rāga in Act II.35 and Act III.3 of the drama. As illustrations let us take two songs in order to show their intrinsic beauty. Act I.28 describes the alluring beauty of lovely Vṛndāvana as follows :

('Vasanta' Rāgeṇa)
aparicitaṁ tava rūpam idaṁ vata paśya divocita khelam/
lalita-vikasvara-kusuma-cayair iva hasati cirād ativelam//
kalaya sakhe bhuvi sāraṁ
tvad upāgamād iva sarasam idaṁ mama
vṛndāvanam anuvāram//
(dhruvam)
mṛdu-pavan āhati cañcala-pallava kara-nikarair iva kāmam/
narttitum upadiśatīva bhavantaṁ santatam idam
abhirāmam//
sukhayatu gajapati rudra manoharam anudinam idam
abhidhānam/
Rāmānanda Rāya kavi-racitaṁ rasika-janaṁ suvidhānam//

In the Act IV.51 how musical and enchanting is the description of Śrī Rādhā proceeding as an *abhisārikā!*

(Mālavaśrīḥ)
cikura-taraṅgaka-phena-paṭalam iva kusumaṁ dadhatī
kāmam/
naṭad apasavyadṛś ādiśatīva ca narttitum atanum
avāmam//
Rādhā Mādhava-vihārā
Harim upagacchati manthara pada gati, laghu laghu
tara-litahārā// (dhruvam)
śaṅkita-lajjita-rasabhara-cañcala-madhura-dṛganta-lavena/
Madhumathanaṁ prati sam upaharantī kuvalaya-dāma rasena
gajapati rudra-narādhipam adhunā tanmadanaṁ madhureṇa/
Rāmānanda Rāya-kavi-bhaṇitaṁ sukhayatu rasa-visareṇa//

These lyrical songs produce desired feelings and emotions in the audience when played to the accompaniment of musical instruments by the artistes. From it we may infer that Rāmānanda was not only dexterous in dance and drama, but also he had considerable command over the science of music.

So far as the *alaṁkāras* (figures of speech) are concerned, Rāmānanda seems to be proficient in handling them. The Sanskrit word *alaṁkāraḥ* is constitued of alaṁ, *kṛ* and suffix *ghañ* and it literally means "that which decorates or adorns" *(alaṁkṛtiḥ alaṁkāraḥ* or *alaṁ kriyate anena iti)*. Just as ornaments decorate human body, in rhetorics *alaṁkāras* are the poetic embellishments, that is to say, they add beauty to poetry. The *alaṁkāra* is divided into three classes namely *śabdālaṁkāra, arthālaṁkāra* and *ubhayālaṁkāra*. Generally *anuprāsa, yamaka, śleṣa* and *vakrokti*, are known as *śabdālaṁkāras; upamā, rūpaka, utprekṣā, apahnuti*, etc., are regarded as *arthālaṁkāras* and the third category equally showing the importance of both word and meaning is called *ubhayālaṁkāra*. Let us take up some figures of speech from the *Jagannātha-vallabha-nāṭaka* for ascertaining the merit of Rāmānanda.

Act I.22 depicting the youthful Śrīkṛṣṇa, Act II.20 and Act III.34 delineating Śrī Rādhā's love-sickness are fine specimens of *anuprāsa* (alliteration).[11]

As regards the arthālaṁkāra, Act I.10[12] of the *Jagannātha-vallabha-nāṭaka* is a good example of *upamā* (simile). In the words of Viśvanātha Kavirāja a semblance between two things expressed by a single sentence and unaccompanied with a difference is called an *upamā*.[13]

In Act I.13 of the drama where king Pratāparudra is identified with Rudra (the formidable aspect of Lord Śiva) and the destructive Fire at the time of deluge for his rival kings and warriors,[14] we meet with the figure of speech called rūpaka *alaṁkāra* (metaphor). According to Viśvanātha, the author of *Sāhitya-darpaṇa*, a *rūpaka* consists in the super-imposition of a fancied character upon an object unconcealed by negation.[15]

Act I.2[16] of the drama describing the countenance of Śrī

Kṛṣṇa provides us with an example of *apahnuti alaṁkāra* (the figure of concealment). According to *Sāhitya-darpaṇa* X.38 the denial of the real nature of a thing and the ascription of another character constitute the figure *apahnuti*.[17]

Similarly in the First Act the speech of Vidūṣaka in Prakrit at the sight of cowherd-maidens advancing towards them as "a number of golden images put to motion by some magicians"[18] represents the *bhrāntimān alaṁkāra* (error). This figure of speech consists of a sort of confusion based on similarity. According to Viśvanātha *bhrāntimān* is the thinking, from resemblance, of an object to be what it is not—suggested by poetical fancy.[19]

We need not multiply further examples. From these it is quite clear that Rāmānanda was not only proficient in dance, drama and music, but also he was thorough in rhetorics, particularly his mastery over figures of speech was commendable. Otherwise as referred to by Kṛṣṇadāsa Kavirāja, Caitanya would never have asked Rūpa Gosvāmin to get his literary productions examined by Rāmānanda (vide supra p. 27).

From historical point of view this drama deserves our attention in so far as it refers to the indomitable valour and prowess of the king Pratāparudradeva. In Act I.10 though the play-wright praīses his patron in highly eulogistic terms, yet his eulogy is not totally baseless. In the first half of the 16th century particularly from 1497 to 1540 A.D. Gajapati Pratāparudradeva ruled over a vast empire extending from the river Kṛṣṇā in the south to the river Hughli in the east. In the *Jagannātha-vallabha-nāṭaka* he is depicted to be one, "having heard of whose name Sekandhara took shelter in the cave, the Kalavarga chief looked at his relatives with tearful eyes, the Gujjara monarch used to consider his city as a forest in decay and the king of Gauḍa thought of sitting in a ship violently shaken by stormy wind in the ocean".[20] When we look at history, these accounts of the play-wright seem to be corroborated by historical data to some extent. The Muslim king Husain Shah was, in fact, the ruler of Gauḍa (Bengal) from 1493 to 1518 A.D. As pointed out by Mukherjee, "he wanted to push back the Oriyas from the banks of the Hughli for the safety of Satagaon".[21] And for this he had started periodical border clashes right from 1500 A.D. Lastly though Husain Shah invaded Orissa, "it is stated in the Idupulupāḍu grant dated November 1500 that Vīra Rudra the king of Utkala completely defeated the king of Gauḍa".[22] Mukherjee again holds—"the Velicherla plates tell us that the huge elephants of Pratāparudra the Gajeśvara, terrified the king of Gauḍa who fled to his capital".[23] Thus the defeat of Husain Shah, the Sultan of Gauḍa (Bengal) at the hands of king Pratāparudradeva was a historical fact.

In the prologue Rāmānanda claims that his drama is a novel creation *(abhinava kṛti);* it does not imitate any other composition *(anya-cchāyayā no nibaddha)* and hence it is original, but there is no doubt about the fact that it has borrowed its theme from the *Śrīmad Bhāgavata* particularly its *Rāsa-pañcādhyāya* (X.Chs.29-33) and the *Gīta-govinda.* In the *Śrīmad Bhāgavata* X.Ch.29 when the cowherd-maidens apporach Śrīkṛṣṇa, in order to know their mind, Śrīkṛṣṇa persuades them to go back to Vraja. He tells the cowherd-maidens that it is their duty to attend upon their husbands; a husband, however poor, ailing,decrepit or dull-witted he may be, should not be abandoned by the wife; for a woman intercourse with a paramour is a bar to heaven[24] and by their absence in the home they must not cause anxiety to their near and dear ones. In the same way in the second Act of the drama at the approach of Śaśimukhi carrying the love-letter, Śrīkṛṣṇa dissuades her from her venture and instructs her on domestic virtues and glorious family traditions.[25] The introduction of the bull-demon Ariṣṭa in the last Act of the drama has been borrowed from the *Harivaṁśa* (II. Viṣṇuparvan, Ch.64), the *Viṣṇu Purāṇa* (Part V, Ch.14), the *Brahma Purāṇa* (Ch.189.46-58) and the *Śrīmad Bhāgavata* (X.36.1-14). In all the three texts—the *Harivaṁśa,* the *Viṣṇu* and the *Brahma* when Śrīkṛṣṇa is engaged in amorous sports with the cowherd-maidens, the terrible demon Ariṣṭa appears there and Śrīkṛṣṇa kills him without any difficulty, but in the *Śrīmad Bhāgavata* after the amorous sports *(rāsa-krīḍā)* is over (X.Ch.33), Śrīkṛṣṇa proceeds to the forest for pasturing the cattle (X.Ch.35.I) and on his return to Vraja he meets the bull-demon whom he routs with ease. Following the Śrīmad Bhāgavata, in the fifth Act the Jagannātha-vallabha-nāṭaka ṣimilary describes that after the amorous sports of Śrī Rādhā and Śrīkṛṣṇa in the lovely bower is over, the demon Ariṣṭa appears and endangers the peace and safety of Vraja and it is Śrīkṛṣṇa who gives a fatal blow to him.

As regards Rāmānanda's imitation of Jayadeva's *Gīta-govinda* the following instances may be cited with profit—

(i) *nindati candanaṁ indu-kiraṇam anu vindati khedam adhīram/*
vyāla-nilaya-milanena garalam iva kalayati malaya-samīram/
G.G.IV.2

ityākalpa-vikalpa-talpa racanā-saṅkalpa-līlāśata-
vyāsaktāpi vinā tvayā varatanur naiṣā niśāṁ neṣyati//
G.G. VI.11

Cf. *induṁ nindati candanaṁ vikirati prālaṁbakaṁ muñcati*
prāleyāt trasati pariyaṁ prijanaṁ nābhāṣate samprati/
Govindas tava viprayoga-vidhūraḥ kiṁ kiṁ na vā ceṣṭate
tat kuñjodaratalpa-kalpanaparaṁ Rādhe tam ārādhaya//
J.V.N. IV.43

(ii) *sarasa-masṛṇam api malayaja-paṅkam/*
paśyati viṣam iva vapuṣi saśaṅkam// G.G. IV.12
Cf. *viṣābhaṁ śrīkhaṇḍaṁ kalayati vidhuṁ pāvaka-samam/*
J.V.N. IV.30

(iii) *tvad abhisaraṇa-rabhasena valantī/*
patati padāni kiyantī calantī// G.G. VI.3
Cf. *niravadhi nayana-salila-bhavasāde/*
patati kṛśā paricalati ca pāde// J.V.N. IV.25

(iv) *tat kiṁ kaṁ api kāminīm abhisṛtaḥ kiṁ vā kalā-kelibhir*
baddho bandhubhir andhakāriṇi vanopānte kimu bhrāmyati/
kāntaḥ klāntamanā manāg api pathi prasthātum ev ākṣamaḥ
saṁketī kṛta-mañju--vañjula-latākuñje'pi yan nāgataḥ//
G.G. VII.11

Cf. *kim eṣā matvā māṁ aparicita-bhāvaṁ vimukhatāṁ*
prayātā viśvāsaṁ kimu sahacarī-vāci na gatā/
atha bhrāntā varttany atitimira-bhājīha vipine
na śaktā tanvaṅgī smara-śara-hatā vā pracalitum//
J.V.N. IV.45

And it is due to all these factors that De comments on the *Jagannātha-vallabha-nāṭaka*—"neither the theme nor its treatment displays much variety or originality".[26] As it deals with the usual traditional *Rādhā-Kṛṣṇa-līlā,* the theme is stereotyped and there is no opportunity for any innovation. No novelty of expression is expected in such plays which solely aim at depicting love at first sight, mutual longings and pangs of separated lovers, love-letter, personal beauty of the hero and the heroine and their final union through the help of some go-between. In these plays we usually notice that for description the author uses conventional words and imageries.

But the absence of novelty or originality should not be taken as a drawback in these playlets. Little romantic plays of this nature with a precise fixed theme always like to present pretty sentiment in a pretty atmosphere. Therefore De again observes that "perhaps in these idyllic and romantic little plays which aim at nothing more than picturing the pretty sentiment in a pretty environment, elegance was more expected than originality, and poverty of invention need hardly be regarded as a defect".[27] Since the sweetness of expression is much more desired, the play-wrights neglect the plot or structure of the drama and give more emphasis on elegance. And in order to depict scenes we very often notice them to be in the habit of utilising conventional words and imageries. For instance the following is a description of Śrīkṛṣṇa presented in the traditional words and imageries by Rāmānanda—

so'yam yuvā yuvati-citta-vihaṅga śākhī
sākṣādiva sphurati pañca-śaro Mukundaḥ/
yasmin gate nayanayoḥ pathi sundarīṇāṁ
nīviḥ svayaṁ śithilatām upayāti sadyaḥ// I.44

Similarly conventional but charming is Act II.19 which hints at the amorous gestures of Śrī Rādhā -

śaśini nayana-pāto nādarād unmadānāṁ
rutam anu ca pikānāṁ karṇa-rodhaś chalena/
prati-vacanam apārthaṁ yat sakhīnāṁ kathāsu
smara-vilasitam asyās tena kiñcit pratītam//

The pangs of separation *(viraha)* of Śrī Rādhā and Śrīkṛṣṇa and their lamentations are described in the same traditional manner, and both of them are delineated like the sentimental hero and heroine; but despite want of novelty or oriiginality, in the language of De it cannot be denied that "the little play is not fluent and graceful".[28] The dramatic situations are often hackneyed and uninteresting, but like other classical dramas they are not over-embellished so as to create aversion in the reader's mind. In the emotional description of dramatic situations Rāmānanda has been careful and he has used the poetical stanzas with such precision that in the words of De we can say, "their poetical stanzas are neither tediously profuse nor inappropriate.[29]

Finally to use the author's own version as stated in the prologue of the drama, "even if there is no slightest merit in this literary composition, still the work praising the lotus-feet of Śrīkṛṣ ṇa, the enemy of demon Madhu is a source of immense pleasure and delight to the heart of connoisseurs of poetry. Hence his attempt at composing or staging the play is not in vain.[30] Rāmānanda was a great devotee by nature and a staunch follower of Vaiṣṇavism. He was delighted to sing aloud the glory and greatness of Lord Viṣṇu. By writing such a little dramatic piece in praise of the Lord and presenting it to the Vaiṣṇavite world, his devout heart considers his labours amply rewarded even if the work lacks in merit.

Thus this little drama has created an appreciable place for itself in the history of Sanskrit literature in general and in the devotional literature of Gauḍīya Vaiṣṇavism in particular. It is so popular in Orissa that in its imitation Raghunātha Parīkṣā an Oriya dramatist of 1795 A.D. writes a drama entitled Gopīnātha-vallabha-nāṭaka in Oriya language with the same theme of the love-sports of Śrī Rādhā and Śrīkṛṣṇa.

REFERENCES

1. Kubba, Raj Kumari, *Kṛṣṇa-kāvyas in Sanskrit Literature,* Introduction, pp.1-5.
2. Mahapatra, K.N., *A Descriptive Catalogue of Sanskrit Manuscripts of Orissa,* Vol.II, p.CXIX.

3. *Ibid.*, p.LIV.
See also Rath, Banamali—*A Study on the Śrīkṛṣṇa-līlāmṛtam* Ch. VIII, p.225.
4. Rath, Banamali, *Ibid.*, pp.295-296.
5. Kubba, Rajkumari, *op.cit.*, Indroduction, pp.3-4.
6. *Rādhā (sāsram)—devi Madanike: kaḥ pratikāraḥ?*
premacchedarujo' vagacchati Harir nāyaṁ na ca prema vā
sthān āsthānam avaiti nāpi Madano jānāti no durvalāḥ/
anyo veda na cānyaduhkham akhilaṁ, no jīvanaṁ vāśravam
dvitrāṇy eva dināni yauvanam idaṁ, hā hā vidhe kā gatiḥ?
J.V.N. Act III.9
7. *induṁ nindati candanaṁ vikirati prālambakaṁ muñcati*
prāleyāt trasati priya-parijanaṁ na bhāsate samprati/
Govindas tava viprayoga-vidhuraḥ kiṁ kiṁ vā na ceṣṭate?
J.V.N. Act IV.43
8. *tām vīkṣya vepathumatī sarasāṅga yaṣṭir*
nikṣepaṇāya padam uddhṛtam udbahantī/
mārgācala-vyatikar ākulit eva sindhuḥ
*śailādhirāja-tanayā na yayau na tasthau// K.S.*V.85
9. Madanikā—*bhagnaḥ kadācit yad ayaṁ pramādāt*
prem āṅkuro yojayituṁ na śakyaḥ// J.V.N. III.30
10. Madanikā—*ayi sarale!*
upadiśati gurur guru-prayatnāt
tad api ca kāla-vaśāt prayāti pākam/
iti kila niyatāḥ samasta-vidyāḥ
surata-kalāḥ svata eva sambhavanti// J.V.N. Act V.28
11. Viśvanātha Kavirāja has defined *anuprāsa* as—
anuprāsaḥ śabdasāmyaṁ vaiṣamye'pi svarasya yat/
(i) *mṛdutara-māruta-vellita-pallava-vallī valita sikhaṇḍam/*
tilaka-viḍambita-marakata-maṇitala-vimbita-śaśadhara-khaṇḍam//
yuvati-manohara-veśaṁ
kalaya kalānidhim iva dharaṇīm any pariṇata-rūpa-viśeṣam/ *(dhruvam)*
khelā-dolāyita-maṇikuṇḍala-ruci rucirānana-śobham/
helā-taralita-madhura-vilocana-janita-vadhū-jana lobham/
J.V.N. Act I.22

(ii) *hari haricandana-māruta pikarutam anu tanur atanu-vikāram/*
tirayitum iva sā kati kati sahasā racayati na śiśuvihāram/
upanata-manasija, bādhā
abhinava-bhāvabharān api dadhatī śiva śiva sīdati Rādhā/
(dhruvam)
aviṣaya niścala-nayana-yugala-galad ambukaṇān anuvāram/
rahasi haṭhād upayāti sakhīm anu racayati sauhṛda-sāram/
J.V.N. Act II.20

(iii) *mañjutara-guñjad ali-kuñjam atibhīṣaṇam/*
manda-marud-antaraga-gandha-kṛta-dūṣaṇam//
sakalam etad īritaṁ
kiñca guru-pañcaśara-cañcalaṁ mama jīvitam// (dhruvam)
matta-pika-dattarujam uttamādhikaraṁ vanam/
saṅgasukham aṅgam api tuṅga-bhaya-bhājnam// J.V.N. Act III.34

12. *mene Gujjara-bhūpatir jarad iv āraṇyaṁ nijaṁ pattanaṁ/ vāta-vyagra-payodhi-potagam iva svaṁ veda Gauḍeśvaraḥ// J.V.N.* Act I.10
13. *sāmyaṁ vācyam avaidharmyaṁ vāky aikya upamā dvayoh// S.D.* X.14
14. *tena pratibhaṭa-nṛpaghaṭā-kālāgnirudreṇa śrīmad Pratāparudreṇa..... .... ādiṣṭo'smi, J.V.N.* Act I.13
15. *Rūpakaṁ rūpit āropād viṣaye nirapahnave/ S.D.* X.28
16. *smitaṁ nu na sita-dyutis taralam akṣi n āmbhoruhaṁ śrutir na ca jagajjaye manasijasya maurvī-latā/ J.V.N.* Act I.2
17. *prakṛtaṁ pratiṣidhy ānya sthāpanaṁ syād apahnutiḥ/ S.D.* X.38
18. *Vidūṣakaḥ—(purato'valokya) bho vaassa! pekkha pekkha keṇāvi indaālieṇa saṁcālido kaṇaa- puttaliā-niara idha jjeva āacchadi. J.V.N.* Act I.39
19. *sāmyād atasmiṁs tad buddhir bhrāntimān pratibhotthitaḥ/ S.D.* X.36
20. *yan nām āpi niśamya sanniviśsate Sekandharaḥ kandaraṁ sva-vargaṁ Kalavarga-bhūmi-tilakaḥ sāsraṁ samud vīksate/*

mene Gujjara-bhūpatir jarad iv āraṇyaṁ nijaṁ pattanaṁ vāta-vyagra-payodhi-potagam iva svaṁ veda Gaudeśvaraḥ// *J.V.N.* I.10

21. *Mukherjee, P., The History of the Gajapati Kings of Orissa,* Ch.V, p.73
22. *Ibid.*
23. *Ibid.*
24. *Bhāg.P.* X.Ch.29.24-26.
25. *J.V.N.* Act II.46.2-3.
26. De, S.K. *Early History of the Vaiṣṇava Faith and Movement in Bengal,* p.578.
27. De, S.K., *op.cit.*, p.579.
28. *Ibid.*
29. *Ibid.*
30. *na bhavatu guṇa-gandho'pyatra nāma prabandhe*
    Madhu-ripu-pada-padm otkīrttanaṁ nas tathāpi/
    sahṛdaya-hṛdayasy āṇanda-sandoha-hetur-
    niyatam idaṁ ato'yaṁ niṣphalo no prayāsaḥ// J.V.N. Act I.18

PART II

THE JAGANNĀTHA-VALLABHA NĀṬAKA :

TEXT WITH ENGLISH TRANSLATION

THE JAGANNĀTHA-VALLABHA NĀṬAKA

प्रथमोऽङ्कः

ACT-I

स्वराञ्चितविपञ्चिका मुरजवेणु सङ्गीतकं
त्रिभङ्ग तनुवल्लरी-वलित वल्गुहासोल्वणं
वयस्य-करतालिका-रणित नूपुरैरुज्ज्वलं
मुरारिनटनं सदादिशतु शर्म लोकत्रये॥१॥

Let the dance of Murāri give perpetual happiness to the three worlds, the dance which is accompanied by instrumental music consisting of the lute played on different tunes (like *niṣāda,* etc.), the drum and the flute, the dance which is gaudy with the sweet smile in the creeper-like tender body in *tribhaṅga* pose (a pose in which the body is bent at three parts), the dance which is lovely being supported by the clappings of companions and the jingling anklets./1/

अपि च-

स्मितं नु न सितद्युतिस्तरलमक्षि नाम्भोरुहं
श्रुति र्नच जगज्जये मनसिजस्य मौर्व्वीलता
मुकुन्द मुखमण्डले रभसमुग्ध-गोपाङ्गना
दृगञ्चल भवोभ्रमः शुभशताय ते कल्पताम्॥२॥

Moreover,

This is not the smile (in the face of Mukunda), but the moon; this is not the tremulous eye, but the lotus; this is not the ear, but the string of the bow of the mind-born god (Cupid) bent upon conquering the world. May this delusion arising in the side-long glances of the cowherd maidens infatuated with the face of Mukunda bring all-round happiness to you./2/

अपि च-

कामं कामपयोनिधिं मृगदृशामुद्भावयन्निर्भरं
चेत:कैरवकाननानि यमिनामत्यन्तमुल्लासयन्
रक्ष: कोक कुलानि शोक विकलान्येकान्तमाकल्पय-
न्नानन्दं वितनोतु वो मधुरिपोर्वक्त्रापदेश: शशी।।३।।

Moreover,

May the moon in the guise of the face of the slayer of Madhu (Kṛṣṇa) give happiness to you all, the moon which intensely augments the ocean of love of the fawn-eyed (cowherd maidens) to their hearts' content, which exceedingly delights the thicket of white water-lilies in the shape of heart of (even) the ascetics, which excessively afflicts the demons like the *Cakravāka* birds with grief./3/

(नटरागेण)

(Sung with Rāga 'Naṭa')

मृदुलमलयजपवनतरलित चिकुरपरिगतकलापकम्।
साचितरलितनयनमन्मथ शङ्कु शङ्कुलचित्त सुन्दरीजनजनितकौतुकम्।।
मनसिजकेलिनन्दितमानसं
भजत मधुरिपुमिन्दुसुन्दरवल्लवीमुखलालसम्।।ध्रुवम्।।
लधुतरलितकन्धरं हसितनवसुन्दरम्।
गजपतिप्रतापरुद्र हृदयानुगतमनुदिनं
सरसं रचयति रामानन्दराय इति चारुसङ्गीतम्[१]।।४।।

Adore this slayer of Madhu (Kṛṣṇa) intent upon kissing the face of cowherd maidens as lovely as the moon, the slayer of Madhu whose feathers of the peacock put on around the hairs (of the head) wave by the gently breeze blowing from the Malaya mountain, whose dart of Cupid in the shape of the side-long glances of his tremulous eyes cause delight to the timid beautiful cowherd maidens, whose mind rejoices in the love-sports (with the cowherd maidens).

Rāmānanda Rāya has composed the sweet and pleasing musical song of (Lord Kṛṣṇa) in which the portion of the neck of the Lord is slightly moving, in which the smile in the face of the Lord is ever fresh and charming, and which day after day appeals, to the king Pratāparudra, the lord of elephants *(Gajapati)*.[2] /4/

(नान्द्यन्ते)

सूत्रधारः– अलमति विस्तरेण। (नेपथ्याभिमुखे) प्रिये! इतः इतः॥५॥

After the Nāndī (prayer to the deities)

The Stage-Manager—Enough of it. (Looking at the dressing room) oh, my dear! this way, this way./5/

(प्रविश्य नटी)

(Enters the actress)

नटी —अज्ज एसहिम णिअ किंकरीअणं चरण-पडिदं विलोअण पसादेहिं पसन्नहिअअं कादुं भट्टा परं पमाणम्॥६॥
(आर्य! एषास्मि। निजकिंकरीजनं चरणपतितं विलोकन-प्रसादैः प्रसन्नहृदयं कर्त्तुं भर्त्ता परं प्रमाणम्।)॥६॥

Actress —My lord! here I am. It behoves, my lord, by your gracious look to make this maid fallen prostrate at your feet happy and contented./6/

सूत्रधारः —(सहर्षम्) चिरसमयं विदग्धोचितवेशेन योवनविलासमनुभवतु भवती।

नटी —अज्जेण कुदो आहूदह्मि?॥७॥ (आर्येण कस्मादाहूतास्मि?)

The Stage-Manager—(With delight) Dressed as a respectable woman you may enjoy youthful pleasure for a long time.

Actress —Why have I been called here by my lord? /7/

सूत्रधारः —प्रिये! न विदितम्? भवत्याः प्रसादकथनमेतत्।

नटी —सम्पदि तां सोदुं मम हिअअं कुदुहलेहिं विप्फारिदं वट्टदि।
(सम्प्रति तत् श्रोतुं मम हृदयं कुतुहलैर्विस्फारितं वर्त्तते)॥८॥

The Stage-Manager—Oh, my dear! did you not know? It is a pleasant affair on your part.

Actress —Now I am extremely curious to listen to that (affair)./8/

सूत्रधारः —प्रिये! शुणु। अद्य खलु वसन्तवासरावसरे तरुण भास्वद्विमुक्त दक्षिणदिग्विलासिनी-स्तन-मलयाचलावलम्बि-वेणी-भुजङ्ग-सङ्गि -समीरण-मूर्छित-विरहिणीजन-जीवातु-वयस्या श्वासवचः प्रसरे। विकसित शीतकिरण प्रसूने च विमलनभोवन प्रोज्जृम्भमाण नव-

नवोन्मीलित-निस्तलमुक्ताफल तुलिततारा मुकुलमध्यावलम्बिनि सासूयनिर्भर निरीक्ष्यमाण विरहिणीजन चञ्चललोचनाञ्चल-लताग्रवर्त्तिनि। निरुपम कान्तिलक्ष्मीलुब्ध लक्ष्मीरमणावस्थानोचित-चित्तदुग्धाव्धिना विभावादिपरिणत- रसरसालमुकुल-रसास्वाद-कोविद-पुंस्कोकिलेन श्रीकण्ठहार-सहचरगुण-मुक्ताफलमण्डित हृदयेन, किं वहुना।।९।।

The Stage-Manager—Oh, my dear! listen to me. The lady of the southern quarters is separated from the morning sun; the braid-like serpent is hanging down the breast-like Malaya-mountain; the women in separation become senseless by contacting the breeze (made poisonous) by its association with the braid-like serpents; this is the evening of spring time when everywhere one hears the words of consolation of the companions acting as the medicine for bringing back the bereaved women to their senses.

The flower-like full-moon brightly shines in the forest-like clear spotless sky; the stars recently visible in the sky looking like round pearls appear as buds; the flower-like moon appearing in the midst of the bud-like stars exists at the tip of the creeper-like side-long glance of the tremulous eyes of the bereaved women looking at it intently with envy.

Whose heart-like milk-ocean worthy of being the residence of the consort of Lakṣmī (Viṣṇu) who is usually fascinated by the matchless splendour of loveliness who is a male cuckoo proficient in relishing the sap of the mango-buds in the form of the poetic sentiments resulting from the delineation of different elements like *vibhāva* etc., whose heart is sublime (lit. ornamented) with pearl-like virtues of Śrī Kṛṣṇa (lit. the necklace and the companion of Rādhā), what more shall I say? /9/

यन्नामापि निशम्य सन्निविशते सेकन्धरः कन्दरं
स्ववर्गं कलवर्गभूमितिलकः सास्रं समुद्वीक्षते।
मेने गुज्जरभूपतिर्जरदिवारण्यं निजं पत्तनं
वात व्यग्रपयोधिपोतगमिव स्वं वेद गौड़ेश्वरः।।१०।।

Having heard of whose name the Muslim king Sekandhara resorts to the caves of the mountain, having heard of whose name the ruler of Kalavarga region looks at his kith and kin with tearful eyes, having heard of whose name the king of Gujjara takes his own city to be a forest in decay, having heard of whose name the king of Gauḍa country regards himself to be seated in a ship sailing in the ocean agitated with storms; /10/

कायव्युहविलास ईश्वरगिरेर्द्वैतं सुधादीधिते–
र्निर्यासस्तुहिनाचलस्य यमकं क्षीराम्बुराशेरसौ।
सार: शारदवारिदस्य किमपि स्वर्व्वाहिनी वारिणो–
द्वैराज्यं विमलीकरोति सततं यत् कीर्त्तिराशिर्जगत्।।११।।

The mass of whose fame is the charm of the physical frame of the mount Kailāsa, is the second moon, is the sap of the snow-capped mountain (the Himalayas), is one of the twins, one being the milk-ocean and the other being the mass of his fame, is the essence of the autumnal cloud, whose fame is shared by the celestial Ganges[3] and the mass of whose glory purifies the world for all time to come. /11/

यद्दानाम्बुकदम्बनिर्मितनदीसंश्लेषहर्षादसौ
रिङ्गं-तुङ्गं-तुरङ्ग निस्वनमिषात् प्रस्तौति यं वारिधि:।
नित्य प्रस्तुत-सप्ततन्तुभिरभिस्युतं मनो नाकिनां
येनैतत् प्रतिमाच्छलेन यदमी मुञ्चन्ति न प्राङ्गणम्।।१२।।
तेन प्रतिभट-नृपघटा-कालाग्निरुद्रेण श्रीमत्प्रतापरुद्रेण
श्रीहरिचरणगधिकृत्य कमपि प्रबन्धमभिनेतुमादिष्टोऽस्मि।।१३।।

Because of the pleasure in embracing (in being united with) the river formed of the huge mass of water collected at the time of making gifts and donations whom thc ocean loudly praises under the pretext of the roaring sound of lofty dancing waves, by whom in the sacrifices *(saptatantu)*[4] performed daily, the celestials have their heart and soul absorbed (as if woven together-*abhisyūta*) and in consequence of which whose courtyard is never deserted by those divinities living there in the form of images, /12/ by that celebrated Pratāparudra who is Rudra (incarnate), the destructive fire at the time of deluge for the hosts of kings—the rival warriors,

I have been ordered to stage some play dealing with the conduct of Śrī Hari. /13/

यदुक्तम्–
मधुरिपुपदलीलाशालि तत्तद्गुणाढ्यं
सहृदय-हृदयानां काममामोदहेतुम्।
अभिनवकृतिमन्यच्छायया नो निवद्धं
समभिनयनटानां वर्य्य किञ्चित् प्रबन्धम्।।१४।।

As I have been told—

With all perfection stage some novel play, agreeable to actors and not adapted from some other composition, a play dealing with the sports of the enemy of the demon Madhu (Kṛṣṇa), abounding in his manifold noble qualities and a source of great aesthetic pleasure to the connoisseurs of poetry. /14/

नटी —तत् कथय।

नट —कथमाराधनीयो विद्यानां निधिः। यत्तोऽस्मिन्नभिधातुकामो, वाक्पतिरपि प्रतिपत्तिमूढः स्यात् (क्षणं विमृश्य) आम् स्मृतम्।।१५।।

Actress —You name that (play).

Actor —How can I adore the treasure of learning! For even the Lord of Speech (Bṛhaspati) intent to speak out would be bewildered in this attempt (to stage a play quite original). (Thinking for a moment) Oh I remember! /15/

नटी —ता किं सो।१६। (तत् किं स्मृतम्?)

Actress —What do you remember? /16/

सूत्रधार: —प्रिये! सर्व्वविद्या- नदी, विलासगाम्भीर्य्यमर्य्यादा स्थैर्य्यप्रसादादिगुण-रत्नाकरस्य सुरगुरुप्रणीतनीतिकदम्बकरम्बित मन्त्राश्रवीकृत प्रगुण पृथ्वीश्वरस्य श्रीभवानन्दरायस्य तनुजेन श्रीहरिचरणालङ्कृतमानसेन श्रीरामानन्दरायेण कविना तत्तत् गुणालङ्कृतं श्रीजगन्नाथवल्लभ नाम गजपतिप्रतापरुद्रप्रियं रामानन्दसङ्गीतनाटकं निर्म्माय समर्पितम-भिनेष्यामि।।१७।।

The Stage-Manager—Oh my dear! Śrī Bhavānanda Rāya is the

ocean of virtues like dignity, propriety of conduct, patience and serenity etc., as the ocean has *gāmbhīrya* (depth), *maryādā* (a limit), *sthairya* (stability) and *prasāda* (purity and clearness) the ocean having the grace of its union with the rivers of all types of learning, whose counsel conforming to the set of principles laid down by the preceptor of gods (Bṛhaspati) is followed by the worthy king (Pratāparudradeva). His son is the poet Śrī Rāmānanda Rāya whose mind is steeped in thought of feet of Śrī Hari. The *saṅgīta nāṭaka* called "*Śrī Jagannātha-vallabha*" endowed with manifold guṇas (like *mādhurya, ojaḥ, prasāda,* etc.) dear to (the king) Pratāparudra, the lord of elephants composed by (the poet) Rāmānanda has been handed over to me and I would like to stage (that play). /17/

तथा चायं कविः सविनयमिदमवादीत्-
न भवतु गुणगन्धोऽप्यत्र नाम प्रबन्धे
मधुरिपुपदपद्मोत्कीर्त्तनं नस्तथापि।
सहृदयहृदयस्यानन्दसन्दोहहेतु-
र्नियतमिदमतोऽयं निष्फलो न प्रयासः॥१८॥

And with humility this poet submits —

Possibly there may not be the slightest merit in this composition; still the work full of praise of the lotus-feet of the enemy of Madhu (Kṛṣṇa) is certainly a source of immense delight to the heart of connoisseurs of poetry. Hence my endeavour (in staging this play) is not futile. /18/

तदादिश्यन्तां कुशीलवा वर्णिकापरिग्रहाय

नटी —(संस्कृतमाश्रित्य) यदाज्ञापयति स्वामी (पुरोऽवलोक्य) पश्य पश्य॥१९॥

Then the actors may be advised to begin their painting and dressing.

Actress —(In Sanskrit) As the Lord commands (Looking in the front) Look, Look. /19/

मृदुलमलयवाताचान्तवीचिप्रचारे
सरसि नवपरागैः पिञ्जरोऽयं क्लमेन।
प्रतिकमलमधूनिपानमत्तो द्विरेफः
स्वपिति कमलकोषे निश्चलाङ्गः प्रदोषे।।

सूत्रधारः —(सहर्षम्)-प्रिये! साधु, साधु। मन्मनः कुतुहलजलनिधिविवर्त्ते निहितं भवत्या। यतो गोपाङ्गनाशताधरमधुपाननिर्भर -केलिक्लमाल-सापघनः क्वचित् प्रौढ़वधू-स्तनोपधानीय-मण्डितहृदयपर्य्यङ्कशायी पीताम्बरो नारायणः स्मारितः।।२०।।

In the lake with its waves moving because of the gentle "Malaya' breeze, this bee assuming a tawny colour with the pollens of the lotus recently in bloom, intoxicated by drinking the honey from each and every lotus is tired and resting firmly in the Lotus-filament in the evening (of spring).

The Stage-Manager—(With delight) Oh my dear! Well-done, well-done, you have put my mind in the whirl-pool of the ocean of curiosity. For

You have reminded me of the yellow-garbed Nārāyaṇa whose body has become slothful because of being tired in his excessive dalliance of drinking the nectar of the lips of hundreds of cowherd maidens and who somewhere has fallen asleep on the couch of the heart of some grown-up cowherd maiden whose breasts have served the purpose of a pillow. /20/

(नेपथ्ये)

द्वात्रिंशल्लक्षणैर्युक्तो देवदेवेश्वरो हरिः।
गोपालबालकैः सार्द्धं जगाम यमुनावनम्।।२१।।

(Behind the curtain)

Endowed with thirty-two[5] auspicious marks on his body Hari, the Lord of gods, in the company of cowherd boys had entered the forest on the bank of the river Yamunā. /21/

(केदाररागेण)

मृदुतरमारुत-वेल्लितपल्लववल्ली-वलितशिखण्डम्।
तिलकविड़म्बितमरकतमणितलविम्बितशशधरखण्डम्।।

युवतीमनोहरवेशं
कलय कलानिधिमिव धरणीमनु परिणतरूपविशेषम्।।ध्रुवम्।।
खेलादोलायितमणिकुण्डलरुचिरुचिराननशोभम्।
हेलातरलितमधुर-विलोचनजनितबधूजन लोभम्।।
गजपतिरुद्रनराधिपचेतसि जनयतु मुदमनुवारम्।
रामानन्दरायकविभणितं मधुरिपुरूपमुदारम्।।२२।।

—Sung with Rāga "Kedāra"—

Take notice of the handsome figure of the enemy of Madhu (Kṛṣṇa) who has put on the charming dress appealing to the young maidens, who has feathers of the peacock (on his head) enclosed within sprouts and creepers moving by the force of the very gentle breeze, the *tilaka* mark on whose forehead ridicules the moon reflected on the surface of the emerald, who appears like the moon in its full beauty and splendour coming down to the earth, the beauty of whose face is enhanced by the lustre emitted from the ear-rings of gem moving to and fro during his sports, who creates longing in the cowherd maidens by his attractive eyes where the pupils keep on moving to the corner amorously.

May that figure as depicted by the poet Rāmānanda Rāya frequently cause delight in the mind of the king (Pratāpa) rudra, the lord of elephants. /22/

सूत्रधारः – (सचकितम्) प्रिये! मत् कनीयान् श्रीकृष्णवृन्दावनगमनमावेदयति। तद्वयमपि स्वनेपथ्योपचिताय याम (इति निष्क्रान्तौ)।।२३।।

The Stage-Manager—(With surprise) Oh my dear! my younger brother informs me that Śrī Kṛṣṇa has left for Vṛndāvana. So let us go for putting on our costumes (necessary for the stage). (With these words both of them leave the stage). /23/

प्रस्तावना।।२४।।

Prologue /24/

(ततः प्रविशति यथानिर्दिष्टः कृष्णः)

(Then enters Kṛṣṇa as depicted before)

कृष्ण: —सखे रतिकन्दल! पश्य, पश्य, रामणीयकं वृन्दावनस्य।।२५।।

Kṛṣṇa —Friend Ratikandala! Look, look at the beauty of Vṛndāvana. /25/

तथाहि –

उद्दामद्युति पल्लवावलि चलत् पाणिस्पृशोऽमीस्फुरत्
भृङ्गालिङ्गितपुष्पसाञ्जनदृशोमाद्यत्पिकानां रवैः।
आरब्धोत्कलिकालताश्च तरवश्चालोलमौलिश्रियः।
प्रत्याशं मधुसम्मदादिव रसालापं मिथः कुर्व्वते।।२६।।

For,

Those trees endowed with beauty in their topmost parts moving hither and thither and creepers in the primary stage of budding, with eyes anointed with collyrium in the form of the flowers embraced by the bees (with bees seated upon them), touching one another with hands moving in the shape of lustrous—young foliage (shaken by the southern breeze) in every direction, intoxicated as they are (with the advent of spring), are as if engaged in conversing among themselves on matters of love in the pretext of the cooing sound of the delighted cuckoos. /26/

विदूषक: —भो वअस्स तुज्झ एदं वुन्दाअणं रमणिज्जं, मम उण भोअणालओ ज्जेवव। जत्थ कहिम्पि सिहरिणी कहिम्पि रसाला कहिम्पि सुरहि घिओं कहिम्पि सालिभओं।।२७।।

(भो वयस्य! तवेदं वृन्दावनं रमणीयं, मम पुनर्भोजनालय एव यत्र कुत्रापि शिखरिणी कुत्रापि रसाला कुत्रापि सुरभिघृतं कुत्रापि शालिभक्तम्।।२७।।)

Vidūṣaka —Oh friend! This Vṛndāvana is beautiful to you, but for me beautiful is a dining hall where there is a dish of curds and sugar with spices *(śikhariṇi rasālā)* in some place, in some place sweet-smelling ghee and fine rice somewhere. /27/

कृष्ण: —सखे!

(वसन्तरागेण)

अपरिचितं तवरूपमिदं वत पश्य दिवोचितखेलम्।
ललित विकस्वरकुसुमचयैरिव हसति चिरादतिवेलम्।।

कलयं सखे भुविसारं
त्वदुपगमादिव सरसमिदं मम वृन्दावनमनुवारम्।।ध्रुवम्।।
मृदुपवनाहतिचञ्चलपल्लव करनिकरैरिव कामम्।
नर्त्तितुमुपदिशतीव भवन्तं सन्ततमिदमभिरामम्।।
सुखयतु गजपतिरुद्र मनोहरमनुदिनमिदमभिधानम्।
रामानन्दरायकविरचितं रसिकजनं सुविधानम्।।२८।।

Sung with Rāga "Vasanta" -

Kṛṣṇa —Oh friend! you are not acquainted with the beauty of this (Vṛndāvana). Hurray! Look at the divine play of nature; with the tender flowers in full bloom this (Vṛndāvana) excessively laughs as it were for a long time. Time after time, Oh friend! take notice of my lovely Vṛndāvana, the essence of the earth.

At your advent, with the hands in the shape of young foliage trembling, being struck by the gentle breeze this eternally pleasing (Vṛndāvana) as if directs you to dance to your heart's content.

May the song depicting this (beauty of Vṛndāvana), nicely composed by the poet Rāmānanda Rāya, pleasing to the heart of king (Pratāpa)rudra, the lord of elephants cause delight to the men of taste day after day. /28/

सखे! अतिमधुरोऽयं कोकिलानां रव:।।२९।।

Oh friend! how sweet is this cooing of the cuckoos? /29/

विदूषक: —भो वअस्स तुज्झ वंसीए रओ इदोवि महुरो। तदोवि अह्माणं कण्ठरओ, ता तुए वंसी वादिअदु मएवि कण्ठरओ कादव्वो।।३०।।
(भो वयस्य! तव वंश्या रव ईतोऽपि मधुर: ततोऽपि अस्माकं कण्ठरव:। तस्मात् त्वया वंशी वाद्यतां, मयापि कण्ठरव: कर्त्तव्य:।) ।।३०।।

Vidūṣaka —Oh friend! the sound of your flute is more sweet than it. And my voice is sweeter than that. Then you play the flute and I will be vocal. /30/

कृष्ण: —यदभिरुचितं वयस्याय (इति वंशीं वादयते)।।३१।।

Kṛṣṇa —As it pleases my friend (with these words he plays the flute). /31/

विदूषकः —भो सुदो दे वंसीरओ ममावि कण्ठरओ सुनीअदु

(भो श्रुतः ते वंश्या रवः, ममापि कण्ठरवः श्रूयताम्।)

(इति मुखवैकृत्य परुषं नदति)।।३२।।

Vidūṣaka —Well, the sound of your flute has been heard, now you listen to my voice. (With these words he changes the form of his face and shouts harshly). /32/

(तरुशिखरानवलोक्य) भो जिदं अह्मेहिं, तुज्झ वंसीए रएहिं एदे दासीए पुत्तआ कोइला निहुदं ट्ठिदा। मह उण कण्ठरएहिं कहिं वि पलाइदा। ता वअस्स मा गव्वो दे होदु।।३३।।

(भो जितं अस्माभिः तव वंश्या रवैरेते दास्याः पुत्रकाः कोकिला निभृतं स्थिताः, मम पुनः कण्ठरवैः कुत्रापि पलायिताः। तत् वयस्य! मा गर्वस्ते भवतु)।।३३।।

(Looking at the summit of the trees) Oh, I have won; these bastard cuckoos rested silently when you played your flute, but when I became vocal, they have flown away somewhere, therefore oh friend! you don't take pride (in playing your flute). /33/

कृष्णः —सखे, पश्य, पश्य, केनाप्यकरुणेन भग्नानि नवाशोकपल्लवानि चेतः खेदयन्ति।।३४।।

Kṛṣṇa —Look, look oh friend! some cruel person has torn off the fresh sprouts from the 'Aśoka' tree and the sight torments me. /34/

विदूषकः —भो वअस्स सुदं मए दासिए धीदाओ गोविआओ एथ्थ कुसुमाणि आहरन्ति। (सपरिहासस्) तुमंपि तदो ज्जेव एदं वुन्दाअणं ण मुञ्चसि।।३५।।

(भो वयस्य। श्रुतं मया दास्या पुत्रिका गोपिका अत्र कुसुमानि आहरन्ति। (सपरिहासम्) त्वमपि तत एव इदं वृन्दावनं न मुञ्चसि।)।३५।।

Vidūṣaka —Oh friend! I heard, these mischievous female-slaves, the cowherd maidens are plucking flowers here. (In jest) And that is why you are not leaving this

Vṛndāvana./35/

(नेपथ्ये)

वृन्दावने विहरतो मधुसूदनस्य
वेणुस्वनं श्रुतिपुटेन निपीय कामम्।
उद्यन्मनोज शिथिलीकृतगाढ़लज्जा
राधा विवेश कुतुकेन सखीकदम्बम्।।३६।।

(Behind the curtain)

Having drunk in through the ears (having heard) to her heart's content the sound of the flute of the slayer of Madhu (Kṛṣṇa) sporting in the Vṛndāvana, Rādhā with her intense feeling of bashfulness given in, due to love-sickness has eagerly joined the company of her friends. /36/

(गोण्डकिरीरागेण)

Sung with Rāga "Goṇḍakirī"—

कलयति नयनं दिशि दिशि वलितम्।
पङ्कजमिव मृदुमारुतचलितम्।।
केलिविपिनं प्रविशति राधा
प्रतिपदसमुदितमनसिजवाधा।।ध्रुवम्।।
विनिदधती मृदुमन्थरपादम्।
रचयति कुञ्चरगतिमनुवादम्।।
जनयतु रुद्रगजाधिपमुदितम्।
रामानन्दराय कविगदितम्।।३७।।

In every direction Rādhā casts her eyes tremulous like the lotus moving with the gentle breeze; struck with love-sickness at every step she enters the pleasure-garden; moving in a languid motion she imitates the gait of an elephant.

May the song composed by the poet Rāmānanda Rāya cause delight to (the king Pratāpa)rudra, the lord of elephants. /37/

विदूषक: —(कर्ण दत्त्वा) भो सुट्ठु मए जाणिदम्। (भो सुष्ठु मया ज्ञातम्)

कृष्ण: —किंम्?

Vidūṣaka —(Listening) Well, now I understand it clearly.

Kṛṣṇa —What did you understand?

विदूषकः —मं ज्जेवव पुच्छसि? ।।३८।। (मामेव पृच्छसि?)

Vidūṣaka —Do you ask me? /38/

(ततः प्रविशति सखीभिरनुगम्यमाना राधिका मदनिका वनदेवता च?)

विदूषकः —(पुरतोऽलोक्य) भो वअस्स! पेक्ख, पेक्ख, केणावि ईन्दआलिएण संचालिदो कणअ पुत्तलिआ निअर इध ज्जेव आअच्छदि। ता एदं एककं गोह्निअ पलाइस्सं मम दरिद्द वडुअस्स एदाए ज्जेव्व किदात्थदा हुविस्सदि। (इति स्वैरं स्वैरं धर्तुमुपसर्पति)।।३९।।

[भो वयस्य! पश्य पश्य केनापि इन्द्रजालिकेन सञ्चारितः कनकपुत्तलिकानिकर इत एव आगच्छति। तत इत एकां गृहीत्वा पलायिष्ये मम दरिद्र-वटुकस्य एतयैव कृतार्थता भविष्यति। (इति स्वैरं स्वैरं धर्त्तुमुपसर्पति।] ।३९।

(Then enters Rādhikā followed by her companions; Madanikā and the sylvan deity also enter)

Vidūṣaka —(Looking in the front) Look, look oh friend! a number of goldern images put to motion by some magician are coming in this direction. I will run away by catching hold of one (of these images). I am a poor boy, my purpose will be achieved only with this single (image) (with these words he slowly approaches to catch hold of one of the images). /39/

कृष्णः —धिङ् मूर्ख! नायं कनकपुत्तलिकानिकरः, किन्तु गोपीकदम्बकमिदम्।।४०।।

Kṛṣṇa —Fie upon you fool! this is not a collection of golden images, but this is a group of cowherd maidens. /40/

विदूषकः —(निरूप्य विहस्य) सुष्ठु तु ए तक्किदं ता फलिदं दे वुन्दाअणागमनं।।४१।।

(सुष्ठु त्वया तर्क्कितम्, तस्मात् फलितं ते वृन्दावनागमनम्)।४१।।

Vidūṣaka —(Observing carefully with a smile) your conjecture is right; the purpose of your coming to Vṛndāvana has borne fruit. /41/

कृष्णः —धिङ् मूर्ख! किं फलं मम वृन्दावनागमनस्य?

विदूषकः —एदाणं दासीए धीदानं सआसादो वुन्दाअण णअपल्लवाणं पडिवालणं त्ति भणामि।।४२।।

(एतासां दास्याः पुत्रिकाणां सकाशाद् वृन्दावननवपल्लवानां प्रतिपालनमिति भणामि।।४२।।)

Kṛṣṇa —Fie upon you fool! what is the consequence of my coming to Vṛndāvana?

Vidūṣaka —The protection of the new foliage of the Vṛndāvana garden is possible because of these female slaves, that is what I say. /42/

राधा —(पुरतोऽवलोक्य) अज्जे मअणिए! को एसो नीलुप्पल दल कोमल छइ कणअ णिअर सरिच्छ वसणो ईसिअ अलम्बिअ कन्धरं महुरमहुरं वेणुं वादेइ।।४३।।

(आर्ये मदनिके! क एष नीलोत्पलदलकोमलच्छविः कनकनिकरसदृशवसनं ईषदवलम्बितकन्धरं मधुरं मधुरं वेणुं वादयति।।४३।।)

Rādhā —(Looking in the front) Oh noble lady Madanikā! This person with the sweet lustre of the petal of a blue lotus and dressed with the attire of a golden hue is sweetly playing the flute slightly hanging down from the neck. Who is he? /43/

मदनिका —सखि! न जानासि यस्तव मया कथितः।

सोऽयं युवा युवतिचित्तविहङ्गशाखी
साक्षदिव स्फुरति पञ्चशरो मुकुन्दः।
यस्मिन् गते नयनयोः पथि सुन्दरीणां
नीविः स्वयं शिथिलतामुपयाति सद्यः।।४४।।

Madanikā —Oh dear friend! Don't you know I told you about this person?

This is that youth, a tree (providing shelter) for the birds—the hearts of young women, Mukunda (name of Viṣṇu) looks splendid as if god of love incarnate; at whose sight the knot of the garmet put on by beautiful women gets automatically loose all at once. /44/

कृष्ण: —(मनागवलोक्य, स्वगतम्) अहो शुभसमयजातत्वं कस्यचिद् वस्तुनः।।४५।।

Kṛṣṇa —[(Looking a little at (Rādhā), aside] Oh! This entity has its birth in an auspicious moment! /45/

तथाहि—

यदपि न कमलं निशाकरो वा
भवति मुखप्रतिमो मृगेक्षणायाः।
रचयति न तथापि जातु ताभ्या
मुपमितिरन्यपदे पदं यदस्य।।४६।।

For,

Neither the lotus flower nor the moon can be an object of comparison with the face of the fawn-eyed (lady). Even then besides those two (the lotus flower and the moon) the creator has not created any other object which can stand comparison with it (the face). /46/

विदूषक: —जाणिदं मए दासिए धीदा एहिं गोविआहिं उक्कण्ठिद हिअओ संवुत्तो भवं। ता एहि एदाणं दशणंपथादो गदुअ सिहरिणीहिं रसालाहिं वि अप्पाणं निव्वुदं करेह्म। पेक्ख, मज्झण्णो जादो।।४७।।

(ज्ञातं मया दास्याः पुत्रीभिर्गोपिकाभिरुत्कण्ठितहृदयः संवृत्तो भवान्। तस्मात् एहि एतासाम् दर्शनपथात् गत्वा शिखरिणीभिः रसालाभिरपि आत्मानं निवृत्तं कुर्म्मः। पश्य, मध्याह्नो जातः।)

Vidūṣaka —I know, for these slave-girls the cowherd-maidens you are feeling uneasy. Therefore let us go; let us get out of the sight of these maidens and be happy with the drink of curds mixed with sugar and spices *(rasālā* and *śikhariṇī)*. Look, it is already mid-day. /47/

कृष्ण: —सखे! सम्यगुपलक्षितम्।।४८।।

Kṛṣṇa —Oh friend! You have rightly noticed. /48/

तथाहि—

कथमिव परिखिन्ना व्योममात्र प्रयातुं
यदिहगलितवेगा वाजिनो यूयमित्थम्।
इति बिततकरान्तः सन्नुपालब्धुमश्वान्
गगनमिव मिमीते मध्यमध्यास्य भानुः।।४९।।

For,

How is it, you horses with your speed decreased by traversing even a little of this sky look so exhausted? Reproaching the horses in these words the Sun with his rays spread all around is, as it were, measuring the sky with its position secured in the centre of it. /49/

विदूषक: —(आकुञ्चितलोचनश्चिरं निरीक्ष्य) वअस्स! मएवि वण्णिदव्वो रइमण्डलो। आरोविअ चक्कभमिं, भमिदो जह विस्सकम्मणा सूरो। अज्जवि तह सक्कार भमिदं रइमण्डलं तक्केमि।।५०।।

(वयस्य! मयापि वर्णयितव्यो रविमण्डलः। आरोप्य चक्र-भ्रमिं भ्रमितो यत् विश्वकर्मणा सूर्यः, अद्यापि तस्य संस्कारभ्रमितं रविमण्डलं तर्कयामि।)

Vidūṣaka —(Looking at the sky for a long time with contracted brows)

Oh friend! let me depict the solar orb. Having set the sun on the potter's wheel Viśvakarman made it rotate; even today I think, the solar orb is rotating as before because of that impression retained in it. /50/

मदनिका —सखि! चिरविहार-परिश्रान्तासि, तदेहि गच्छाव। (इति निष्क्रान्ताः सर्व्वे)।।५१।।

Madanikā —Oh friend! You are tired and exhausted because of your pleasure-walk long since. So let us go. /51/

(Exeunt all)

इति पूर्वरागो नाम प्रथमोऽङ्कः।

Thus ends Act I entitled "the Dawning of Love".

REFERENCES

1. It is in the text of Śarmā that we come across this word सङ्गीतम्; in all other five texts used by us the musical song ends with चारु।
2. *Gajapati*—In ancient India the kings were in the habit of using

four honorific titles just to denote their greatness-*Aśvapati* (lord of horses), *Gajapati* (lord of elephants), *Narapati* (lord of people) and *Chatrapati* (lord of a horde of armies or soldiers). The emperors of Madradeśa were using the title *Aśvapati,* the emperors of Kalinga (Utkala) were using *Gajapati,* whereas the kings of Kāśī and Mahārāṣṭra were respectively designated as *Narapatis* and *Chatrapatis* (*Utkala Itihāsar Eka Ajñāta Adhyāya,* p. 19).

These titles *Aśvapati, Narapati* or *Gajapati* indicated sovereign status and prowess of a king. As pointed out by Prabhat Mukherjee, "Kapilendra and his descendants styled themselves as Gajapati or lord of the elephants and this became their dynastic title". Kapilendra, Puruṣottama and Pratāparudra were the Sūryavaṁśī kings of Orissa and they ruled Orissa for a period of hundred and five years.

The eminent historian Mukherjee again holds that "the title of Gajapati was unknown in Orissa before the 10th century A.D. Anantavarman Coḍagaṅga and his sons did not use this title". However, from South Indian Inscriptions it is known that Bhānudeva I was called *Gajaghotapati* (the lord of elephants and horses) and Narasiṁha IV and Bhānudeva IV, the last Gaṅga king bore the title Gajapati.

In the Jagannatha temple inscription of Kapilendradeva dated April 1450 A.D. the first Sūryavaṁśī king uses the term Gajapati for the first time (pp. 14, 168). In the Velicherla inscription (N.12 of 1920-21) recording the achievements of Gajapati kings it is mentioned that "Pratāparudra's huge elephants terrified the king of Gauḍa who fled to his capital" (p. 98). So it is clear from the above references that after Kapilendradeva, the first Sūryavaṁśī king the title *Gajapati* has come to be a normal epithet for the succeeding kings of this dynasty (For details vide Mukherjee, Prabhat—*The History of Gajapati Kings of Orissa,* Ch.1, pp. 1-3, 14, 98, 168).

3. Only the celestial Ganges brought down to the earth by Bhagīratha could purify Sagara's sons dead because of the curse of sage Dadhīci.

4. *Saptatantu*—It is an adjective which literally means "containing seven threads"; it is a metaphysical description of *yajña*. In commenting on this word Sāyaṇa takes it to be an epithet of *yajña* and his interpretation is "*saptabhiś chandomayaiḥ stutibhir vistṛtam*" (RV.X. 52.4)—the sacrifice in which the *mantras* are expanded into seven different Vedic metres like Gāyatrī, Uṣṇik, Anustup, Bṛhatī, Paṅkti,Tristup and Jagatī. In RV.X.124.1 this word is repeated and Sāyaṇa takes it as an epithet of *yajña,* the individual names of the basic sacrifices are—Agniṣṭoma, Atyagniṣṭoma, Ukthya, Ṣoḍaśī, Vājapeya, Atirātra and Aptoryāma. Further the other interpretation of Sāyaṇa is—"*sapta vaṣaṭ-karttāraḥ*"—the sacrifice in which seven priests are engaged in making the oblations with the exclamation '*vaṣaṭ*'.
5. Thrity-two marks—Rūpa Gosvāmin's *Ujjvala-nīlamaṇi* happens to be a supplement of his earlier work *Bhakti-rasāmṛta-sindhu* (1541 A.D.) *Ujjvala-nīlamaṇi* in its first chapter verses 5-8 refers to twenty-five qualities of Śrī Kṛṣṇa; commenting on the same verses Jīva Gosvāmin in his *Locana-rocinī* commentary explains and enumerates thirty-two auspicious qualities of the Lord (p.9). It is *Śrīmad Bhāgavata,* I.16.26-29 that speak of forty qualities of Kṛṣṇa. Referring to this particular portion of the *Bhāgavata, Bhakti-rasāmṛta-sindhu* goes on giving the list of sixty-four qualities of Lord Kṛṣṇa in its text, Part II.I verses 23-29, 37-44.

द्वितीयोऽङ्कः

ACT-II

(ततः प्रविशति मदनिका)

(Then enters Madanikā)

मदनिका —(पुरतोऽवलोक्य) कथमियमशोकमञ्जरी?।।१।।

Madanikā —(Looking in the front) Well, is it Aśokamañjarī? /1/

अशोकमञ्जरी —देइ! वन्दिज्जसि। गहिदकज्जभारव्व किम्पि चिन्तअन्ती कहिं पत्थिदासि।।२।।

(देवी वन्द्यसे। गृहीतकार्य्यभारेव किमपि चिन्तयन्ती कुत्र प्रस्थितासि?)

Aśokamañjarī—My greetings to you oh, revered lady! Having undertaken a responsibility, where are you proceeding in a thoughtful mind? /2/

मदनिका —वत्से! महती खल्वियं वार्त्ता।।३।।

Madanikā —My dear! it is a serious undertaking indeed. /3/

अशोकमञ्जरी —कथम्विअ? ।।४।। (कथमिव?)

Aśokamañjarī—How is it? /4/

मदनिका —वत्से! न जानासि प्रियसखीं राधामादाय कुसुमविहारार्थं गताः स्म?।।५।।

Madanikā —My dear! don't you know that in the company of dear friend Rādhā, I had been to the flower-garden? /5/

अशोकमञ्जरी —अध इं तत्थ?।।६।। (अथ किं तत्र?)

Aśokamañjarī—Then what happened there? /6/

मदनिका — तत्राशोकतरूमूले तया लोचनातिथिकृतोऽयं मुकुन्दः।।७।।

Madanikā —There at the foot of the Aśoka tree, she chanced to look at Mukunda. /7/

अशोकमञ्जरी –ण क्खु विलसिदं किम्पि कुसुमाउहेण?॥८॥
[न खलु विलसितं किमपि कुसुमायुधेन?]

Aśokamañjarī—Didn't the Cupid manifest any amorous pleasure at the time? /8/

मदनिका –अथ किं?॥९॥

Madanikā —Exactly so. /9/

अशोकमञ्जरी –ता एत्थ किं पडिवण्णं तत्थ भोदीए॥१०॥
(तस्मादत्र किं प्रतिपन्नं तत्र भवत्या?)

Aśokamañjarī—Therefore what did the revered lady infer from it? /10/

मदनिका –अयि सरले! अत्रापि[१] प्रष्टव्यास्मि?॥११॥

Madanikā —Oh, simple-minded! Is it proper to ask me on this point? /11/

अशोकमञ्जरी –अणुसरिदव्वो मुउन्दो?॥१२॥ (अनुसर्तव्यो मुकुन्दः?)

Aśokamañjarī—Shall we seek for Mukunda? /12/

मदनिका –अथ किं ॥१३॥

Madanikā —Yes, indeed! /13/

अशोकमञ्जरी –अध कधं ताए लज्जातरलाए हिअअं तुए ण्णादं?॥१४॥
[अथ कथं तस्या लज्जातरलाया हृदयं त्वया ज्ञातम्?]

Aśokamañjarī—Then how did you know the heart of that bashful lady? /14/

मदनिका –वत्से!

तावदेव त्रपावर्म्म बालानां हृदये स्थिरम्
यावद्विषमबाणस्य न पतन्ति शिलीमुखाः॥१५॥

Madanikā —My dear! Listen. The armour of bashfulness is steady in the hearts of young women so long as the shafts of Cupid *(Viṣamabāṇa)*[2] do not pierce them. /15/

अशोकमञ्जरी –तहवि किं ताए ज्जेव स्फुड़ीकिदं तुह्मेहिं वा अणुमिदं?॥१६॥
(तथापि किं तयैव स्फुटीकृतं युष्माभिर्वा अनुमितम्?)

Aśokamañjarī —Then did she reveal her heart to you or did you infer it? /16/

मदनिका —मयैवानुमितम्।।१७।।

Madanikā —I have inferred it. /17/

अशोकमञ्जरी —कधं विअ?।।१८।। (कथमिव?)

Aśokamañjarī—How so? /18/

मदनिका —शशिनि नयनपातो नादरादुन्मदानां
रुतमनु च पिकानां कर्णरोधश्छलेन
प्रतिवचनमपार्थं यत्सखीनां कथासु
स्मरविलसितमस्यास्तेन किञ्चित प्रतीतम्।।१९।।

Madanikā —Aversion to look at the moon with love or affection, closing her ears against the sweet note of intoxicated cuckoos, giving meaningless reply in course of conversation with her companions—all these somewhat suggest the amorous gesture of this maiden. /19/

(गान्धाररागेण)

—Sung with Rāga "Gāndhāra" -

हरि हरिचन्दनमारुत पिकरुतमनुतनुरतनु विकारम्।
तिरयितुमिव सा कति कति सहसा रचयति न शिशुविहारम्।।१।।
उपनतमनसिजवाधा
अभिनवभावभरानपि दधती शिवशिव सीदति राधा।।ध्रुवम्।।
अविषय[3] निश्चल नयनयुगल गलदम्बुकणाननुवारम्।
रहसि हठादुपयाति सखीमनुरचयति सौहृदसारम्।।२।।
गजपतिरुद्रमनोहरमहरहरिदमनुरसिकसमाजम्
रामानन्दराय कवि भणितं विहरतु हरिपदभाजम्।।३।। ।।२०।।

In order to conceal the love-sickness caused by the breeze blowing in association with the *Haricandana* tree and by the sweet note of the cuckoos, the slender-maiden inconsiderately many a time behaves like a child (lit; how many times does she not show childish behaviour?). With the torment of Cupid fallen to her lot, Rādhā remains dejected bearing the excess of youthful love. With the drops of tears streaming down from both of her steady motionless eyes, turned away from sense-objects all on a sudden with great frequency she repairs to a solitary place and makes friendship with her companion. May this (song) composed by the poet Rāmānanda Rāya, pleasing to the king (Pratāpa)rudra, the lord of elephants constantly amuse the assembly of the men of taste who adore the feet of Hari. /20/

त्वं पुनः कुत्र प्रस्थितासि?।।२१।।

And where are you going? /21/

अशोकमञ्जरी —अहं पि ताए भणिदा, सहि! अहिणअपउमदलसेज्जा पज्जुसुअह्मि। ता उवणेहि तारिसाइं पउमदलाइं। अदो तदत्थं पत्थिदाह्मि।।२२।।

(अहमपि तया भणिता—सखि! अभिनव पद्मदलशय्यापर्य्युत्सुकास्मि। तस्मादुपनय तादृशानि पद्मदलानि। अतस्तदर्थं प्रस्थितास्मि।)

Aśokamañjarī—She also told me —O friend! I am anxious to have a bed of new lotus-leaves; so procure those lotus-leaves. Hence I am going for that. /22/

मदनिका —(स्वगतं) अये, अतिनिष्ठुरं विलसति पुष्पचापः श्रुतं मया—

सा दक्षिणानिल कुहुरुत भृङ्गनाद
व्याजृम्भमाणमदना सुचिरं विचार्य्यम्।
किञ्चित् सखीं शशिमुखीं सुमुखी विविक्ते
पर्य्याकुलाक्षरमिदं निजगाद राधा।।२३।।

Madanikā —(aside) As I hear, Cupid appears to be very cruel.

With love-sickness intensely manifested due to the southern breeze, the sweet note of cuckoos and the humming of the black-bees, lovely Rādhā pondered for a long time and said some of these confounded words to her companion Śaśimukhī.

(तोड़ीवराड़ीरागेण)

—Sung with Rāga "Toḍīvarāḍī" —/23/

विदलित सरसिजदलचयशयने।
वारितसकलसखीजननयने॥१॥
वलति मनो मम सत्वर रचने।
पूरय काममिमं शशिवदने॥२॥
अभिनवविस-किशलय-चय-वलये।
मलयजरसपरिसेवितनिलये॥ध्रुवम्॥
सुखयतु रुद्रगजाधिपचित्तम्।
रामानन्द राय कविभणितम्॥३॥ ॥२४॥

My mind is yearning for a bed formed of quite open lotus-leaves. encircled with fresh lotus-stalks and young tender foliage in an apartment with sandal paste applied therein. Away from the sight of all my companions, O moon-faced lady! immediately you please prepare the bed, and fulfil this desire of mine. May this composition of the poet Rāmānanda Rāya delight the heart of the king (Pratāpa)rudra, the lord of elephants. /24/

मदनिका —साधय, शिवाः सन्तु ते पन्थानः। अहमपि मुकुन्दमनुसरिष्यामि॥२५॥

Madanikā —Proceed, God bless you on your journey, I will also look for Mukunda (lit. I will also follow Mukunda). /25/

अशोकमञ्जरी —ता वन्दिज्जसि (इति निष्क्रान्ता)॥२६॥
(तस्मात् वन्द्यसे।)

Aśokamañjarī—I bow to you (she departs). /26/

मदनिका —(परिक्रम्य, आकाशे लक्ष्यं वद्धवा) भोः शुकाः। जानीत कुत्रायं द्रष्टव्यो मुकुन्दः? (श्रुतिमभिनीय) किं ब्रूत, भाण्ड़ीर तरुमूले शशिमुखीद्वितीयः प्रतिवसति? भवतु, नियोजिता मयैव तत्र शशिमुखी। (प्रेत्य) किं ब्रूत, "त्वं कुत्र प्रस्थितासि" इति? तत्रैवात्मानमपवार्य्य "श्रोतव्योऽयं वृत्तान्तः" इति तत्रैव गच्छामि (इति निष्क्रान्ता)॥२७॥

Madanikā —(Going round, concentrating her attention in the sky) O parrots! Do you know where I can find Mukunda? (Acting as if hearing something) Do you say, he is there at the foot of *Bhāṇḍīrą* tree in the company of Śaśimukhī? Alright, Śaśimukhī has been deputed there. (Going forward) Do you say, where are you going? Having concealed myself there, I will listen to this news. Let me go there (leaves the stage). /27/

विष्कम्भकः।।२७।।

An interlude[4] /28/

(ततः प्रविशति शशिमुखीद्वितीयः कृष्णः)

(Then enters Kṛṣṇa in the company of Śaśimukhī)

कृष्णः —इतः इतः।

शशिमुखी —(अनङ्गपत्रिकामर्पयति)

कृष्णः —(वाचयति)—सुदिढं विज्जसि हिअअं लम्भइ मअणो क्खु दुज्जसं वलिअं दीससि सअल दिसासु तुमं, दीसइ मअणो ण कुत्तावि।।२९।।

(सुदृढं विध्यसि हृदयं, लभते मदनः खलु दुर्यशोवलीयः।
दृश्यसे सकलदिक्षु त्वं, दृश्यते मदनो न कुत्रापि।।२९।।)

Kṛṣṇa —This way, this way.

Śaśimukhī —(Hands over the love letter).

Kṛṣṇa —(reads aloud) Very intensely you pierce my heart; but ill-repute goes to Cupid. I behold you in all directions, but nowhere Cupid is to be seen. /29/

कृष्णः —(स्वगतम्) अये! अतिभूमिं गतोऽस्या रागः। तदाकलयाम्यौदास्येनास्या हृदयस्थैर्यं (प्रकाशं, सावहित्थं) सखि! को वाऽयं मदनाभिधः कथमितः किं वापराद्धं तया येनायं हृदयं दुनोति सुदृशः कंसस्य किं कोऽप्यसौ? (साटोपम्) तदादेशय क्वासौ।

अद्यैनं भुजयुग्ममात्रशरणः सम्मर्द्य बालामिमा-
मभ्यग्रां रचयामि किं मयि सति त्रासो व्रजस्त्रीजने?।।३०।।

(aside) Oh! (Her) love has reached the climax! By remaining indifferent let me then test the fortitude of this (maiden) (concealing his inner feelings, openly)

Friend! who is this Madana? Why he is here? What is her fault for which this (Madana) torments the heart of the pretty woman (lit. having beautiful eyes)? Is he somehow related to Kaṁsa? (With pride) then tell me, where is he? Only with the support of both of my arms, today I will vanquish this (Madana) and make this maiden free from anxiety. When I am there, can there be any alarm to the women of Vraja? /30/

विदूषकः —(अपटीक्षेपेण प्रविश्य) भो वअस्स! ण क्खु एसो कंसस्स कोवि, अहं ज्जेव्व मअणाभिहो, ता तुए किं मह वह्मणसस कादव्वं।।३१।।

[भो वयस्य! न खलु एष कंसस्य कोऽपि, अहमेव मदनाभिधस्तत् किं त्वया मम ब्राह्मणस्य कर्त्तव्यम्?]

Vidūṣaka —(enters, tossing aside the curtain)
Oh friend! This (Madana) is no way related to Kaṁsa; my name is Madana; then what can you do to me, a Brahmin?/31/

कृष्णः —धिङ् मूर्ख! अलं परिहासेन।

विदूषकः —भोदि! अह्माणं पिअवअस्सस्स हत्थे लड्डुअजुअलं तुए दादव्वं, पिअ वअस्स तत्थ गदुअ मअणं निराकरिस्सदि।।३२।।

(भवति! अस्माकं प्रियवयस्यस्य हस्ते लड्डुकयुगलं त्वया दातव्यम्, प्रियवयस्य तत्र गत्वा मदनं निराकरिष्यति।)

Kṛṣṇa —Fie upon you, fool! enough of jest!

Vidūṣaka —Oh revered lady! you hand over two sweet-meats to our dear friend. (Our) dear friend will go there and vanquish Madana. /32/

मदनिका —(कर्णं दत्त्वा) अये! निसृष्टार्थेयं दूती, यतः—
इयं तत्तत्वचो वृन्दावने माधवसन्निधौ।
राधारूपकथाव्याजादुवाचासत्तिकोविदा।।
(निरूप्य, विहस्य)
अमुष्याः प्रोन्मीलत् कमलमधु धारा इव गिरो
निपीय क्षीवत्वं गतइव चलन्मौलिरधिकम्।

उदञ्चत् कामोऽपि स्वहृदयकलागोपनपरो
हरिः स्वैरं स्वैरं स्मितसुभगमूचे कथमिदम्।।

तद् भवतु,
अतिभूमिं गतो रागो। माधुर्य्यमावहति।।३३।।

Madanikā —(Listening) This confidante has been entrusted with the task of uniting the youth and the maiden *(nisṛṣṭ-ārthā dūti)*[5]. For, under the pretext of depicting the beauty of Rādhā, in Vṛndāvana this (Śaśimukhī) expert in bringing about the union of the youth and the maiden has told many things to Mādhava.

(Observing carefully, with a smile)

Drinking in her words (sweet) like a stream of honey flowing down from a lotus in full bloom, Kṛṣṇa shaking his head (in appreciation) gets highly excited as it were. Even though his feeling of love is in ascendancy, proficient in concealing all the emotions of his heart, Hari in a relaxing mood spoke this pleasantly with a smile. How is it? Let that be so. Love which has reached the climax, leads to sweetness. /33/

कृष्णः —(पुनरपि पत्रिकां वाचयित्वा) सखि! सम्यगिदं नावकलितम्।

गोपालवालकवृतो यमुनातटान्ते
वृन्दावने किमपि केलिकलां भजामि।
कस्मादियं दिशिदिशि स्फुटरूपभाजं
मामेव पश्यति कुरङ्गकिशोरनेत्रा?।।३४।।

Kṛṣṇa —(again reading aloud the letter) Oh friend! I cannot make it out thoroughly.

In the outskirts of the banks of the river Yamunā in Vṛndāvana, surrounded by the cowherd-boys I resort to some love-sports. How is it that this fawn-eyed maiden beholds me everywhere in my visible form! /34/

(सामगुज्जरीरागेण)
गोपकुमारसमाजमिमं सखि पृच्छ कदानुगतोऽहम्।
कथमिव मामनुपश्यति दिशिदिशि कथमिव कलयति मोहम्।।१।।
सखि! परिहर वचनविलासं
गोपशिशूनां विदितमिदं मम जनयति गुरुपरिहासम्।।ध्रुवम्।।
यदिच कुलाचलयापि[६] कुलस्थितिरनयापरिहरणीया।
किमिति तदा मयि रति रतिविकला वाले किल करणीया।।२।।
गजपतिरुद्रमुदे मधुसूदनवचनमिदं रसिकेषु।
रामानन्दरायकविभणितं जनयतु मुदमखिलेषु।।३।। ।।३५।।

(Sung with Rāga "Sāmagujjarī")

Oh friend! ask this host of cow-herd boys when I have followed her. But how is it that she beholds me everywhere and why does she fall into a swoon? Oh friend! away with (your) jugglery of words. Once the cow-herd boys know of it, they would highly ridicule me. When this maiden used to family traditions is not supposed to abandon her family honour, how is she justified in making a show of her deep excitement in love before me, a mere boy! May these words of Madhusūdana (the destroyer of the demon Madhu) composed by the poet Rāmānanda Rāya for the pleasure of the king (Pratāpa)rudra, the lord of elephants delight all men of taste. /35/

शशिमुखी —(स्वगतम्) अहो! पिअसहीए अत्थाणाणुराओ। ता किं एत्थ कादव्वं।।३६।।

(अहो! प्रियसख्या अस्थानानुरागः। तत् किमत्र कर्त्तव्यं)

Śaśimukhī —(aside) Alas! my dear friend is attached to a wrong person! Then what is the remedy here? /36/

विदूषकः —भो! किं एदाए दुट्ठ गोवीधीदाए भणिदाए? वअस्स पेक्ख पेक्ख—

रइअरचलिदाहंसी मग्गइ छाअं कमलगुच्छस्स।
मारु-अ धुअ अरआत्ता पेक्खसि जं तं निआरेदि।।३७।।

(भो, किमेतया दुष्टगोपी-पुत्रिकाया भणित्या? वयस्य! पश्य पश्य-
ऽविकरचलिता हंसी मृगयति च्छायां कमलगुच्छस्य।
मारुतधूततरात्मा पश्यसि यत्तां निवारयति)।।३७।।

Vidūṣaka —Oh! what is the use of these words of this wretched cow-herd maiden? Oh friend! Look, look—Agitated by the rays of the sun, the female-swan seeks for the shade of the cluster of lotus-flowers, but you see, shaken by the breeze the cluster of lotus-flowers prevents her (from taking shelter). /37/

कृष्णः —(स्वगतम्) अहो वचनभङ्गी धूर्त्तस्य (प्रकाशम्) धिङ् मूर्ख! किमप्रस्तुतमालपसि?।।३८।।

Kṛṣṇa —(aside) Oh! the rogue speaks in a round about way, (aloud) Fie upon you, fool! Why do you talk irrelevant? /38/

विदुषकः —भो वअस्स! मए ज्जेव पत्थुदं भणिदं।।३९।।
(भो वयस्य! मयैव प्रस्तुतं भणितम्)

Vidūṣaka —Oh friend! what I say is relevant. /39/

मदनिका —(स्वगतम्) सर्वथा कृतार्थासि अये राधिके!।।४०।।

Madanikā —(aside) Oh Rādhikā! You have achieved your object in every respect. /40/

शशिमुखी —(प्रकाशम्) महाभाअ असरिसं तुह्मारिसाणं अनुगदवञ्चणं।।४१।।
(महाभाग! असदृशं त्वादृशानामनुगतवञ्चनम्।)

Śaśimukhī —(aloud) It is not proper for people of your type, revered sir! to disappoint somebody attached to you. /41/

कृष्णः —भद्रे! अन्यदप्याकलय।
दयितो दयितस्तस्या बालेयं कुलपालिका
अकाण्डे किमसौ मुग्धे धत्तामाचारविप्लवम्।।४२।।

Kṛṣṇa —My good lady! Please think over it from a different angle. This maiden born in a noble family is dear to her lover. Oh simple-minded lady! Why should she deviate from her course of conduct all on a sudden? /42/

विदूषक: —भोदि, अह्माणं पिअवअस्सो धम्मसरणो ता ओसरदु भोदी। (कृष्णस्य हृदि हस्तं दत्त्वा) भोदि! मा उत्तम्म सा ज्जेव्व पिअवअस्सस्स हिअए कुरकुराअदि। ता मए ज्जेव फुडं कादव्वं सव्वं। (कर्णे) भो वअस्स! तुह्मेहिंपि सा सिविणे वारसहस्सं दिट्ठा। एहिंन कीस अत्थिज्जन्तो अप्पा अत्थाविज्जदि?।।४३।।

(भवति! अस्माकं प्रियवयस्यो धर्म्मशरणः, तदपसरतु भवती। (कृष्णस्य हृदि हस्तं दत्वा) भवति! मा उत्ताम्यसैव। प्रियवयस्यस्य हृदये कुरकुरायते। तस्मात् मयैव स्फुटं कर्त्तव्यं सर्व्वम्। (कर्णे) भो वयस्य! युष्माभिरपि सा स्वप्ने वारसहस्रं दृष्टा। इदानीं कस्मादर्थ्यमान आत्मा अर्थापयसि?)

Vidūṣaka —Our dear friend is attached to righteousness. Your ladyship! Please be off (move away). (Placing his hand on the chest of Kṛṣṇa). Your ladyship! Don't get suffocated. She is the cause of excitement of my friend. Therefore let me make everything clear. (In the ears) Oh friend! You have dreamt of her a thousand times. Now even though sought after by her, what is the reason of your double-dealing? /43/

कृष्णः —धिङ् मूर्ख! मम स्वप्नवृत्तान्तः कथं त्वया ज्ञातः?

Kṛṣṇa —Fie upon you, fool! How did you know of my dream?

विदूषकः —सिविणेवि किं परिहरसि? तहिं ज्जेव अह्मेहिंपि दिट्ठं।।४४।।

(स्वप्नेऽपि किं परिहरसि, तस्मिन्नेवास्माभिरपि दृष्टम्।)

Vidūṣaka —Do you ever desert us even in a dream?/44/

Therefore we have also seen you in the dream.

श्रीकृष्णः —(स्वगतं) यद्यप्यनेन वाचाटवटुना परिहासशीलतया आलापितं, तथापि सद्वादो वृत्तः। भवतु, तथापि जिज्ञासनीयस्वभावा हि बालारमण्यः। (प्रकाशम्) भद्रे! तन्निवर्त्त्यतां असदृशात् साहसादियं वाला। (विदूषकं प्रति) वयस्य! तदेहि वयमपि वत्साहरणाय यामः। भद्रे! त्वमपि सानुनयमेनां निवर्त्तय इति।।४५।।

Kṛṣṇa —(aside) Even though this garrulous chap talks in jest, yet he speaks the truth. Alright, still it is worth-knowing the innate desire of the young women. (Openly) My good lady! so let this young maiden be restrained from unbecoming rashness. (To Vidūṣaka), Friend! Therefore you come, let us go to bring together the calves. My good lady! Through friendly persuasion you too restrain this (maiden). /45/

(मल्लाररागेण)
शशिनि न रागं भजते नलिनी।
रविमनु नैव वृषस्यति रजनी॥१॥
कुलवनितानामिदमाचरितम्।
परपुरुषाधिगमे गुरुदुरितम्॥२॥
शशिमुखि! वारय वारिजवदनां।
अनुचितविषय विकस्वरमदनाम्॥ध्रुवम्॥
सा यदि गणयति न कुलचरित्रम्।
किमिति वयं कलयाम न चित्रम्॥३॥
उदयतु रुद्रगजाधिपहृदये।
रामानन्दभणितमति सदये॥४॥ ॥४६॥

—Sung with Rāga "Mallāra"

The lotus does not have any love for the moon; the night does not long for union with the sun; this conduct of women of high birth to approach strangers is a heinous sin. Ward off the lotus-faced maiden intoxicated with love, Oh Śaśimukhī! from the ugly affair. Is it not a thing to be surprised, if she does not stick to her family traditions?

May this composition of Rāmānanda exalt the very compassionate heart of king (Pratāpa)rudra, the lord of elephants. /46/

इति निष्क्रान्ता सर्वे॥

इति भावपरीक्षा नाम द्वितीयोऽङ्कः।

(Exeunt all)

Thus ends Act II entitled "The Testing of Sentiment of Love".

REFERENCES

1. Another reading here is तत्रापि।
2. *Viṣamabāṇa* —Cupid, the god of love is known as *Pañceṣuḥ*. The flowers like *Aśoka* (saraca indica), *Aravinda* (nelumbo pucifera), *Cūta* (mangifera indica), *Mallikā* (jasminum sambac) and *Nīlotpala* (nymphaea stellata) constitute the five arrows of Cupid. Five is an uneven number. So the god of love is called *Viṣamabāṇaḥ*.
3. Even though we find the reading "अविधय" in four texts such as edited by Vidyāratna, Śarmā, Brahmacārī and Otā, the word "अविषय" is most appropriate here and it is supported by Orissa Museum text and the text of Senagupta. (See also translation p. 111 for it.)
4. A *Viṣkambhaka* or an interlude indicates that portion of the plot which intervenes between what has already happened and what is to happen. Couched up in brief words it is set in the beginning of an Act.
5. *nisṛṣṭārthā dūtī*—Vatsyāyana (400 A.D.), the author of *Kāmasūtra* speaks of eight types of female-messengers in his text. *Nisṛṣṭārthā dūtī* being the first type of female messenger is defined as *—nāyakasya nāyikāyāśca yathāmanīṣitam artham upalabhya svabuddhyā kāryasampādinī nisṛṣṭārthā/*

   Kāmasūtra, V.4.46
6. In the five texts we come across this reading. कुलाचला here means-कुले अचला, a woman steadfast in domestic virtues. Further the word अचला suggests that like an immovable mountain (अचल) Rādhā is unswerving in her family customs, but Senagupta's reading अबला is not suggestive.

तृतीयोऽङ्कः

ACT-III

(ततः प्रविशति अशोकमञ्जरी)

(Then enters Aśokamañjarī)

अशोकमञ्जरी –अए! सुदं मए मअणिआए वनदेअदाए ससिमुहीए सद्धं किम्पि रहस्सं कुणन्ती माहवीलदामण्डवसआसे पिअसही चिट्ठदि, ता पेक्खिअ गमिस्सं। (अग्रतोऽवलोक्य समुपसर्प्य च) अए! एदाओ लहु लहु किम्पि जप्पन्ति, ता ण जुज्जदि एत्थ पविसिदुं। (इति निष्क्रान्ता)॥१॥

[अये! श्रुतं मया–मदनिकया वनदेवतया शशिमुख्या च सार्द्धं किमपि रहस्यं कुर्वती माधवीलतामण्डपसकाशे प्रियसखी तिष्ठति, तत्प्रेक्ष्य गमिष्यामि। (अग्रतोऽवलोक्य समुपसर्प्य च) अये, एता लघु लघु किमपि जल्पन्ति, तन्न युज्यतेऽत्र प्रवेष्टुम्। (इति निष्क्रान्ता)]

(ततः प्रविशति शशिमुख-मदनिकाभ्यां प्रवोध्यमाना राधा)

Aśokamañjarī—Oh! I hear, in the bower of Mādhavī creepers there is (our) dear friend (Rādhā) conversing on something secret with Madanikā, the sylvan deity and Śaśimukhī. After meeting them let me go. (Looking in the front and approaching) They are talking something in a low voice, so it is not proper to enter here. (Exit) /1/

(Then enters Rādhā consoled by Śaśimukhī and Madanikā)

राधा –(दीर्घमुष्णञ्च निःश्वस्य) सच्चवकं ज्जेब्व गरिहिदहि माहवेण॥२॥

[सत्यकमेव परिहतास्मि माधवेन?]

Rādhā —[Breathing a long feverish sigh (of bereavement)] Is it a fact that Mādhava has abandoned me? /2/

(संस्कृतमाश्रित्य)-सामगुज्जरीरागेण-
कुलवनिताजन घृतमाचारम्।
तृणवदगणयं गलितविचारम्।।१।।
शिव शिव किं वा चरितमशस्तं।
विधिरधुना वद वशयतु कस्तम्।।ध्रुवम्।।
शिशुरपि युवतिरिवाहितभावा।
विगलितलज्जितमहमिव का वा।।२।।
गजपतिरुद्रमुदे समुदीतम्।
रामानन्दराय कवि गीतम्।।३।। ।।३।। (In Sanskrit)
—Sung with Rāga "Śāmagujjarī" -

Deprived of my conscience I considered the conduct of women of high birth as worthless as grass. Alas! What an indiscreet act have I not done! Now say, what is to be done, who can win him (Kṛṣṇa) over. Even though a girl, I behaved like a young maiden; who is there so shameless like me! This song of the poet Rāmānanda Rāya is recited for the pleasure of the king (Pratāpa)rudra, the lord of elephants. /3/

शशिममुखी —वण्णिदो ज्जेव्व सव्वो वुत्तन्तो, ता सअं ज्जेव्व विआरीअदु।।४।।
(वर्णित एव सर्ववृत्तान्तः। तत् स्वयमेव विचार्य्यताम्।)

Śaśimukhī —All the facts have been put (before you), so you are the person to decide. /4/

राधा —(संस्कृतमाश्रित्य) श्रावं श्रावं सुसाम श्रुतिसमितपरब्रह्म वंशीप्रसूतं
दर्शं दर्शं त्रिलोकीवरतरुण-कलाकेलिलावण्यसारम्।
ध्यायं ध्यायं समुद्यद्द्युमणि कुमुदिनीबन्धुरोचिः सरोचि
श्च्छायं श्रीकान्तसङ्गं दहति मम मनो मां कुकूलाग्निदाहम्।।५।।

Rādhā —(In Sanskrit)

In the sound produced from the flute repeatedly I heard the voice of the Supreme Spirit resembling the perfect chanting of the Sāmaveda; at every sight I noticed the essence of beauty of the skillful amorous sport of the most beautiful youth of the three worlds;

repeatedly I meditated upon (my) association with lovely and beautiful Śrīkānta endowed with the glow of the rising sun and the moon. My heart torments me like fire made of chaff. /5/

शशिमुखी –सहि! मुञ्च अत्थाणागहं ॥६॥ (सखि! मुञ्च अस्थानाग्रहम्)

Śaśimukhī —Oh friend! Give up your interest in a wrong place. /6/

(संस्कृतमाश्रित्य)

यद् यद् व्यञ्जितमञ्जन-प्रतिकृतौ कृष्णे तदर्थं मया
तत्तत्तेन निवारितं शिशुदशाभाव-प्रकाशैरलम्।
आस्तामुत्कलिका-प्रसून-विगलन्माध्वीकनद्धं विषं
कृष्ण ध्यानमितोऽन्यतः सुवदने सङ्कल्पमाकल्पय॥७॥

(In Sanskrit)

For that (For your union with Kṛṣṇa) whatever indications I gave to Kṛṣṇa, an image of collyrium, were totally rejected by him by a show of childish pranks. The honey existing in the flower of your longing is but poison. Give up your longing for Kṛṣṇa, Oh lovely maiden, divert your thought to some other person. /7/

(सुहयीरागेण)

हीनं पतिमपि भजते रमणी।
केशरिणं किमु कलयति हरिणी॥१॥
राधिके, परिहर माधवरागगये॥ध्रुवम्॥
क्षीणे शशिनि च कुमुदवनीयम्।
भजति न भावं किमु रमणीयम्॥२॥
सुखयतु गजपतिरूद्र नरेशम्।
रामानन्दराय गीतमनिशम्॥३॥ ॥८॥

—Sung with Rāga "Suhayī"

A woman betakes herself to her husband however vile and mean he may be, a female-deer does not long for union with a lion; Oh Rādhikā! Give up your attachment for Mādhava. Is it not a fact that this cluster of white water lilies is delighted even when the moon is on the wane? May the song of Rāmānanda Rāya incessantly delight the king (Pratāpa)rudra, the lord of elephants. /8/

राधा —(सास्रं) देविमदनिके! कः प्रतिकारः?[१]

प्रेमच्छेदरुजोऽवगच्छति हरिर्नायं न च प्रेम वा
स्थानास्थानमवैति नापि मदनो जानाति नो दुर्ब्बलाः।
अन्यो वेद न चान्यदुःखमखिलं नो जीवनं वाश्रवं
द्वित्राण्येव दिनानि यौवनमिदं, हा हा विधेः का गतिः।।९।।

Rādhā —(With tears) Oh revered lady Madanikā! What is the remedy? (How is it that) this Hari neither knows of love nor even of the pangs of separation in love? Cupid never takes note of proper or improper place. Neither Cupid knows us to be frail. One does not feel all the sorrows and sufferings of the other. Our life is a flowing stream and this youth lasts only for two or three days. Alas! What the providence ordains for me? /9/

मदनिका —कथमेवं उत्ताम्यसि? यतः—

समाकृष्टा दूराद् किमपि यदि सा केतकिवन—
प्रसूनेनोन्मीलत् सुरभि भरसारेण नियतम्।
अथ भ्रामं भ्रामं रजसि रसमालोक्य न मना—
गपि प्रान्तप्राप्ता परिहरति तन्नो मधुकरी।।१०।।

Madanikā —Why do you gasp for breath? For, invariably attracted from a distance by the essence of fragrance of the flower blooming in the forest of *Ketakī* plants, does not the female-bee hovering over the flower abandon it by merely touching its tip when she does not get even a drop of honey in the pollens? /10/

राधा —(धैर्य्यमवलम्ब्य) परित्यक्त एव (इत्यर्द्धोक्तेन) (ससाध्वसोत्कम्पं) देवि! नायं ममापराधः। यतः—

यदायातो दैवान्मधुरिपुरसौ लोचनपथं
तदास्माकं चेतो मदनहतकेनाहृतमभूत्।

(क्षणं स्थित्वा दीर्घमुष्णञ्च निःश्वस्य)
पुनर्यस्मिन्नेष क्षणमपि दृशोरेति पदवीं
विधास्यामस्तस्मिन्नखिल-घटिकारत्नखचिता॥११॥

Rādhā —(With patience) Am I to be deprived of Kṛṣṇa? (in a broken voice). (Trembling with fear) Oh revered lady! It is not my fault. For,

When that (Kṛṣṇa), the enemy of the demon Madhu accidentally came within the range of my sight, my mind was fascinated by the wretched Cupid.

[Waiting for a moment and breathing a long feverish sigh (of bereavement)]

Were this (Kṛṣṇa) to come within the range of sight once again for a moment, I would store that moment in my mind as invaluable treasures. /11/

मदनिका —(स्वगतम्) अतिभूमिं गतोऽस्या अनुरागस्तददति प्रियकथनेनान्यमानसां[2] रचयामि। (प्रकाशम्) वत्से! पश्य, पश्य—

योऽयं त्वया स्वकरपुष्करसिक्तमूलं
सम्बर्द्धितः सुतनु बालरसालशाखी।
जातः स ते मुकुलदन्तुरमौलिरीष-
न्मन्ये तदेव मधुपाः प्रियमालपन्ति॥१३॥

Madanikā —(aside) The love of this (maiden) has reached the climax. Let me then divert her mind by speaking something pleasant. (Aloud) My dear! Look, look— The young mango tree which had been reared by you with water poured at its root by your lotus-like hands, Oh lovely maiden, has its top covered a little with the cluster of buds. So I think, the black bees are conversing pleasantly (the humming sound of the black bees is taken to be their pleasant conversation). /13/

राधा —(सत्रासोत्कम्पम्) हला शशिमुखि! स्मर्त्तव्यास्मि।

मदनिका —(स्वगतम्) अहो!! केयमनर्थपरम्परा स्वयमुपस्थिता? (प्रकाशम्) वत्से!

मातिविक्लवा भूः। उपलक्षितमेवास्य सानुरागहृदयम्॥१४॥

Rādhā —(Trembling with fear) Friend Śaśimukhī! Keep me in your mind.

Madanikā —(aside) Ah, what a series of calamities has befallen (her)! (Aloud) My dear! Don't be so helpless. We have already observed the heart of this (Kṛṣṇa) intense in love. /14/

(देशागरागेण)
सरसकथासु कथं पुलकाचितमाननकमलमजस्रम्।
कलयति चारुहसितनववलितं[3] परिहृतकेलिसहस्रम्।।१।।
मुग्धे! परिहर शङ्कितमधिकमये।।ध्रुवम्।।
आदरमधुरमिमामनुवेलं कथमालपति ससारम्।
सुमुखि सखीं तव तदपि मनो वत कलयति किमु न विचारम्।।२।।
गजपतिरूद्रनराधिपहृदये वसतु चिरं रस-सारे।
रामानन्दरायकविभणितं परिचित केलिविचारे।।३।। ।।१५।।
—Sung with Rāga "Deśāga"

In course of sweet conversation (with Śaśimukhī) how is it that a thrill of joy perpetually spreads over the lotus-like face (of Kṛṣṇa)? How is it that the face of Kṛṣṇa, even though he has forgone thousands of amorous sports, recently gets wrinkled owing to sweet smile? Oh simple-minded lady! Do not be too much apprehensive. Why does he pleasantly converse ever and anon with so much attention with this friend of yours in a true and genuine spirit? Oh lovely lady! even then how is she not able to judge his mind? May (this song) composed by the poet Rāmānanda Rāya get a lasting place in the heart of king (Pratāpa)rudra, the lord of elephants, the heart acquainted with love-sports and filled with nectar of love. /15/

राधा —देवि!
अनुमितमम्बुपयोदे, तनु परिकलिता दावानलज्वाला।
वपुरतिललितं बाला शिवशिव भविता कथं हरिणी।।१६।।

Rādhā —Oh revered lady! Scorched by the blaze of the forest-conflagration, how will the fawn with a very tender and delicate frame survive? Alas! Can it remain alive only by thinking that the cloud which has arisen, will cause a shower? /16/

मदनिका —वत्से! नियोजितापि मया माधवी तत् परिज्ञानाय त्वत् प्रतिच्छन्दक सनाथ चित्रफलकहस्ता।।१७।।

(ततः प्रविशति चित्रफलकहस्ता माधवी)

Madanikā —My dear! In order to know his heart I have engaged Mādhavī and handed her over a portrait with your picture drawn on it. /17/

(Then enters Mādhavī with the portrait in her hand)

माधवी —देवि! वन्दे! ।।१८।।

Mādhavī —Oh revered lady! I bow to you. /18/

मदनिका —वत्से! स्वागतं, ते अपि विदितं रहस्यम्।।१९।।

Madanikā —My dear! Welcome to you, did you know of the secret? /19/

माधवी —अथ किम्।।२०।।

Mādhavī —Yes, indeed, /20/

मदनिका —तदावेदय।।२१।।

Madanikā —Then you speak out. /21/

माधवी —(फलकमावेदयति)।।२२।।

Mādhavī —(Offers the portrait). /22/

राधा —(सल्लजं फलकं याचते)।।२३।।

Rādhā —(Bashfully asks for the portrait). /23/

माधवी —देहि मे पारितोषिकम्।।२४।।

Mādhavī —Give me my reward. /24/

मदनिका —(स्वगतम्) ध्रुवं तदस्या हृदयं प्रतीत्य
स्फुटं मुकुन्दोऽपि चकार रागम्।
भग्नः कदाचिद् यदयं प्रमादात्
प्रेमाङ्कुरो योजयितुं न शक्यः।
(प्रकाशम्) वत्से! उपनय फलकम्।।२५।।

Madanikā —(aside) It is a fact that convinced of the intention of this (maiden), Mukunda has also openly declared his love. Once the sprout of love is broken by mistake, it is not so easy to join. (Aloud) My dear! Bring the portrait. /25/

माधवी –(मनाग् दर्शयित्वाञ्चलेनाच्छादयति)।।२६।।

Mādhavī —(Having shown a little of it she covers up the portrait with the hem of her garment). /26/

शशिमुखी –(बलाद्गृहीत्वावलोकयति) अए कधं एदाइं अक्खराइं।
(अये, कथमेतानि अक्षराणि!)
(इति वाचयति)
मा शङ्किष्ठाः सुमुखि विमुखिभावमेतस्य, न स्या-
दानन्दाय प्रथममुकुला पद्मिनी कस्य कामम्।
आघ्रायैव प्रशिथिलधृतिर्गन्धिमस्यास्तथापि
नालम्बेत क्षणमपि युवा किं नु मध्यस्थभावम्?।।२७।।

Śaśimukhī —(Forcefully snatches away and looks at it) Oh, how come, these letters are here? (reads aloud) Don't be apprehensive, Oh lovely maiden, of the attitude of aversion of this (Kṛṣṇa). Who is not delighted at the sight of the lotus, blooming forth with; Having sufficiently inhaled the fragrance of this Padminī-nāyikā,[4] does not the youth, with all his fortitude gone, remain indifferent for a moment? /27/

माधवी –सहि! सुहं वडढ़से पिआणुराएण।।२८।।
(सखि! सुखं वर्द्धसे प्रियानुरागेण)

Mādhavī —Friend ! you are happy with the gesture of love shown by your lover. /28/

राधा –(दीर्घमुष्णं च निःश्वस्य) हला! कहिदाणीं अह्माणं ईरिसं भाअधेअं। (मदनिकां प्रति) एत्थ को अत्थो।।२९।।
(हला! कथमिदानीमस्माकमीदृशं भागधेयम्? (मदनिकां प्रति) अत्र कोऽर्थः?)

Rādhā —[Breathing a long feverish sigh (of bereavement)]

Friend! how am I now so fortunate! (To Madanikā) What's the purport here? /29/

मदनिका —तवैतदेव हृदयं प्रतीत्य

स्फुटं मुकुन्दोऽपि चकार रागम्।
भग्नः कदाचित् यदयं प्रमादात्
प्रेमाङ्कुरो योजयितुं न शक्यः।।
तद् वत्से! मातिविक्लवा भूः।
फलितोऽस्माकं मनस्कामतरुः।।३०।।

Madanikā —Convinced of this intention of yours Mukunda has also openly declared his love. Once this sprout of love is broken by mistake, it is not so easy to join. Therefore don't be so helpless. Oh my dear! the tree of our desire has borne fruit. /30/

राधा —अज्जवि ण पच्चेमि, ता एत्थ भोदी ज्जेव्व-सरणं।।३१।।
[अद्यापि न प्रत्येमि, तदत्रभवत्येव शरणम्]

Rādhā —Even now I do not believe it; you revered lady are (my) sole resort here. /31/

मदनिका —एषाहं चलितास्मि, तदनुमन्यस्व।।३२।।

Madanikā —Let me go now; be pleased to permit. /32/

राधा —(सप्रणामं, संस्कृतमाश्रित्य) भगवति!

निकुञ्जोऽयं गुञ्जन्मधुकरकदम्बाकुलतरः
प्रयातः प्रायोऽयं चरमगिरिशृङ्गं दिनमणिः।
मरुन्मन्दं मन्दं तरलयति गल्लीमधुकरान्
किमन्यद्वक्तव्यं विधुरपि विधातासमुदयम्।।३३।।

Rādhā —(Paying obeisance) (in Sanskrit)

Oh revered lady! this bower gets more disturbed with the swarms of humming bees; the sun has almost gone over to the peak of the western mountain; the breeze makes the bees and the jasmine flowers move very gently; what more shall I say? Even the moon is about to rise. /33/

(कर्णाटरागेण)

—Sung with the Rāga "Karṇāṭa"—

मञ्जुतरगुञ्जदलिकुञ्जमतिभीषणम्।
मन्दमरुदन्तरगगन्धकृतदूषणम्।।
सकलमेतदीरितं
किञ्च गुरु पञ्चशरचञ्चलं मम जीवितम्।।ध्रुवम्।।
मत्तपिक-दत्तरुजमुत्तमाधिकरं वनम्।
सङ्गसुखमङ्गमपि तुङ्गभयभाजनम्।।
रुद्रनृपमाशु विदधातु सुखसङ्कुलम्।
रामपदधामकविरायकृतमुज्ज्वलम्।।३४।।

The swarm of bees humming so sweetly excites terror; the fragrance innate in the gentle breeze affects me; moreover, pierced by the five shafts of Cupid my life is very unsteady (i.e., any moment I may give up my life); the sweet note of the intoxicated cuckoos physically afflicts me; the thicket of trees is the cause of my intense mental anguish; my body longing for the pleasure of the company (of my lover) is affected by excessive fear; I have told you everything; (now it is left to you to devise means to save me).

May the beautiful song constituting a series of amusing words of the poet (Rāmānanda) Rāya immediately delight the king (Pratāpa) rudra. /34/

मदनिका —वत्से ! अस्मिन् वकुलपादपोपकण्ठे द्रष्टव्यास्मि । (इति निष्क्रान्ता)।।३५।।

Madanikā —My dear! you can meet me in the vicinity of this *Vakula* tree. (Exit)

इतरा अपि निष्क्रान्ताः।

इति भावप्रकाशो नाम तृतीयोऽङ्कः।

(Others leave the stage)

Thus ends Act III entitled "Exposition of Sentiment of Love".

REFERENCES

1. When in all other texts the reading is प्रकार: which carries no meaning, in the Orissa Museum text the reading is प्रतिकार: which seems to be appropriate here.
2. Another reading here is अन्यमनसम्।
3. Another reading here is ललितम्।
4. *Padminī-nāyikā* —The writers on erotical science divide women into four classes, the *Padminī-nāyikā* being the first of them. The *Ratī-Śāstram* (p. 17) defines the term as follows :
   bhavati kamalanetrā nāsikākṣudrarandhrā
   aviralakucayugmā dīrghakeśī kṛśāṅgī/
   mṛduvacanasuśīlā nṛtyagītānuraktā
   sakalatanusuveśā padminī padmagandhā//

चतुर्थोऽङ्कः

ACT-IV

(ततः प्रविशति मदनिका)

(Then enters Madanikā)

मदनिका —अये! श्रुतं मदनमञ्जरीमुखात्, यद्वकुलपादपोपकण्ठे वटुद्वितीयो निवसति मुकुन्दः। तत्तत्रैव गच्छामि। (पुरतोऽवलोक्य) अये! मुकुन्दोऽयं वटुना सह किमपि मन्त्रयन् सविषादमास्ते। तद्ध्रुवमेव विलसितमत्र कुसुमशायकेन। तन्माधवीगुच्छान्तरिता[१] शृणोमि। (इति आत्मानम् अपवार्य्य स्थिता)

(ततः प्रविशति मदनावस्थां नाटयन् विदूषकेण सहालपन् कृष्णः।)

Madanikā —Oh! I heard from Madanamañjarī that in the neighbourhood of the *Vakula* tree Mukunda is resting in the company of a boy. Well, let me go there. (Looking in the front) Oh! This Mukunda engaged in some secret conversation with the boy is found to be remorseful. Therefore I am sure, Cupid reigns supremely here. Alright, let me listen to them hiding myself behind the *Mādhavī* bower. (Thus she remains hiding herself).

(Then gesticulating love-sickness enters Kṛṣṇa engaged in conversation with Vidūṣaka.)

मदनिका —(स्वगतम्) (मालवरागेण)

वदनमिदं विधुमण्डलमधुरं विधुरं वत सुचिरेण।
कलयदनङ्ग शराहतिमनिशं नलिनमिवेन्दुकरणे।।१।।
माधववपु रतिखेदं।
जनयति चेतसि शतधा भेद्म्।। (ध्रुवम्)
परिहृतहारं हृदयमुदारं धूसरितं विरहेण।
मरकतशैलशिलातलमाहतमहह किमिन्दुकरेण।।२।।

गजपदिरूद्रं सुकृतसमुद्रं शशिकिरणादपि शीतम्।
रामानन्दरायकविभणितं सुखयतु रुचिरं[२] गीतम्॥३॥ ॥२॥

Madanikā —(aside) —Sung with Rāga "Mālava"-This facial appearance (of Kṛṣṇa) is as sweet and charming as the orb of the moon; but alas! pierced by the shafts of Cupid long since it always remains pale like the lotus-blossom fading in the rays of the moon. Mādhava's person is very much distressed. My heart is rent asunder a hundred-fold (at this sight). His broad and extensive chest with the necklace cast aside, turned whitish due to separation, ah, looks like the slab of the rock of emerald spread over with the rays of the moon. May this sweet song, composed by the poet Rāmānnda Rāya delight the king (Pratāpa) rudra who, the ocean of meritorious deeds, is even more soothing than the moon-beams./2/

कृष्ण: —सा चेदुत्पललोचना सहचरीवक्त्रेण मे निर्भरं
प्रेमाणं प्रकटीचकार-तदयं हासो मया कल्पित:।
हा हा शुक्तिधिया महामणिरभूत् त्यक्तो मया दैवतो
यायाल्लोचनगोचरं पुनरियं पुण्यैरगणैर्मम॥३॥

Kṛṣṇa —That lotus-eyed maiden confidently expressed her love in me through her companion, but I took it in jest. Alas! I have abandoned the precious jewel mistaking it to bc a shell. May I have the good fortune of meeting her again by virtue of my countless meritorious deeds in the past!/3/

विदूषक: -भो वअस्स! भणिदं ज्जेव्व मए मा एसा अणुराइणी परिहरि अदुत्ति एहिंन कीस उत्तम्मसि? भोअणेच्छाए निउत्ताए लड्डुअमोदएहिं किं कादव्वं?
ता एत्थ अहं ज्जेव्व उवाओ॥४॥
(भो वयस्य! भणितमेव मया-मा एषा अनुरागिणी परिह्नियतामिति। इदानीं कस्यादुत्ताम्यसि? भोजनेच्छायां निवृत्तायां लड्डुकमोदकै: किं कर्त्तव्यं? तदत्राहमेव उपाय:।)

Vidūṣka —Oh friend! I had already told you—let not this maiden in love be forshaken. Now why are you in distress? What is the use of sweetmeats when there is no appetite? So I am to find out some means./4/

कृष्ण: –कथमिव?

Kṛṣṇa —What is the means?

विदूषक: –अहं बह्मणो मन्तं आवट्टिअ आवट्टिअ इमं आअड्ड इस्ससं।।५।।

(अहं ब्राह्मणो मन्त्रमावर्त्त्य आवर्त्त्य इमामाकर्षयिष्यामि।)

Vidūṣaks —Being a Brahmin I will seduce this maiden by repeatedly reciting some *mantra.*/5/

कृष्ण: –ज्ञातं ते ब्रह्मण्यम्। तदाकलय मदनिकाम्।।६।।

Kṛṣṇa —I am aware of your Brahminhood. Send for Madanikā./6/

मदनिका –(प्रविश्य) स्वस्ति वत्साय।।७।।

Madanikā —(Having entered) May good betide you, my dear!/7/

कृष्ण: –(पुरतोऽवलोक्य) कथमियं मदनिका?(सप्रश्रयम्) देवि! स्वागतं ते।।८।।

Kṛṣṇa --(Looking in the front) Oh! is it Madanikā? (with humility) Oh revereed lady! Welcome to you./8/

मदनिका –(सस्मितम्) महाभाग! तव मुखचन्द्रदर्शनेन।।९।।

Madanikā —(Smilingly) My Lord! I am very pleased to see your moon-like face./9/

विदूषक: –कुसुमशरोवेत्थिदो अह्माणं पिअवअस्स ता आणीअदु सा ज्जेव गोवकुमारिआ।।१०।।

(कुसुमशरव्यथितोऽस्माकं प्रियवयस्यस्तस्मादानीयतां सा एव गोपकुमारिका।)

Vidūṣaka —My dear friend has been tormented by the shafts of Cupid. So please fetch that cowherd maiden./10/

कृष्ण: –(सल्लजम्) धिङ्मूर्ख! मैवं भण।।११।।

Kṛṣṇa —(Bashfully) You fool! Don't talk like that./11/

विदूषकः —अह्मे बह्मणा उज्जुआ फुडंज्जेव भणाम॥१२॥

(वयं ब्राह्मणा ऋजवः स्फुटमेव भणामः।)

Vidūṣaka —We Brahmins are straight forward; we speak clearly and distinctly./12/

मदनिका —(सस्मितम्) वत्स! अपि नाम अमिथ्यावचनोऽसि॥१३॥

Madanikā —(Smilingly) Well, my dear; I know, you never tell a lie./13/

विदूषकः —अधइं? पेक्ख, पेक्ख, एदाइं पउमपत्ताइं।

(अथकिम्। पश्य पश्य, एतानि पद्मपत्राणि।)

(इति मर्म्मरपत्राणि दर्शयति।)॥१४॥

(संस्कृतमाश्रित्य)

(दुःखीवराड़ीरागेण)

नलिनवनं वनमालिकृते कृतमुज्झितकुसुमपलाशम्।

पल्लवमपि वृन्दावनमनु कलयसि ललितविकासम्॥१॥

सरले! पश्यसि किमु नहि कृष्णं?

त्वयि निहिताशं गलितविलासं चातकमिव धनतृष्णम्॥ ध्रुवम्॥

विधुमेववीक्ष्य विधुन्तुदमानय चपलमिति[3] प्रतिवेलम्।

वदति कथं वद यदि मदनो हृदि न वसति विरचितखेलम्॥२॥

गजपतिरुद्रमुदं तनुतामिति रामानन्दरायसुगीतम्।

निभृतमनोभव-विशिखपराभव हरिविरहेण समेतम्॥३॥ ॥१५॥

Vidūṣaka —What else? Look, look at these lotus leaves. (Shows the dry lotus-leaves producing rustling sound). (In Sanskrit) Sung with Rāga "Duḥkhīvarāḍī" For sake of *Vanamālin*[4] the lotus-bed has been made bare of leaves and flowers. Have you ever noticed in Vṛndāvana any flower lovely and in full bloom? Oh, simple-minded lady! Don't you look at Kṛṣṇa, who, like the *cātaka* bird longing for the cloud, with his hopes reposed in you, has lost all his grace and beauty. If Cupid causing the sport of love has not taken his position in the heart (of Kṛṣṇa), how is it that every moment he is quick to invite the presence of Rāhu at the sight of the moon? May the sweet song of Rāmānanda Rāya depicting the separation of Hari, secretly tormented by the shafts of Cupid, enhance the pleasure of king (Pratāpa) rudra,the lord of elephants./15/

मदनिका —किमेतावता?॥१६॥

Madanikā —What is the use of talking like this ?/16/

विदूषक: —तुमं पि पिअवअस्स जादो, जाणिदम्पि ण जाणासि; ता सअंज्जेव्व गदुअ मए आणिदव्वा। अहम्पि णिसिट्ठात्थो दूदो (इति गन्तुमिच्छति)॥१७॥

(त्वमपि प्रियवयस्यो जात:, ज्ञापितमपि न जानासि? तत् स्वयमेव गत्वा मया आनेतव्या। अहमपि निसृष्टार्थो दूत:। (इति गन्तुमिच्छति।)

Vidūṣaka —You also behave like (my) dear friend; even though informed of it, you don't realise. So personally I will go and guide her (to this place). Of my own accord as an emissary . I will also bring about their union *(nisṛṣṭārtha dūta)*[5]./17/

(Saying so he wants to go).

कृष्ण: —(उत्तरीये गृह्णाति)॥१८॥

Kṛṣṇa —[Pulls the upper-garment (of the Vidūṣaka)]./18/

मदनिका —वत्स कृष्ण! किमिति मय्येव गोपयसि?॥१९॥

Madanikā —Dear Kṛṣṇa! Why do you conceal facts from me?/19/

कृष्ण: —देवि! किञ्चिद् प्रष्टव्यासि[६]॥२०॥

Kṛṣṇa —Revered lady! I have to ask something./20/

मदनिका —विश्रब्धमभिधीयताम्॥२१॥

Madanikā —Please speak out in confidence./21/

कृष्ण: —तवास्यादेतस्या वदनरुचमाकर्ण्य शशिन:
कृतावज्ञा यस्मादयमपि रुजं तद्वितनुताम्।
तदंगेनासंगं भजत इति यो मे बहुमत:
कथं सोऽपि प्राणैर्मम मलयवातो विहरति॥२२॥

Kṛṣṇa —I neglected the beauty of the moon-like face of this

(maiden) even though I heard of it from you. And that is why even this (moon) torments me. How is it that the *Malaya* breeze for whom I had a very high regard for its close association with her limbs, takes away my life!/22/

मदनिका –(स्वगतम्) कृतार्थास्माकं मनोरथेन सार्द्धं राधिका। तदस्या अपि विरहावस्थां प्रकाशयामि। (प्रकाशम्) वत्स! सापि लावण्यमात्रशेषा कल्याणी। ।२३।

Madanikā —(aside) Along with our desire Rādhikā's desire has been fulfilled. Then let me speak out the pangs of separation of this (maiden). (Aloud) That blessed (maiden) has only loveliness left in her body./23/

तथाहि।

शिलापट्टे हैमे तुहिनकिरण-चन्दनरसै-
रियं तन्वी पिष्ट्वा तनुमनुविलेपं मृगयते।
क्षणं स्थित्वा हा हा सरसविसिनीपत्रशयने
समुत्तस्थौ यावज्ज्वलति न चिरान्मर्म्मरमिदम्।२४।
(सामतोड़ीरागेण)
निरवधि नयनसलिल-भवसादे।
पतति कृशा परिचलति च पादे।।
माधव! गुरुतर मनसिज बाधा
हरिहरिकथमपि जीवति राधा।।ध्रुवम्।।
निवससि चेतसि कथमिव वागम्।
शिव शिव शमयसि तदपि न कामम्।।
गजपतिरुद्र नृपतिमविगीतम्।
सुखयतु रामानन्दरायसुगीतम्।।२५।।

For,

With the sandal paste, the moon-beam as it were, prepared by rubbing on the slab of snow, this slender (maiden) seeks to anoint her body. She remains for a while on the watery bed of lotus-stalks and lotus leaves, but alas! all on a sudden she gets up when the bed dried up (because of the excessive heat of the body of the maiden) catches fire as it were./24/

—Sung with Rāga "Sāmatoḍī"-

With tears trickling down from her eyes without any interruption, the slender maiden falls down when she steps out. Torment of Cupid is intense indeed, Oh Mādhava! Somehow Rādhā is alive, Even though you have taken a seat in her heart, you are not able to pacify the torment of love. May Rāmānanda Rāya's song sweetly recited without discord delight the king (Pratāpa) rudradeva, the lord of elephants./25/

विदूषकः —भोदि, साहसिआओ गोविआओ होन्ति त्ति तक्केमि। जं चन्दचन्दणेहिं अणुलेवणं मग्गेन्ति। अह्माणं पिअवअस्सो उण चन्दं पेक्खिअ दिणअरं बिअ उलुओ कहिंबि उवारिदसरीरो णअणजुअलं मुद्दिअ चिट्ठदि। चन्दणाणं बाअंपि लम्भिअ सिद्धतण्णं बिअ भुअङ्गो इदोतदोओसरेदि।२६।

(भवति, साहसिका गोपिका भवन्तीति तर्कयामि। यच्चन्द्रचन्दनैरनुलेपनं मृगयन्ति। अस्माकं प्रियवयस्य पुनः चन्द्रं प्रेक्ष्य दिनकरमिव उलुकः कुत्रापि अपवारित-शरीरो नयनयुगलं मुद्रयित्वा तिष्ठति। चन्दनानां वातमपि लब्ध्वा सिद्धतन्त्रमिव भुजङ्ग इतस्ततोऽपसराति।)

Vidūṣaka —Oh revered lady! I think the cow-herd maidens are brave, as they are anxious to anoint their bodies with camphor and sandal. On the other hand, like an owl hiding itself from the sun, at the sight of the moon our dear friend covers his body and lies down with his eyes closed. As the snake though coming in contact with the breeze of the sandal wood trees lies benumbed because of the magic spell, our dear friend (thoughtlessly) moves here and there./26/

कृष्णः —(स्वगतम्) साधु भणितम्। (प्रकाशम्) धिङ् मूर्ख! मातिवाचालो भव।२७।

Kṛṣṇa —(aside) You have spoken aright. (aloud) Fie upon you fool! Don't be so garrulous.

मदनिका —एतस्या हृदयपरीक्षणाय कति कति प्रकाशिता न धर्म्माः।२८।

Madanikā —To know the mind of this (maiden) how many tricks have not been adopted? [Quite a few devices have been adopted to know the mind of this (maiden)]./28/

कृष्णः —(स्वगतं साशङ्कम्) अपि नाम निवृत्तेयं मदभिलाषतः?।२९।

Kṛṣṇa —(aside, with apprehension) Is it then that this (maiden) is disinclined to me?/29/

मदनिका —तदस्तु।

यदा नासौ दोषं गणयति गुरुणां कुवचने
न वा तोषं धत्ते सरसवचने नर्म्मसुहृदाम्।
विषाभं श्रीखण्डं कलयति विधुं पावकसमं
तदस्यास्तद्वृत्तं त्वयि गदितुमत्राहमगमम्।३०।

Madanikā —That may be.

Neither she finds fault with the harsh words of revered people nor she gets any delight in the sweet talk of her pleasure-companions. She takes sandal paste to be poison and for her the moon is like fire. So I have come here to report to you the (changed) behaviour of this (maiden)./30/

कृष्णः —(सोच्छ्वासम्)

त्वं चेदवञ्चनपरे स्मरवारिराशे
रुद्धर्त्तुमेषि तदकारणवत्सलासि।
तत् केशरद्रुमनिकुञ्जगृहे प्रसाद्य
तामानयस्व नयकोविदतां तनुष्व। ।३१।

Kṛṣṇa —(with a sigh of relief) O simple-minded lady (not skillful in deceit)! Surely you are so affectionate to me for nothing if you are interested in rescuing me from the ocean of love. So pacify her and lead her to the bower of *Vakula* trees; prove your prudence in policy matter./31/

मदनिका —वत्स! सत्यमेवेदम्।३२।

Madanikā —My dear! It is true indeed./32/

विदूषकः —भोदि, उज्जुए सच्चकं ज्जेव्व एदं। एत्थ अहं ज्जेव्व पड़िभू बह्मणो।३३।

(भवति! ऋज्जुके सत्यमेवेदम्। अत्राहमेव प्रतिभूर्ब्राह्मणः।)

Vidūṣaka —Revered lady! Oh, simple-minded, it is a fact. In this case a Brahmin like me stands surety (for Kṛṣṇa)./33/

कृष्णः —अलमन्यथा सम्भावनया, कुरु मत्प्रतिकारम् ।३४।

Kṛṣṇa —Don't take it otherwise. Do something for my relief. /34/

मदनिका —इयं प्रस्थितास्मि। स्वस्ति वत्साय। (इति निष्कान्ता।) ।३५।

(ततः प्रविशति संकेतोचितवेशा राधिका)

Madanikā —Right away, I start (on my errand). May good betide you, my dear! (Exeunt omnes)./35/

(Then enters Rādhikā fittingly dressed for the rendezvous)

राधा —सहि माहवि। विप्पलम्भिदह्मि भवदीहिं।

(सखि माधवि! विप्रलम्भितास्मि भवतीभिः।)।३६।

(संस्कृतमाश्रित्य)

(रामकेलिरागेण)

तिमिरतिरोहित-सरणी।

गिरिषु दरीषु समेव हि धरणी।।

चिरयति किं सखि देवी।

विधिरपि मयि किमु नहि हितसेवी।।ध्रुवम्।।

अतिवाहितमतिभीमम्।

विफलमिदं किमु गहनमसीमम्।।

सुखयतु रुद्रगजेशम्।

रामानन्दरायकृतमनिशम्। ।३७।

Rādhā —Friend Mādhavī! All of you have deceived me./36/

(sung with Rāga "Rāmakelī")

The path remains covered with darkness. The earth everywhere looks the same whether in hills or caves.

Friend! Why is the revered lady late? Is not fate favourable to me? Is it in vain that I crossed over this boundless and very dreadful forest! May the song composed by Rāmānanda Rāya incessantly delight the king (Pratāpa) rudra, the lord of elephants!/37/

माधवी —सखि! अलमन्यथासम्भावनया, आगतामिव देवीमवधारय ।३८।

(ततः प्रविशति मदनिका)

Mādhavī —Don't take it otherwise, friend! the revered lady is definitely coming./38/

(Then enters Madanikā)

मदनिका —वत्से! दिष्ट्या वर्द्धसे ।३९।

Madanikā —Oh dear! fortune favours you./39/

राधा —(सहर्षोच्छ्वासम्) देवि! अध को तत्थ वुत्तन्तो? ।४०।

(देवि! अथ कस्तत्र वृत्तान्तः?)

Rādhā —(breathing a sigh of relief with pleasure) Revered lady! What is the matter there?/40/

मदनिका —वलवति मदनज्वरे यः स्यात्। ।४१।

Madanikā —Whatever is expected in a case of extreme love-sickness./41/

राधा —कथम्विअ? (कथमिव?)।४२।

Rādhā —How indeed?/42/

मदनिका —इन्दुं निन्दति चन्दनं बिकिरति प्रालम्बकं गुञ्यति
प्रालेयात्त्रसति, प्रियं परिजनं न भाषते सम्प्रति।
गोविन्दस्तवविप्रयोगविधुरः किं किं न वा चेष्टते
तत् कुञ्जोदरतल्पकल्पनपरं राधे तमाराधय।।४३।।

(अथ निकुञ्जे कृष्णः)

Madanikā —He reproaches the moon, throws about the sandal paste, casts aside the pearl-necklace. He is afraid of dew-drops. At present he does not converse with his favourite attendants. What is there which Govinda distressed because of separation from you, does not do? Gratify him, Oh Rādhā! who has the sole idea of preparing a bed inside that bower of creepers./43/

(Kṛṣṇa in the bower of creepers)

कृष्ण: —सखे! कथं चिरयति मदनिका?

(सातङ्कं) इयं तन्वी पीनस्तनजघनभारालसगति-
र्विदूरे कुञ्जोऽयं ममरचितसंकेतवसति:।
स्वतो भीरुर्वाला, गहनमपि घोरान्धतमसं
कथंकारं सा मामभिसरतु को मेऽत्र शरणम्।।४४।।

Kṛṣṇa —Friend! Why does Madanikā delay? (with apprehension). Due to plump breasts and heavy hips this slender maiden is of slow-gait. And this bower, the rendezvous fashioned by me, is at a great distance. The young woman is fearful by nature; and also the forest is frightful, enveloped in deep darkness. How will she come to meet me in the rendezvous? Who will come here for my rescue?/44/

(क्षणं चिन्तां नाटयित्वा दीर्घमुष्णं च नि:श्वस्य)
किमेषा मत्वा मामपरिचितभावं विमुखतां
प्रयाता, विश्वासं किमु सहचरी वाचि न गता?
अथ भ्रान्ता वर्त्मन्यतितिमिरभाजीह विपिने
न शक्ता तन्वङ्गी स्मरशरहता वा प्रचलितुम्।।४५।।

[Gesticulating anxiety for a moment and breathing a long feverish sigh (of bereavement)]

Not being cognizant of my affection for her, has this maiden become disinclined to me!

Is it that she did not believe in the words of her companion (Madanikā)! or has she lost her way in this forest enveloped in utter darkness! Or pierced by the shafts of Cupid (extremely tormented by love) is the slender-limbed maiden unable to move!/45/

(पुरोऽवलोक्य)। अये! कथमुदितप्रायोऽयं चन्द्र:।

तथाहि,

यथेदं कोकानां प्रसरतितरां काकुविरुतं
यथा स्फीतं स्फीतं भवति परितः कैरवकुलम्।
यथामूर्च्छन्मूर्च्छत् प्रतिपदमिदं वारिजवनं
तथा शङ्के चन्द्रः प्रथमगिरिवीथ्यां विहरति।।४६।।

(Looking in the front)

O, this moon is about to rise. For, the sweet note of ruddy geese intensely spreads all around; in all directions the white water-lilies are in full bloom; every-where the petals in the cluster of lotus flowers are closed; therefore I think, the moon is taking a pleasure-walk in the range of the Eastern mountain./46/

(सखेदम्)

सख्या वाचि कथञ्चन प्रतियती बालान्धकारोचिते
नैषा वेशभरेण वागतवती वर्त्मन्यथार्द्धे मम।
अस्मिन् शक्रदिशं शशाङ्कहतके संदूषयत्युन्मना
नागन्तुं न च गन्तुमद्य चतुरा किंवा करिष्यत्यसौ।।४७।।

(sorrowfully)

Somehow believing in the words of her comapanion, she had been coming to me putting on the dress fitting to the evening twilight; but in the mid-way when this wretched moon totally soiled the eastern quarter (*Śakradiś*[9]), the maiden was perplexed in not deciding wheather to come or to go back. Now what will that clever maiden do? (In other words, she is helpless)./47/

(सविनयाञ्जलिं वद्ध्वा)

रे पूर्वपर्वत सखे कृपया मम त्वं
तुङ्गान्यमूनि तनु शृङ्गशतानि कामम्।
याते विलोचनपथं शशिनि, प्रयाणे
विघ्नो भवेन्मृगदृशो मम जीविते च।।४८।।

(humbly bringing both the palms together)
On my friend Eastern mountain! Have pity on me

and stretch those hundreds of lofty peaks as far as possible. If the moon comes within her sight, the fawn-eyed will face obstacles in her movement and also my life will be at stake./48/

विदूषक: —(कर्णं दत्त्वा) भो सुणीअदु। किं रुणु रुणु सद्दं कुणइ। ।४९।।

(भो श्रूयतां, किं रुणु रुणु शब्दं करोति)

Vidūṣaka —(Listening) Oh! listen, some jingling sound is heard. /49/

कृष्ण: —(श्रुतिमभिनीय नेपथ्ये)

तन्मञ्जीररव: किमेष किमु वा भृङ्गावलीनिस्वन-
स्तत् काञ्चीरणितं नु मन्मथवतां किं सारसानां रुतम्।।
एवं कल्पयतो विकल्पमचिरादालम्ब्य सख्या: करं
गोविन्दस्य निकुञ्जकेलिसदने भूषाभवद्राधिका।।५०।।

Kṛṣṇa —(Gesticulating that he hears something behind the curtain)

Is it the sonorous sound of her anklets or the humming sound of a swarm of black-bees? Is it the jingling sound of her girdle or the sweet note of cranes intoxicated with love? Thus while Govinda fancied in many different ways, supported by the hand of her companion Rādhikā added to the beauty (lit. ornamented) of his pleasure —apartment, the bower of creepers./50/

(मालवश्री:)

Sung with Rāga 'Mālavaśrī.

चिकुरतरङ्गक[१०]-फेनपटलमिव कुसुमं दधती कामम्।
नटदपसव्यदृशा दिशतीव च नर्त्तितुमतनुमवामम्।।
राधा माधवविहारा।
हरिमुपगच्छति मन्थरपदगति, लघु लघु तरलितहारा।।ध्रुवम्।।
शङ्कित लज्जित रसभरचञ्चल मधुरदृगन्तलवेन।
मधुमथनं प्रति समुपहरन्ती कुवलयदामरसेन।।
गजपतिरूद्रनराधिपमधुना तन्मदनं मधुरेण।
रामानन्दरायकविभणितं सुखयतु रसविसरेण।।५१।।

Like a mass of foam on tremulous waves, with flowers

in abundance on the wavy hairs of her head, Rādhā who has undertaken a pleasure-walk for Mādhava, as if commands the Cupid to dance favourably with the movement of her playful right eye. And with her necklace sparkling gently, she proceeds to Hari slowly. Afraid and abashed, with her side-long glances sweet and tremulous due to excess of love, she presents a garland of blue water-lilies to Kṛṣṇa, the destroyer of the demon Madhu. Through the diffusion of sweet sentiment may (this song) composed by the poet Rāmānanda Rāya now delight the king (Pratāpa) rudra, the lord of elephants, Cupid as it were. /51/

विदूषक: –(पुरतोऽवलोक्य) भो वअस्स जिदं अह्मेहिं। एषा तत्थ भोदी आअच्छदित्ति लक्षीअदि।।५२।।

(भो वयस्य! जितमस्माभि:। एषा तत्रभवती आगच्छतीति लक्ष्यते।)

Vidūṣaka —(Looking in the front) O friend! We have won; I notice that this revered maiden is coming. /52/

(तत: प्रविशति मदनिका)

(Then enters Madanikā)

मदनिका –वत्सौ! सम्पन्नश्चिरेण सुहृदां मनोरथ:।
तन्मामनुमन्यस्व स्थानान्तरवासगमनाय।।५३।।

Madanikā —Dear ones! At long last the desire of the loving friends has been fulfilled. Then let me be permitted to go for staying in some other place./53/

विदूषक: –मम्पि निउंजांतर-गमणाय।।५४।। [ममापि निकुञ्जान्तरगमनाय।]

Vidūṣaka —Let me also go to some other bower./54/

(इति निष्क्रान्ता: सर्वे)

इति राधाभिसारो नाम चतुर्थोऽङ्क:।

(Exeunt all)

Thus ends Act IV entitled "Rādhā Proceeding to meet her lover in the rendezvous".

REFERENCES

1. In the Orissa Museum Text the reading is लतान्तरिता; Senagupta has also shown लतान्तरिता as another reading in the footnote of his text. (p. 20)
2. In the Orissa Museum Text the reading is सुचिरम्; Senagupta has noted down this reading in the footnote of his text. (p. 21)
3. In Orissa Museum text the reading is चपलमति; Senagupta has also given this reading in the footnote of his text. p. 22
4. *Vanamālin* —Kṛṣṇa puts on a garland called *Vanamālā; so he is called* Vanamālin. The definition of *Vanamālā as given in the Practical Sanskrit-English Dictionary,* p. 828, by V. S. Apte is as follows:
   ajānulambinī mālā sarvartukusumojjvalā/
   madhye sthūlakadambāḍhyā vanamāleti kīrtitā//
5. *nisṛṣṭārtha dūta*—Authors on poetics speak of three types of emissaries. The first type of emissary referred to by Viśvanātha in *Sāhitya-darpaṇa* (III.48) is defined:
   ubhayor bhāvam unnīya svayaṁ vadati cottaram/
   suśliṣṭaṁ kurute kāryaṁ nisṛṣṭārthastu sa smṛtaḥ//
6. Though in the text of Vidyāratna, Śarmā, Brahmacārī and Otā the reading is द्रष्टव्यासि, the correct reading here is प्रष्टव्यासि. And it is seen in the Orissa Museum text and the text of Senagupta. p. 23
7. Here another reading is पिष्टा in most of the texts used by us.
8. Another reading is भ्रान्त्या which Senagupta has pointed out in the footnote of his text. p. 26.
9. *Śakradiś* —Since Śakra or Indra is the guardian deity of the eastern quarter, the latter is popularly known as *Śakradiś*.
10. Though the reading here is तरङ्गक in all the texts, Senagupta has given another reading करम्बित in the footnote of his text. p. 27.

पञ्चमोऽङ्कः

ACT V

(ततः प्रविशति शशिमुखी)

(Then enters Śaśimukhī)

शशिमुखी -अए! अज्ज णिउंजे कल्लाणाहिनिवेसाणं को वुत्तन्तो त्ति ण जाणीअदि। ता देई अणुसरिअ जाणिससं। (पुरतोऽवलोक्य) अए! कधं एसा णिद्दामुउलिदलोअणा लहु लहु इध ज्जेव्व आअच्छदि।।१।।

(अये! अद्य निकुञ्जे कल्याणाभिनिवेशयोः को वृत्तान्तः इति न ज्ञायते। तत् देवीमनुसृत्य ज्ञास्यामि। (पुरतोऽवलोक्य) अये! कथमेषा निद्रामुकुलितलोचना लघु लघु इहैवागच्छति।)

Śasimukhi —Oh, I don't know what has happened today to the pair of noble resolve in the bower. Then I would follow the revered lady (Madanikā) and ascertain the fact. (Looking in the front) Oh, how is it that this revered lady with her eyes closed due to drowsiness is slowly coming in this direction?/1/

(संस्कृतमाश्रित्य)

(in Sanskrit)

स्वैरं स्वैरं कथमपि दृशौ मन्दनिष्पन्दतारे[१]
विन्यस्यन्ती शिथिलितभुज द्वन्द्व सन्नामितांसा।
मन्दन्यासस्खलितचरणव्यस्तमञ्जीरघोषा
देवी-निद्राकुलतरतनुर्मोदमाविष्करोति।।२।।

(सुखसिन्धुडारागेण)

दरमुकुलारुण लोचनमानन इहगतकान्ति विकाशे।
कमलमिवारुणमुषसि विधावनुविम्बितमम्बुसकाशे।।
किमिदमियं प्रविशन्ती
भजति मनो मम रतिविरताविव वनिता कापि चलन्ती।।ध्रुवम्।।

शिथिलभुजा मृदुरणितकनकमणिकङ्कणमिदमनुवारम्।
विसकलपाद-निवेश निवारित नूपुर ललित विहारम्।।
गजपति रुद्र नराधिप हृदये मुदमिदमातनुतेति।
रामानन्दरायकवि भणितं विलसति रसिकजनेति।।३।।

Somehow gently looking with eyes where pupils have become steady and motionless, with her pair of arms hanging loosely from the shoulders bent down, with the disorderly jingling sound of the anklets produced from the wavering foot-steps during her lazy gait, the revered lady with a body languid due to drowsiness, diffuses pleasure as it were./2/

—Sung with Rāga "Sukhasindhuḍā"

In the manifestation of its beauty (i.e., of Madanikā) the face with small budlike reddish eyes resembles the reddish lotus flower reflected in the water when the moon shines in the sky at dawn. Oh! how is it that this revered lady enters just as a tired and exhausted woman moves ahead after the enjoyment of sexual pleasure.

The golden bracelet studded with gems frequently produces sweet tinkling sound as her arms hang loosely down; her wavering footsteps prevent the anklets from producing gentle and pleasing sound. This (song) composed by the poet Rāmānanda Rāya highly amuses the men of taste and enhances great delight in the heart of the king (Pratāpa) rudra, the lord of elephants./3/

(ततः प्रविशति यथोक्तवेशा मदनिका)

(Then enters Madanikā dressed as said before)

मदनिका —(चक्षुषी विमृज्य, पुरतोऽवलोक्य) अहो! रमणीयता वसन्तयामिनी परिणामस्य।।४।।

तथाहि—

इतो मन्दं मन्दं सरसिजवनीवातलहरी
ततश्चुतास्वादप्रमुदितपिकानां कलकलः।

क्वचितफुल्लां वल्लीमनुमधुकराणां स्वरकथा
कुतश्चित् कोकानां मृदुमधुरमानन्दलपितम्।।५।।

Madanikā —(Rubbing the eyes and looking in the front) Oh, how charming it is when the night dawns in the spring season!/4/

For,

Here gently blows the breeze wafting the fragrance of the cluster of lotus-flowers; there one hears the sweet note of the cuckoos delighted by feasting on the mango-blossoms; somewhere is heard the humming sound of the bees hovering over the creepers in full bloom; and somewhere one hears the soft sweet and pleasing note of ruddy geese./5/

(द्वित्राणि पदानि परिक्रम्य आनन्दमभिनीय)
उद्दामस्मरचातुरीपरिचयादन्योन्यरागादिमां
रात्रिं जागरितानि सद्मनि-युवद्वन्दानि यच्छेरते।
तत्तेषां श्वसितानिलेन तुलनामासादयिष्यन्निव
प्रोन्मीलत्-कमलावलीषु वलते श्रीखण्ड़वीथीमरुत्।।६।।

(going round two or three steps and gesticulating pleasure)

Because of love and affection for each other, acquainted with the art of unrestrained amorous sport, the young pairs in the dwelling (of the bower) are asleep after spending the sleepless night; with the desire of being equal with the breath of the young pairs, the *Malaya* breeze (the breeze blowing over the forest of sandal trees) resorts to the cluster of lotus-flowers in full bloom./6/

(पुरतोऽवलोक्य सविस्मयम्)
चकितचकितं क्वापि क्वापि प्रमोदनिरन्तरं
क्वचनवनिताकुण्ठोत्कण्ठं निधाय विलोचने।
कलयति तथावस्थामेषा रथाङ्गकुटुम्बिनी
भवति न यया चान्तेवासी विदग्धवधूजनः?।।७।।

(looking in the front with amazement)

Sometimes the male-*cakravāka* bird with excess of pleasure is found trembling; this male-*cakravāka* is found centring its eyes upon the female-*cakravāka* with great anxiety. Which young wife would not like to be the disciple of this female-*cakravāka* who has been the butt of attention of her mate?/7/

(क्षणमन्यतो गत्वा साश्चर्य्यम्)
अये! अतिरमणीयमिदं वर्त्तते।
तथाहि–
उन्मीलत् कमलोदरे मधुभरे दृष्ट्वानुविम्बं निजं
मन्वाना दयितं कथाञ्चिदधुना नोत्कण्ठया धावति।
उत्कण्ठोपनतं पुनः सहचरं दृष्ट्वा विलक्षामुहु
र्न स्थातुं न च गन्तुमत्रचतुरा भृङ्गी चिरं भ्राम्यति॥८॥

(For a moment going in the other direction with amazement)

Oh, it looks very lovely!

For,

Having noticed its own reflection in the large quantity of juice stored inside the lotus in full bloom and having mistaken it to be its lover, now the female black-bee no more runs with anxiety, (but) when again she meets her lover (companion) approaching with all eagerness, the witty female black-bee abashed and perplexed in not deciding whether to stay or to go frequently hovers around (the lotus) for a long time.

शशिमुखी —इयमतिप्राभातिकरामणीयकाहृतचित्ततया न मामवलोकयति। तदुपसृत्य वन्दे। (इत्युपसृत्य) देवि! वन्द्यसे?॥९॥

Śaśimukhī —The (revered) lady with her heart fascinated by the beauty of the dawn fails to notice me. So let me approach and greet her (then approaching) Oh, revered lady! I bow to you./9/

मदिनका —कथं शशिमुखि? वत्से! मे चिरमन्यचित्ततया नावधारितासि॥१०॥

Madanikā —Oh, is it Śaśimukhi? Long since I was absent-minded; therefore my dear! I could not notice you./10/

शशिमुखी —देवि! कथं निद्राकुलामिव भगवतीं तर्कयामि?॥११॥

Śaśimukhī —Oh, revered lady! I guess, the illustrious lady looks languid with drowsiness./11/

मदनिका —वत्से! इवेति कथम्? तथैव॥१२॥

Madanikā —Why do you guess? My dear! It is exactly so./12/

शशिमुखी —अथ, कथमिव?

Śaśimukhī —Why is it so?

मदनिका —राधामाधवयोरद्य निकुञ्जमधितिष्ठतोः।
तत्तत् कुतुकितालोकान्निशेयमतिवाहिता॥१३॥

Madanikā —Today while curiously observing the various amorous sports of Rādhā and Mādhava putting up together in the bower, this (whole) night passed./13/

शशिमुखी —अथ कीदृशस्तत्रत्यो वृत्तान्तः?॥१४॥

Śaśimukhī —Then what's the news there?/14/

मदनिका —शृणु (नयने प्रमृज्य) वत्से! जानासि निकुञ्जप्रवेशावधि॥१५॥

Madanikā —Listen. (rubbing both the eyes)

Oh, my dear! You know everything till their entry into the bower./15/

शशिमुखी —अध किं? (अथ किम्?)॥१६॥

Śaśimukhī —Yes, indeed./16/

मदनिका —तदनन्तरम्

यस्तम्भो मुरविद्विषः समभवत्तेनापि तस्या मनो
माध्यस्थं परिशङ्कते भयमनोजन्मत्रपानिर्भरम्।
कामेषु व्रजपक्षवात[2] विसर प्राप्तोदयो न क्षणा-
दाश्वासं हरिणीदृशो वितनुते तस्य प्रकम्पो यदि॥१७॥

Madanikā —Thereafter—

When the enemy of Mura (Kṛṣṇa) was stupefied at

the sight of Rādhā, her mind violent with fear and bashfulness arising out of love, would have led to a state of indifference *(mādhyastha)*, had not the violent tremor of the development of love on the part of Kṛṣṇa comparable to the blowing wind, immediately given comfort and solace to the deer-eyed./17/

शशिमुखी —प्रियं मे प्रियम्, कृतार्थाऽस्मि।।१८।।

Śaśimukhī —A good service done to me. I have my object fulfilled./18/

मदनिका —इतः परमपि सुहृदां कृतार्थता।।१९।।

Madanikā —Besides, the object of friends like us has been fulfilled./19/

शशिमुखी —अपि नाम दृष्टं देव्या अन्यदपि?।।२०।।

Śaśimukhī —Has revered lady noticed anything else?/20/

मदनिका —समस्तमेव।।२१।।

Madanikā —Exactly everything./21/

शशिमुखी —ततस्ततः?।।२२।।

Śaśimukhī —What next?/22/

मदनिका —वत्से!

साशङ्कं समनोभवप्रहसितं सापत्रपं सस्मयं
सासूयं समनोहरात्मकपदं सप्रेम सोत्कण्ठितम्।
राधायाः मधुसूदनस्य च तदा कुञ्जे तदासीद्रतं
येनासीन्मदनोऽपि विस्मयरसस्निग्धान्तरो निर्भरम्?।।२३।।

Madanikā —My dear! In the primary stage there was apprehension (in both Rādhā and Kṛṣṇa); then they cheered up with love; no more there was that bashfulness; then there was the sense of pride (in each of them); next each detracted the merits of the other in jest; then followed the conversation in sweet and pleasing words; also there developed affection for each other and finally there was intense longing for each other. At that time in that bower there was the union of

Rādhā and the slayer of Madhu (Kṛṣṇa) at the sight of which the god of love was completely overtaken with a sense of wonder./23/

आहिररागेण-

मृदुमञ्जीररवानुगतं गतमनया शयनसमीपम्।
मधुरिपुणापि पदानि कियन्त्यपि चलितं कियदनुरूपम्।।
शशिमुखि! किं तव वत कथयामि
राधामाधवकेलिभरादहमद्भुतमाकलयामि।।ध्रुवम्।।
मिलितमिदं किल तनुयुगलं पुनरपि न कञ्चन भेदम्।
विषमशशशुग कीलितमिव सखि गलितचिरन्तनखेदम्।।
नखररदावलि खण्डितमपि गुरु निःश्वसितायतभीतम्[3]।
रुद्रगजाधिपमुदमातनुतां रामानन्दरायसुगीतम्।।२४।।

—Sung with Rāga "Āhira"-

To the accompaniment of the soft and gentle sound of the anklets (worn in her feet) this Rādhā went near the bed, likewise Kṛṣṇa (the slayer of Madhu) also went ahead a few steps. Oh Śaśimukhī! What shall I tell you? I think to be a great surprise to notice the love-sport of Rādhā and Mādhava in full form, As if pierced by the shafts of Cupid, both of them were physically united; and moreover there was aboluetly no gap in between the two. Oh friend! the pangs of separation existing in them long since vanished. Both of them had their bodies hurt because each pierced the other with nails and bit with teeth. And both of them breathed long and heavy sighs as if in fear. May the sweet song of Rāmānanda Rāya enhance the pleasure of king (Pratāpa) rudra, the lord of elephants./24/

शशिमुखी —देवि! असम्बन्धमिवेदं प्रतिभाति माम्।।२५।।

Śaśimukhī —O revered lady! it seems absurd to me./25/

मदनिका —कथमिव?।।२६।।

Madanikā —Why so?/26/

शशिमुखी —तयोः कथमीदृशं सौरतकौशलं जातम्?।।२७।।

Śaśimukhī —How is it that both of them could be so proficient in the art of sexual union?/27/

मदनिका —अयि सरले!

उपदिशति गुरुर्गुरुप्रयत्ना-
त्तदपि च कालवशात् प्रयाति पाकम्।
इति किल नियता: समस्तविद्या:,
सुरतकला: स्वतएव सम्भवन्ति॥२८॥
अत्रान्तरे सुरतकेलिकलासु तासु
प्रायेण शिक्षित इवैष शशी चिरेण।
योग्यां तत: किमपि कर्त्तुमिव प्रकामं
संसेवते स्म चरमां दिशमादरेण॥२९॥

Madanikā —Oh, simple-minded lady!

A preceptor imparts instruction; through strenuous efforts in course of time that (instruction) attains maturity in the pupil. Indeed this is the permanent feature in all types of learning, but the art of sexual union is learnt by oneself automatically (without the help of a preceptor)./28/

In the meanwhile this moon almost trained in the art of those love-sports (of Rādhā and Mādhava) at long last affectionately resorted to the Western quarters[4]-his fitting companion to have an affair with her to his heart's content./29/

शशिमुखी —सम्प्रति च कल्याणिनो:-

अभिमतसुरतप्रमोदलक्ष्मी परिचय निर्वृतिमायतोश्चिरेण
नखपददशनाङ्क चारुभूषाललिततमं वपुरीक्षितुं मनो मे॥३०॥
(तत: प्रविशति सत्वरा राधिका, कतिचिद्दूरे कृष्ण:)

Śaśimukhī —Now at last the long-cherished sexual pleasure of the blessed pair has been consummated. How much I desire to look at the most graceful body bearing marks of nails and teeth of the maiden charming with beautiful ornaments!/30/

(Then enters Rādhā in a hurry and Kṛṣṇa quite at a distance)

राधा —(पुरतोऽवलोक्य) आपसन्नाइं दिसा मुहाइं, ता कधं उव्वारिदसरीरा गमिससं।

(आप्रसन्नानि दिशां मुखानि। तत् कथमपवारितशरीरा गमिष्यामि?)

(सत्वरं द्वित्राणि पदानि परिक्रम्य वलितग्रीवमवलोकते)॥३१॥

Rādhā —(Looking in the front) The quarters of the sky are quite clear and bright; then how can I go bare-bodied? (hastily walking about two or three steps she turns round and looks back)./31/

कृष्ण: —(क्षणं निर्व्वण्य) अहो! भयमन्मथसम्वलना मृगाक्षी।
द्वित्राण्येवपदानि गच्छति जवात् द्वित्राणिमन्दं पुन-
स्त्रासोत्कम्पमथापि पश्यति दिश: साकूतमेता पुन:।
यो न स्यादपि गोचरे नयनयोर्नेर्दिष्टमेतं जनं
संप्रत्येति पदे पदे व्यवहितं मामन्तिकेऽपि प्रिया॥३२॥

Kṛṣṇa —(Observing carefully for a moment) Ah! the fawn-eyed maiden is seized with fear and love. Hastily she proceeds two or three steps; again in a slow gait she proceeds two or three steps; then again trembling with fear pathetically she remains looking at these quarters. Even though this man never came within the range of the sight of the beloved, now the so called beloved at every step takes this man, that is, me to be at a distnce when he is so close to her./32/

राधा —(पुन: सत्वरं परिक्रामति)॥३३॥

Rādhā —(Again walks about hastily) /33/

मदनिका —वत्से! पश्य, पश्य, पुरतो राधिकां, कतिचिद्दूरे माधवञ्च। इयं हि-

न व्यालादपि संविभेति पुरत: स्थाणोर्यथा दूरतो
नोदविग्ना करिगर्जितादपि यथा काकाबलीनि:स्वनात्।
नैवेयं तिमिरेऽपि मुह्यतितरां कामं प्रकाशे यथा
तन्मन्ये विरहेऽपि नैव विधुरा कान्तस्य योगे यथा॥३४॥

Madanikā —Oh my dear! Look, Look, there is Rādhikā in the front, and at a little distance there is Mādhava.

For,

This (Rādhikā) is not so much afraid of even a snake in her presence as she is afraid of looking at a stump of a tree at a distance; she is not perturbed to listen to the roaring of an elephant as she is to listen to the cawing of the crows; this (Rādhikā) is not more perplexed in pitch-darkness as indeed she is perplexed in sun-shine; so I think, she is not at all afflicted even in separation as she is in union with her lover./34/

ललितरागेण–

अभिमत गाढ़मनोरथ–समुचितरतिपति समरविशेषे।
विजय-पराजय-परिचयविमुषित चेतसि वलदभिलाषे।।
लुलितमनोहरदेहा
कथयति परिचयमियमतिनिपुणं मृदुपदकमललवेहा।।ध्रुवम्।।
कुसुमशरासन-शरनिकर-ध्वनिमणित मनोहर घोषे।
गुणपरिपाटितया परिकल्पित नखदशन क्षतदोषे।।
गजपतिरुद्रनराधिपविदिते रसिकजनहिततोषे।
रामानन्दरायकविभणिते हृदयं कुरुत विदोषे।।३५।।

—Sung with Rāga "Lalita"

In the peculiar love-sport which is a natural consequence of the deep youthful longing for each other, where each is bent upon forcibly stealing the heart of the other because of acquaintance arising out of victory and defeat (in the sexual union), where the tinkling sound of the anklets (of Rādhā) is the sound produced by the shafts let loose from Cupid's bow with the string tightened to the ends, where the blemish of scratches due to biting with teeth and piercing with nails turns to a type of merit, this (Rādhā) with her delicate body in a drooping state and her tender lotus-feet slightly moving, very clearly indicates her sexual relation (with Kṛṣṇa).

Be attentive to the song free from any blemish, composed by the poet Rāmānanda Rāya, the song pleasing to the men of taste and acknowledged by the king (Pratāpa) rudra, the lord of elephants./35/

मदनिका —तदतिभये कातरेयं वत्सा। तत् उपसृत्य संभावयामस्तावदेनाम् (इति उपसृत्य) वत्से! स्वागतं ते।।३६।।

Madanikā —This maiden seems grieved through excessive fear. Then let us approach and honour her. (with these words approaching) Oh, my dear! You are welcome./36/

राधा —(ससंभ्रममवलोक्य) अए! कधं एसा देई? (अये! कथमेषो देवीति)

(सल्लज्जं वन्दते)।।३७।।

Rādhā —(looks frightfully) Oh, how is it, the revered lady is here?

(bashfully greets her)/37/

(नेपथ्ये कलकल:)। अब्रह्मण्यं, अब्रह्मण्यम्।।३८।।

(सर्वा: श्रुतिमभिनयन्ति)

(Indistinct sound behind the curtain)—Horrible, horrible! (All act as if they hear something.)/38/

(पुनर्नेपथ्ये)

शृङ्गाभ्याञ्च खुराञ्चलेन च बलादेष क्ष्मामुल्लिखन्
कल्पान्त स्तनयित्नु गर्जित घनध्वानैर्दिशोदारयन्।
उल्कार्च्चि: प्रतिमल्लमक्षियुगलं क्रोधादिवान्दोलय-
न्नेष व्यापदि मज्जयन् व्रजमभूद्दैवादरिष्टोऽग्रत:।।
(सर्वे निकुञ्जोदरे आत्मानमपवार्य्य पश्यन्ति।)।।३९।।

(again behind the curtain)

Forcibly by digging out the earth with both of his horns and hoofs, by rending the quarters by thundering sound resembling the sound at the time of dissolution, in anger moving to and fro both of his eyes looking like the flame of a meteor, this demon Ariṣṭa all on a sudden appears there in the front endangering this Vraja (the cow-herd village).

(Having concealed themselves inside the bower of creepers all keep on looking at the havoc caused by the demon Ariṣṭa)./39

कृष्णः —(साटोपमुपसर्पन्) अभयं घोषनिवासिनाम् (सगर्व्ववाहुमुद्यम्य।)॥४०॥

दृप्यद्दानव शीर्ण शैलवलय क्षौणीमहालम्बने
वैरिव्याकुल शक्रशान्तिकमखप्रोद्दामयूपेऽपि च।
अस्मिन् कृष्णभुजेऽपि जाग्रति भयं नित्यं तदेकाश्रयान्
घोषस्थानपि संस्पृशेदहहकिं प्राणैर्मम क्रीड़ति॥
(इति साटोपं परिक्रामति।)॥४१॥

Kṛṣṇa —(Approaching with pride)

Safety to the residents of the cow-herd village (by raising aloft his arms in arrogance)./40/

As long as this (mighty) arm of Śrīkṛṣṇa is raised aloft, the arm which is the great support of the earth with the range of its mountains shattered by the haughty demons, the arm which frightens the host of enemies, the arm which is the most formidable sacrificial post in the sacrifice performed for subduing Indra, how can fear have its hold upon the residents of the cow-herd village who have always taken refuse in him alone? Alas! How does this demon play havoc with my life! (with these words haughtily turns around)./41/

(नेपथ्ये)
भो! कष्टं, कष्टम्
याभ्यां गिरीणामपि शृङ्गवत्त्वं
सोढुं न्वशक्तेन विदारितास्ते।
तयोरनेनोत्पल कोमलाङ्गो
लक्ष्यीकृतो वालतनुर्मुकुन्दः॥४२॥

(behind the curtain)

Alas! What an evil! Tender-bodied Kṛṣṇa with his soft and sweet limbs like a blue-lotus has been the centre of attention of the (evil) eyes of the demon who, unable to bear with the great height of the mountains with jealous looks, had torn them asunder./42/

मदनिका —(विलोक्य साश्रम्)

अद्य क्षौणि सहस्व भारमतुलं देवा जयाशा कुत:
श्रीदेवि! ब्रतमाचर व्रजजना: क्वानन्दवार्त्तापि व:।
मात देवकि! किं भविष्यसि गता नन्दादयो राधिके
शून्यं ते जगदद्य जातमधुना हा हा हता: स्मो वयम्।।४३।।

Madanikā —(Looking with tears in her eyes) Oh Earth! today you bear very great burden; Oh divinities! where is the hope of your victory? Oh goddess Śri! You undertake austerities; Oh residents of cow-herd village! What pleasing news is there for you! Oh mother Devakī! What will happen to you! Nanda and his family are ruined! Oh Rādhikā! Today the world has become desolate for you! Alas! now we are dead and gone!/43/

राधा —(श्रुतिमभिनीय सातङ्कम्)—हद्धि मह मन्दभाइणीए एआरिसं दुद्देव्वविलसिदं जादं। (हा धिक्! मम मन्दभागिन्या एतादृशं दुर्दैवविलसितं जातम्।)।।४४।।

Rādhā —(Frightfully she acts as if she hears something). Fie upon me! Such a misfortune has fallen to my lot, the ill-fated as I am./44/

शशिमुखी —सखि! समाश्वसिहि समाश्वसिहि एष खलु मुकुन्द:।।४५।।

Śaśimukhī —Oh friend! Take courage, take courage, here indeed there is Mukunda./45/

(नेपथ्ये)

यत्रोन्मीलति मीलितं त्रिभुवनं यत्रोन्नमत्यानतं
यस्मिन् भ्राम्यति न भ्रमन्ति वियति प्रायेण वाता अपि।

क्षिप्त्वा कन्दुकलीलया तमधुना वृन्दावनाद्दूरतो
हत्वारिष्टमरिष्टमेतदकरोत् श्रीमान् मुकुन्दो जगत्॥४६॥

(behind the curtain)

When the demon Ariṣṭa is awake, all the three worlds go to sleep (the activity in the three worlds comes to a halt). When he is in ascendancy, the three worlds stoop. When he is on the move, the wind in the sky almost becomes motionless. Having killed the demon Ariṣṭa and thrown him out of Vṛndāvana to a distance, like playing with a ball Lord Mukunda now made the world safe and secure./46/

(ततः प्रविशति कृष्णः सर्व्वाः सस्पृहमालोकयन्ति।)॥४७॥

(Then enters Kṛṣṇa. All the females-Rādhā, Madanikā and Śaśimukhī eagerly look at Kṛṣṇa)./47/

मदनिका–अहो रामणीयकं जयश्रीभूषणस्य वत्सस्य!
तथाहि–
विश्रस्तालकवल्लरी परिमिलत् स्वेदोदविन्दूत्कर
व्यालिप्तालिकचन्दनः क्रमगलत्केकिच्छदोत्तंसकः।
पादक्षेप-समुच्छलत् क्षितिरजो रम्याङ्गरागश्चिरा-
दानन्दं वितनोत्ययं नयनयोराविर्भवन्माधवः॥४८॥
(उपसृत्य) दिष्ट्या दृष्टोऽसि वत्स! जयश्रीस्वयम्बरालिङ्गितः॥४९॥

Madanikā —Oh, embellished with the glory of victory how beautiful does our dear (Kṛṣṇa) appear?

For,

This Kṛṣṇa whose faded curly hairs have got mixed up with quite a few drops of water-like perspiration, over whose forehead the sandal paste applied to the curls of hair has spread, from whose crown (of the head) the crest of feathers of the peacock is gradually slipping down, who seems to have applied perfumed unguents to his body in the form of dust-particles of the earth raised high in the air because of being kicked with feet, appears before us and for a long time spreads delight to both of the eyes./48/

	(approaching) Oh my dear! I am fortunate to see you embraced by the goddess of victory of her own choice./49/
कृष्णः	–(दृष्ट्वा सहर्षम्) देवि! स्वागतं ते।।५०।।
Kṛṣṇa	—[Looking at her (Madanikā) with pleasure] Oh, revered lady! Welcome to you./50/
मदनिका	–स्वागतमधुना वत्सेन जयश्रीभूषणेन दृष्टेन। तद्वत्स! क्षणमिह वकुलपादपोपवीथ्यां विश्राम्यताम्।।५१।।
Madanikā	—Now my dear (Kṛṣṇa) whom I have just seen and who has been embellished with the glory of victory, welcomes me. So my dear! please take rest here beneath the *Vakula* tree for a while./51/
कृष्णः	–यदभिरुचितं देव्यै। (इत्युपविशति)।।५२।।
Kṛṣṇa	—As the revered lady likes. (with these words he sits down).
मदनिका	–(सस्नेहमङ्गं स्पृशति) वत्स! कृतदुष्करकर्मणः किमपि पारितोषिकं दित्सामि।।५३।।
Madanikā	—(Affectionately touches the body of Kṛṣṇa) Oh, my dear! I would like to give you some reward for the daring act you have done./53/
कृष्णः	–यदभिरुचितं देव्यै।।५४।।
Kṛṣṇa	—As thc revered lady likes./54/
मदनिका	–(निष्क्रम्य राधामादाय प्रविश्य) वत्स! नवाभिसङ्गविधुरां त्रासोन्मीलितलोचनां मधुरालोकनेनैनां संभावय चिरादिव।।५५।।
Madanikā	—(Goes out and enters in the company of Rādhā) Oh, my dear! By your pleasing sight for ever honour this maiden who, distressed because of recent union has her eyes closed due to fear./55/
कृष्णः	–(सस्पृहमालोकयति।)।।५६।।
Kṛṣṇa	—(Longingly looks at Rādhā)./56/
मदनिका	–वत्से! क्रूरसङ्गर-परिश्रमोल्लसत् स्वेदविन्दुनिकरैः करम्वितं, अञ्चलेन निजवाससः प्रियं वीजय प्रियगिराभिनन्द्य[6] च।।५७।।

Madanikā —Oh, my dear! with sweet and pleasing words welcome your dear and with the hem of your garment fan him whose body is marked with streaming drops of sweat arising due to exertion in the terrible fight (with the demon Ariṣṭa)./57/

राधा —(संस्पृहं वीजयति)।।५८।।

Rādhā —[Fans (Kṛṣṇa) with eagerness]./58/

मदनिका —इत: परं किं ते प्रियं सम्पादयामि?।।५९।।

Madanikā —What is more pleasing than it that I can do for you?/59/

कृष्ण: —देवि! इत: परं किमपि प्रियमस्ति?

पञ्चेषोर्विशिखावलीभिरभितो निस्तक्ष्यमाणेन चे-
दानन्दैकनिदानमेणनयना प्राप्ता प्रसादात्तव।
भूय: सेयमलम्भि काचन दृशो: पीयूषधारा मया
किं वात: परमस्ति देवि भूवने किञ्चित् प्रियं मादृशाम्।।६०।।

Kṛṣṇa —Oh, revered lady! is there anything more pleasing than it?

When being hit by the shafts of Cupid all around I was extremely distressed, through your favour I got the company of (this) fawn-eyed lady, the sole cause of my pleasure. Moreover, this maiden whom I have got as my company, is a stream of nectar to my eyes; Oh, revered lady! for person like me, in the world is there anything more pleasing than it!/60/

मङ्गलगुज्जरीरागेण-

परिणतशारदशशधरवदना।
मिलिता पाणितले गुरुमदना।।
देवि किमिह परमस्ति मदिष्टं।
वहुतरसुकृतफलितमनुदिष्टम्।।ध्रुवम्।।
पिक विधु मधु मधुपाबलि चरितम्।
रचयति मामधुना सुख भरितम्।।
प्रणयतु रुद्रनृपे सुखममृतम्।
रामानन्दभणितहरिरमितम्।।६१।।

—Sung with Rāga "Maṅgalagujjarī"

The maiden having a face —the full autumnal moon, intensely struck with passion is so easily at hand. Oh, revered lady! is there anything more agreeable to me? As destined, the lot of good deeds has borne fruit.

The activities of the cuckoo, the moon, the spring season and the swarm of bees now make me extremely happy. May this song composed by (the poet) Rāmānanda dealing with the rejoicings of Hari give ever-lasting pleasure to the king (Pratāpa) rudra./61/

तथापीदमस्तु।

श्रद्धावद्धमतिर्मम प्रतिदिनं गोपाललीलस्य यः
संसेवेत रहस्यमेतदतुलं लीलामृतं लोलधीः।
तस्मिन् मद्गतमानसे किल कृपादृष्ट्या भवत्या सदा
भाग्यं येन निजेप्सितां व्रजवने सिद्धिं समाप्नोति सः॥६२॥

Further let it be so ordained.

A man of restless mind who, with faith and devotion, everyday ardently listens to this mystery of the incomparable nectar-like amorous pastime of mine sporting with cow-herds, with all his attentions centred on me, would get all his desires fulfilled in the forest of cow-herds, Through your favour, (Oh, revered lady!) it is sure to happen for all time to come./62/

मदनिका —तथास्तु॥६३॥

इति निष्क्रान्ता सर्वे॥६४॥

इति राधासङ्गमो नाम पञ्चमोऽङ्कः।

इति श्रीरामानन्दरायविरचितं श्रीजगन्नाथवल्लभनाम नाटकं समाप्तम्।

समाप्तश्चायं ग्रन्थः।

Madanikā —let it be so./63/

(Exeunt all)/64/

Thus ends Act V entitled "The union of Rādhā with Kṛṣṇa". Here ends the drama "Jagannātha-vallabha" composed by (the poet) Rāmānandə Rāya.

REFERENCES

1. Another reading which Senagupta has mentioned in the footnote of his text p. 28 is भावे।
2. Another reading found in the Orissa Museum text is पद्मवात। Senagupta however has mentioned two readings – पद्मवात and पक्षपात in the footnote of his text p. 30.
3. Senagupta has noted down here another reading – "नि:श्वसितादिव भातम्" in the footnote of his text p. 31.
4. In Sanskrit language the word signifying quarters (*diś*) is always feminine. That is why the dramatist refers to the union of the moon (*śaśin*) always masculine approaching the Western quarters (*caramā diś*) like a lover going to his beloved.
5. In the Orissa Museum text the reading is सम्पन्ना। Senagupta has given this reading in the footnote of his text, p. 32.
6. Senagupta has given another reading प्रियगिराभिनन्दय in the footnote of his text, p. 35.

INDEX OF SANSKRIT VERSES IN THE DRAMA

INDEX OF MUSICAL SONGS IN THE DRAMA

BIBLIOGRAPHY

(A) VEDIC AND PURĀṆIC TEXTS

Atharva-Veda Saṁhitā Vol. II (Text with Eng. Trans.) W.D. Whitney, Nag Publishers, Delhi, 1987.

Ṛg-Veda Saṁhitā (Text) Arya Sahitya Mandal Ltd., Ajmer, 1952.

Bṛhad-devatā—Pat I (Introduction & Text), Part II (Eng. Trans. & Notes), A.A. Macdonell, Motilal Banarsidass, Delhi, 1994.

The Nighaṇṭu and Nirukta (Text with Eng. Trans.) L. Sarup, Motilal Banarsidass, Delhi, 1984.

Agni Purāṇa-Edited by Acharya Baladeva Upadhyaya, The Chowkhamba Sanskrit Series Office, Varanasi, 1966.

Brahma Purāṇa (Text with Hindi Trans.) —Edited by Tarinisa Jha, Hindi Sahitya Sammelana, Prayaga, 1976.

Brahma-Vaivartta Purāṇa Part II —Edited by Vasudev Sastri Marathe & Purrusottama Sastri Ranade, Anandasrama Sanskrit Series, Pune, 1935.

Brahmāṇḍa Purāṇa —Edited by K.V. Sarma, Krishnadas Academy, Varanasi, 1983.

Bhaviṣya Purāṇa Part I, Nag Publishers, Delhi, 1984.

Bhāgavata Purāṇa Parts I & II (Text with Eng. Trans.) C.L. Goswami, Gita Press, Gorakhpur, 1982.

The Harivaṁśa—The Mahābḥārata (Cr. Edn.) Vol. V. BORI, Poona, 1976.

Mārkaṇḍeya Purāṇa—Edited by Jivananda Vidyasagar Bhattacharya, Calcutta, 1979.

Padma Purāṇa (VI. Uttarakhaṇḍa) Part V Gurumandala Series, Calcutta, 1959.

Śiva Purāṇa—Edited by Pandey Ramateja Sastri, Pandit Pustakalaya, Kasi, Saṁvat 2020.

Vāyu Purāṇa, Nag Publishers, Delhi, 1983.

Viṣṇu Purāṇa, Gita Press, Gorakhpur, Saṁvat 2033.

ORIGINAL SANSKRIT WORKS ON POETICS AND DRAMATURGY

Bhāva-prakāśana (Text with Hindi Trans.)—Edited by Madan Mohan Agrawal, Chowkhamba Surabharati Prakashan, Varanasi, 1983.

Daśa-rūpaka—Edited by A.N. Pandey, Bharatiya Vidya Prakashan, Varanasi, 1979.

Nāṭaka-Candrikā (Text with Hindi Trans.), Babulala Sukla Sastri, Chowkhamba Sanskrit Series Office, Varanasi, 1964.

Nāṭaka-lakṣaṇa-ratnakośa (Text with Hindi Trans.), Babulala Sukla Sastri, Chowkhamba Sanskrit Series Office, Varanasi, 1972.

Nāṭya-darpaṇa Vol. I (only Text) Edited by Gajanan Kushaba Shrigondekar and Lalchandra Bhagawandas Gandhi, Oriental Institute, Baroda, 1929.

Nāṭya-śāstra (C.S.S.) Part II (Text with Hindi Trans.) Babulala Sukla Sastri, Chaukhamba Sanskrit Sansthan, Varanasi, 1978.

_________., Part III (Text with Hindi Trans.), Babulala Sukla Sastri, Chaukhamba Sanskrit Sansthan, Varanasi, 1983.

Nāṭya-śāstra (G.O.S.) —Vol. III (with the commentary of Abhinava Gupta) Edited by M. Ramakrishna Kavi, Oriental Institute, Baroda, 1954.

Nāṭya-śāstra (K.S.S.) Edited by Batuk Nath Sharma and Baladeva Upadhyaya, Chowkhamba Sanskrit Series Office, Benaras City, 1929.

The Nāṭya-śāstra —Vol.I (only Eng. Trans.) Manomohan Ghosh, Manisha Granthalaya Pvt. Ltd., Calcutta, 1967.

The Nāṭya-śāstra —Vol.II (only Eng. Trans.) Manomohan Ghosh, The Asiatic Society, Calcutta, 1961.

Rasārṇava-sudhākara (only Text) Edited by T.Ganapati Sastri, Government Press, Trivandrum, Maharajah of Travancore, 1916.

Sāhitya-darpaṇa (with Lakṣmī Commentary), Acharya Kṛṣṇa-mohan Sastri, Chowkhamba Sanskrit Series Office, Varanasi, 1967.

The Sāhitya-darpaṇa or Mirror of Composition (only Eng. Trans.) J.R. Ballantyne and Pramoda Dasa Mitra, Motilal Banarsidass, Delhi, 1994.

Ujjvala-nīlamaṇi —Edited by M.M. Pandit Durga Prasad and V.L. Shastri Panashikar, Chaukhamba Sanskrit Pratisthan, Delhi, 1985.

OTHER SANSKRIT, ORIYA AND BENGALI TEXTS

Bhakti-rasāmṛta Sindhu (Text with Oriya Trans.) —Edited by Nityananda Gosvami, Bhakti Vinoda Asrama, Berhampur, Ganjam, Orissa, 1995.

Caitanya-Caritāmṛta, Madhyalīlā, Part I, A.C. Bhakti Vedanta Svami, Oriya Trans. from English by Priyanatha De, Bhakti Vedanta Book Trust, ISKCON,Bhaubaneswar, 1988.

________., Madhyalīla, Part II, Antyalīlā Parts I-II, Oriya Trans. from English by Priyanatha De and Devaki Devi Dasi, Bhakti Vedanta Book Trust, ISKCON, Bhubaneswar, 1988.

Caitanya-Candrāmṛta (Text with Eng. Trans.) —Bhakti Prajnan Yati Maharaja, Sree Gaudiya Math, Madras, 1978.

Caitanya-Candrodaya-nāṭaka (Text with Hindi Trans.), Acharya Ramachandra Mishra, Chowkhamba Sanskrit Series Office, Varanasi, 1966.

The Gīta-govinda of Jayadeva (Text with Eng. Trans. & Criticism) Edited by Barbara Stoler Miller, Motilal Banarsidass, Delhi, 1984.

Gopīnātha-vallabha-nāṭaka of Raghunatha Parīkṣā (Oriya), Orissa Sahitya Akademi, Bhubaneswar, 1966.

Inscriptions of Orissa, Vol. V, Part I, S.N. Rajaguru, Orissa State Museum, Bhubaneswar, 1975.

Jagannātha-vallabha-nāṭaka (only Text in Oriya), Orissa State Museum Manuscript, S.M.S. No.66.

________,. (Text with Oriya Trans.) Pt. Puruṣottama Brahmacārī Bhakti Vinoda Ashrama, Berhampur, Ganjam, Orissa, 1979.

________,. (Text with Oriya Trans.) Viṣṇupriyā Otā, Published by Damodar Ota, Barachana, Cuttack, 1982.

________,. (Text with Bengali Trans. & Padāvalī of Locana Dāsa Ṭhākura), Rāmanārāyaṇaa Vidyāratna, Murshidabad, Berhampur, Calcutta, 1289 Agrahāyaṇa.

________,. (Text with Bengali Trans.), Jyotiścandra Śarmā, Published by Nirmala Kumara Raya, Calcutta, Caitanya Era 450.

________,. (Text with Bengali Trans. & Preface), Gaurāṅga Gopāla Senagupta, Baulman Prakashan, Calcutta, 1992.

Kāma-sūtra (Text with Hindi Trans.), Sri Devadatta Sastri, Chowkhamba Sanskrit Sansthan, Varanasi, 1996

Kumāra-sambhava (Cantos I-VIII), M.R. Kale, Motilal Banarsidass, Delhi, 1981.

The Padāvalī —Edited by S.K. De, Navrang, New Delhi, 1990.

Rati-śāstram (Text with Eng. Trans.), Abinash Chandra Ghose, Nag Publishers, Delhi, 1977.

Rāya Rāmānanda Padyāvalī (Oriya), Edited by Smt. Pramila Misra, Directorate of Culture, Orissa, Bhubaneswar, 1992.

Śrī Kṛṣṇa-Caitanya-Caritāmṛta or *Murāri Guptera Kaḍacā* (only Bengali Trans.), Madan Mohan Goswami, Published by Pusparani Mandal, Calcutta, 1986.

Śrī Kṛṣṇa-Caitanya-Caritāmṛta mahākāvya of Kavi Karṇapura Paramananda Sena—Ed. by Prankishor Goswami, Sri Gauranga Mandir (Sribhumi), Calcutta-48.

DICTIONARY

Apte, V.S. *The Practical Sanskrit-English Dictionary,* Motilal Banarasidass, Delhi, 1978.

SECONDARY LITERATURE

Banerji, R.D. —*History of Orissa,* Vol. I, R. Chatterjee, Calcutta, 1930.

Bhat, G.K. —*Sanskrit Drama : Problems and Perspectives,* Ajanta Publications, Delhi, 1985.

De, S.K. —*Early History of the Vaiṣṇava Faith and Movement in Bengal,* Firma KLM Private Ltd., Calcutta, 1986.

Devī, Saralā —*Rāya Rāmānanda* (Oriya), Orissa Sahitya Akademi, Bhubaneswar, 1963.

Goswami, Bhakti Sidhanta Saraswati —*Rāi Rāmānanda* (English) Bhakti Vinod Ashram, Berhampur, Ganjam, Orissa, 1986.

Keith, A.B. —*The Sanskrit Drama,* Motilal Banarsidass, Delhi, 1992.

Kinsley, David —*Hindu Goddesses,* Motilal Banarsidass, Delhi, 1987.

Kubba, Raj Kumari —*Kṛṣṇa-kāvya in Sanskrit Literature,* Eastern Book Linkers, Delhi, 1982.

Mahapatra, Cakradhara —*Utkala Itihāsara Eka Ajñāta Adhyāya* (Oriya) Friends' Publishers, Cuttack, 1989.

Mahapatra, K.N. —*A Descriptive Catalogue of Sanskrit Manuscripts of Orissa.* Vol. II. Orissa Sahitya Akademi, Bhubaneswar, 1960.

Mainkar, T.G. —Sanskrit Theory of Drama and Dramaturgy, Ajanta Publications, Delhi, 1985.

Mukherjee, Prabhat —*The History of Medieval Vaiṣṇavism in Orissa,* Asain Educational Services, New Delhi, 1981.

________., *The History of the Gajapati Kings of Orissa,* Kitab Mahal, Cuttak, 1981.

Mukerjee, S.C. —*A Study of Vaiṣṇavism in Ancient and Medieval Bengal,* Punthi Pustak, Calcutta, 1966.

Rath, Banamali —*A Study on the Śrī Kṛṣṇa-līlāmṛtam,* Kalyani Prakasan, Berhampur, Orissa, 1983.

Rosen, Steven J. —*Vaiṣṇavism :* Contemporary Scholars discuss the Gauḍīya Tradition, Motilal Banarsidass, Delhi, 1994.

Sastri, Asoke Chatterjee —*Caitanya,* Sahitya Akademi, New Delhi, 1990.

Trivedi, K.H.—*The Nāṭya-darpaṇa of Rāmacandra and Guṇacandra—A Critical Study, L.D. Institute of Indology, Ahmedabad, 1996.*

Vidyabhusana, Rasika Mohan —ŚrīRāya Rāmānanda (Bengali), Manjulika Bandopadhyaya, Calcutta, 1984.

SELECTED ARTICLES

Rajaguru, S.N. —"Śrīmandira Śilpakalāre Vaiṣṇava Saṁskṛti", (Oriya), *Srimandir,* June 1995.

Dash, K.C.—"Puruṣottama O Jagannātha" (Oriya), *Śrīmandir,* June, 1995.

INDEX

Y

THE PATH TO VICTORY

Delia Steinberg Guzmán

First published in Spanish as *Camino a la Victoria in 2021.*

Translated from Spanish by Julian Scott.
Re-designed for English edition by Janki Shah,
Neha Mehta and Sanjana Nanodkar

Published in 2022 by

NEW ACROPOLIS

New Acropolis Cultural Organization.
Mumbai, India.

www.acropolis.org.in
info@acropolis.org.in

ISBN: 978-81-949468-4-7